OpenMind

Advanced
Teacher's Book

Vinodini Murugesan
Adam Worcester

Concept development:
Mariela Gil Vierma

MACMILLAN

C1

Macmillan Education Limited
4 Crinan Street
London N1 9XW
Companies and representatives throughout the world

ISBN 978-1-786-32122-0

Text, design, and illustration © Macmillan Education Limited 2016 Written by Vinodini Murugesan and Adam Worcester

The authors have asserted their rights to be identified as the authors of this work in accordance with the Copyright, Designs and Patents Act 1988.

This edition published 2016
First edition published 2010

All rights reserved; no part of this publication may be reproduced, stored in a retrieval system, transmitted in any form, or by any means, electronic, mechanical, photocopying, recording, or otherwise, without the prior written permission of the publishers.

Designed by MPS Limited, India
Cover design by emc design limited

The publishers would like to thank the following educators and institutions who reviewed materials and provided us with invaluable insight and feedback for the development of the *Open Mind* series:

Petra Florianová, Gymnázium, Praha 6, Arabská 14; Inés Frigerio, Universidad Nacional de Río Cuarto; Alison Greenwood, University of Bologna, Centro Linguistico di Ateneo; Roumyana Yaneva Ivanova, The American College of Sofia; Táňa Jančaříková, SOŠ Drtinova Prague; Mari Carmen Lafuente, Escuela Oficial de Idiomas Hospitalet, Barcelona; Alice Lockyer, Pompeu Fabra University; Javier Roque Sandro Majul, Windmill School of English; Paul Neale, Susan Carol Owens and Beverley Anne Sharp, Cambridge Academy of English; Audrey Renton, Dubai Men's College, Higher Colleges of Technology, UAE; Martin Stanley, British Council, Bilbao; Luiza Wójtowicz-Waga, Warsaw Study Centre; Escuela Oficial de Idiomas de Getxo; Cámara de Comercio de Bilbao; Universidad Autónoma de Bellaterra; Escuela Oficial de Idiomas EOI de Barcelona; University of Barcelona; Escuela Oficial de Idiomas Sant Gervasi, Isidro Almedarez, Deniz Atesok, Monica Delgadillo, Elaine Hodgson, Mark Lloyd, Rufus Vaughan-Spruce, Kristof van Houdt, Rob Duncan, James Conboy, Jonathan Danby, Fiona Craig, Martin Guilfoyle, Rodrigo Rosa.

These materials may contain links for third party websites. We have no control over, and are not responsible for, the contents of such third party websites. Please use care when accessing them.

Printed and bound in the UK by CLOC Ltd

2020
11 10 9 8

CONTENTS

	INTRODUCTION TO THE COURSE	page iv
	DIGITAL STUDENT'S BOOK	page xviii
	KAGAN STRUCTURES: A MIRACLE OF ACTIVE ENGAGEMENT	page xix
	STUDENT'S BOOK SCOPE AND SEQUENCE	page xxii
	GRAMMAR REVIEW AND REFERENCE	page xxvi
UNIT 1	MONEY-FREE	page 1
UNIT 2	WATCH THIS SPACE …	page 11
UNIT 3	PASSWORD PROTECTED	page 21
UNIT 4	A NEW LOOK AT LEARNING	page 31
UNIT 5	ON THE WILD SIDE	page 41
UNIT 6	MORE THAN MACHINES?	page 51
UNIT 7	THE CRITICAL CONSUMER	page 61
UNIT 8	ARTISTIC LICENCE	page 71
UNIT 9	JUST PLAYING?	page 81
UNIT 10	FACT OR FICTION	page 91
UNIT 11	MUSIC TO MY EARS	page 101
UNIT 12	DOWN TO EARTH	page 111
	AUDIOSCRIPT	page 121
	WORKBOOK ANSWER KEY	page 134

INTRODUCTION TO THE COURSE
Welcome to the *Open Mind* Teacher's Book!

Course philosophy

The philosophy that underlies *Open Mind* is that language is a life skill – a skill for communicating and connecting with others in our everyday lives. As with other life skills, competence in a foreign language opens up possibilities and enables us constantly to expand our potential and our ability to function effectively within the wider social, cultural and economic worlds.

This course is designed to enable students to interact effectively with others in English in a wide variety of communicative situations: in their learning environment, at work, when travelling, online and so on. The authors recognise that the majority of students studying English in their countries will never live or work in an English-speaking country. Instead, they will be using English in the context of their jobs or studies in their own country. For example, they will probably not need to speak English to a doctor; however, they may have to help a foreign visitor to their country talk to a doctor. The activities in *Open Mind* are designed to reflect the reality of how the majority of students will actually use English in their everyday lives.

The authors are fully aware that students do not come to the classroom as blank slates. Instead, they bring ideas, opinions, feelings and experiences, all of which enrich the learning process. The course is designed in such a way that the students are given as many opportunities as possible to share these ideas and experiences through pair and group work, and in their writing and communicative work. All this ensures that the students relate to the material and make it their own. They are no longer mere users, but active participants, expressing their own points of view. The progression of tasks in each unit allows the students to relate what they have learnt to their own experiences and to express their ideas and opinions in English confidently. Specifically devised unit features ensure this smooth transition.

The course title, *Open Mind*, is a direct reflection of this underlying philosophy. It refers to the way in which mastering a new language enables learners to become acutely aware of the social, cultural and economic activities that take place in that new language. It also reflects the way in which acquiring communicative competence enables learners to engage with those activities, opening doors, both personal and professional, that may otherwise have remained closed. Finally, the title resonates with the fact that learning a new language opens a new channel for meaningful communication, allowing the students to express themselves accurately, creatively, and effectively, while maintaining an open mind towards other people's opinions and ideas.

Methodology and unit structure

The creation of *Open Mind* has been a rigorous and carefully researched process. Starting with the overall concept and then underpinning it with specific decisions has ensured that we are presenting you with a course that is meticulously thought-through, market-informed, and theoretically solid, and that it works pedagogically to achieve high learning outcomes in a demanding classroom environment.

Each unit in *Open Mind* is written and designed in sections. The sections reinforce each other, but are not interdependent. This adds unrivalled flexibility and allows for variety in the lesson structure. The unit sections can be taught sequentially, or they can be arranged to meet course requirements, e.g. number of hours per term. Of course, you can decide to use any other parameters you deem relevant.

Approaches to teaching language

A Grammar

Most students embarking on a language course expect to find grammar; they see it as the basis of the language they are learning. The teaching of grammar has traditionally involved a deductive approach in which a grammar rule is presented first (either by the teacher or by the textbook) and then practice exercises are given that allow students to apply the rule. In contrast, throughout *Open Mind* an inductive approach is applied, in which the target grammar is first presented in context, thus raising awareness of the structure in use. Students are then encouraged to observe, compare and analyse in order to identify the principles or rules of the new structure. Finally, students are presented with exercises that ensure comprehension of the grammar form in contexts that elicit the target language. To this end, each Grammar section in *Open Mind* follows a dynamic five-step structure approach that activates the students' learning potential, as shown opposite.

In each unit, there are two Grammar sections. The grammar has been selected to 1) reflect the needs of the students at their present level of English and 2) be relevant to the topic of the unit, ensuring that the practice is natural and meaningful. After completing a Grammar section, the students will encounter that grammar again as they work through the remainder of the unit, which reinforces the point and aids retention.

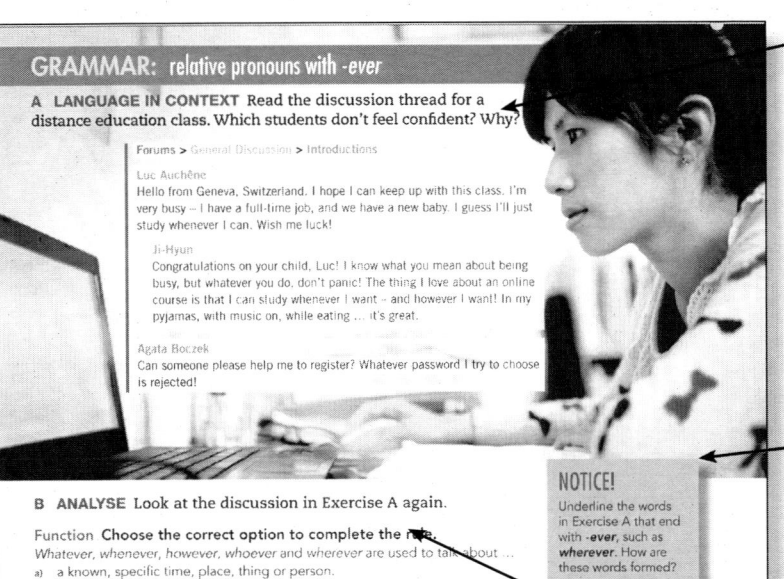

Step 1 – Language in context
This stage introduces students to the target grammar in a realistic reading or listening context. A simple comprehension activity ensures that the students have understood the main idea of the text/audio material. Usually this takes the form of a general comprehension question or questions. At this stage, students are not expected to produce the target language, but they are made aware of the structure in a real-life context.

Step 2 – Notice!
This feature consists of one or two simple questions to help the students notice something simple about the form or function of the new structure as it appears in the text.

Step 3 – Analyse
This stage focuses on a guided inductive presentation that uses examples from the text in the previous step. It usually consists of two subsections: Form and Function. Tasks elicit from the students the rules about the new structure. Having done the tasks, the students are left with a complete grammar presentation on the page.

What's right?
A feature that inductively draws the students' attention to common learner errors in the use of the new structure.

Step 4 – Practise
This stage is a written exercise that enables the students to apply and confirm their inferences from the *Analyse* stage and gives them controlled practice in the use of the target grammar.

Step 5 – Now you do it
The final step of each Grammar section is a one-step communicative activity that allows the students to practise the new grammar in a personalised context. The aim of this stage is to give the students the opportunity to employ the new structure in ways meaningful to them, thereby making it both more relevant and more memorable.

Introduction to the course

B Vocabulary

Language students can make rapid progress in a foreign language if they are able to assimilate and use items of vocabulary quickly and effectively. Traditional methods of teaching vocabulary relied heavily on memorisation of items, which were frequently presented in lists with an accompanying translation. While generations of students learnt vocabulary with some degree of success in this way, more recent approaches have focused on the communicative function of vocabulary, and particularly on the way words combine with other words to form chunks of meaningful language, as described in the Lexical Approach. The question of how people store and recall items of vocabulary has also become relevant, and the importance of associating words with a context, an experience, an image, or indeed with other words, is seen by practitioners as central to this process. When creating a course, there is the inevitable question of what vocabulary to present and in what order. The seemingly random approach adopted in the past has been quantified with the latest corpus linguistics tools, which in turn has enabled us to identify words that are used most frequently and words that are therefore most useful to students.

In *Open Mind*, the authors have adopted a corpus-based approach to selecting and presenting vocabulary. Information on frequency and collocation patterns has been sourced from the corpus work created for the *Macmillan English Dictionary*. The underlying philosophy to teaching vocabulary is that we should introduce students to the words and phrases that are most frequent and useful in general standard English. To this end, each Vocabulary section focuses on lexical terms that the students can use actively in everyday oral and written communication.

There are no independent vocabulary sections in *Open Mind*. Instead, Vocabulary is integrated into existing skills sections. The rationale behind this is that vocabulary useful to higher levels is more likely to relate to a specific text (such as a listening or reading text) or a productive need and function (such as a Speaking or Writing section). Each unit contains two integrated Vocabulary sections, each consisting of six to eight words which stem from the relevant reading, listening, speaking or writing text. Within each of these sections, there are two vocabulary activities – one to present the language, and a communicative task to put it into practice. The aim is to teach students the words that are most frequent and useful within a given topic and also to highlight collocations wherever possible or relevant.

Students at this level often have a good store of words already. To help them boost their vocabulary, you can encourage them to: look at words and phrases that go together (*make a mistake, a decision, a mess*); look at how words and phrases are used in context; make word webs for different word families; look at the connotations of a word (*helpful – positive; poorly made – negative*).

Suggest to the students that they keep a vocabulary notebook to record new items of vocabulary and examples of their use in context.

Step 1 The skills task presents the target vocabulary in context functioning as the engaging stage. At this stage, the students are not expected to use the items actively. There are tasks to check students' comprehension before they focus on the language.

Step 2 This step gives the students the opportunity to use the new vocabulary items in a controlled practice activity. They are often asked to compare options, categorise, complete phrases and sentences, and so on.

Step 3 With this last step, the students are encouraged to use the vocabulary items actively in a speaking activity, such as a discussion or roleplay.

C Pronunciation

Accurate pronunciation is a key element of successful communication. Mastering pronunciation requires awareness and practice at three key prosodic levels: sound, word and sentence – all of which are focused on in *Open Mind*.

First of all, there are the individual sounds (phonemes) of English. Here it is important to focus on those sounds that are different from those in the students' mother tongues and that therefore cause the greatest difficulty, both in terms of recognition (listening and understanding) and in terms of production (speaking and being understood). Second, there is the area of word stress, where English, with its numerous word stress patterns, may differ considerably from the students' mother tongues. Finally, there is the question of rhythm and intonation, where English is characterised by a relatively high number of falling tone patterns in comparison with many other languages. Level-appropriate aspects of these three areas of pronunciation are carefully developed and presented.

As with Grammar, Pronunciation in *Open Mind* is taught inductively. Each Pronunciation section in *Open Mind* typically consists of two or three steps. The Pronunciation sections are supported by audio for the presentation and sometimes additionally for the practice steps.

> **Step 1** Students are given a task which draws their attention to a specific sound or stress pattern. They are always asked to repeat the words or phrases to practise.

PRONUNCIATION: linking words with a /w/ or a /j/ sound

A 1.29 Listen to the phrases. Which ones are joined by a /w/ sound? Which ones are joined by a /j/ sound? Write the correct sound.

go on _____ high altitude _____ no idea _____ two apples _____
he isn't _____ I often _____ true answer _____ we allow _____

B 1.30 Listen to the sentences. Then practise in pairs.
1 If robots go on developing as they have been, I have no idea what it will lead to.
2 I often think that there'll be problems if we allow robots to become intelligent.

> **Step 2** This step provides the students with an opportunity to practise the pattern and to compare and check their grasp of the pronunciation point.

Approaches to teaching the four skills

The four language skills – listening, reading, speaking and writing – are informed by the two modes of communication: spoken and written language. Each of these has a receptive and a productive aspect. To ensure fluency, it is essential that learners of a language get practice in all four skills. However, mere practice alone is not enough. The four skills need to be developed in a planned, coherent way, something that many textbooks have neglected up to now.

Each skill consists of a number of different abilities, or 'sub-skills'. For example, the skill of reading consists of the meaningful use of sub-skills such as scanning, skimming, recognising the main idea, etc. In actual use, we employ a variety of skills and sub-skills simultaneously. Consequently, in order to develop the students' reading and listening skills, it is important to identify and focus on sub-skills in turn. In *Open Mind*, we have devised a skills syllabus that is methodically researched, carefully planned and balanced, and which focuses on sub-skills that are most likely to be of use to learners at their respective levels.

All four skills are present in every unit of *Open Mind*. However, in order to ensure a balanced development of the four main language skills, we have deployed an alternate pattern of 'on' and 'off' skills: 'on' skills are the ones that are developed through subskills, and 'off' skills are the ones that are practised. So every unit includes two types of skills sections:
1) skills development sections for the 'on' skills, and
2) skills practice sections for the 'off' skills. Their pattern is alternate; for example, the two 'on' skills that are developed in Unit 1 are then practised in Unit 2 as 'off' skills, while the two 'off' skills that are practised in Unit 1 are developed in Unit 2 as 'on' skills, and so on.

This alternate pattern of 'on' and 'off' skills sections is clear in the layout of the contents pages, with the two 'on' skills sections in every unit highlighted.

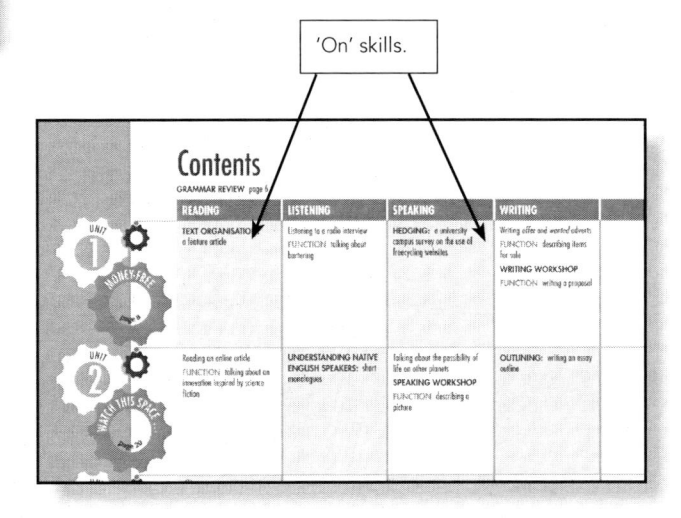

Introduction to the course

1 Teaching sub-skills (skills development sections – 'on' skills)

Each skills development section starts with a skills panel, which informs the students in clear, direct terms what the sub-skill is, why it is important and how to apply it. The sub-skill section builds on the information provided in this feature. The students are always given the opportunity to apply the sub-skill at the end of the section.

'On' skill indicated by cog.

LISTENING: understanding native English speakers

English speakers from different countries or regions might speak with different accents. Pay attention to an unfamiliar accent when you hear one and find out where it comes from. The more familiar you are with a range of accents, the better prepared you are to communicate with many different people.

In each level of the course, three sub-skills are covered for reading and listening. Each of these is covered twice, the second time in further detail or in a more challenging context. There are six sub-skills for speaking and writing per level. Further practice of the sub-skills is provided in the Workbook.

Recycled 'on' skill indicated by cog and page reference.

READING: text organisation page 10

Recognising the structure of a text you are reading helps you understand the text more quickly. Persuasive texts (texts which try to convince the reader of an opinion) often follow a cause-effect structure. The writer presents causes and explains the effects in order to convince the reader of his/her opinion.

Reading

In *Open Mind Advanced*, training is given in the Reading sections in the development of the following key sub-skills:
- text organisation (Units 1 and 3)
- understanding definitions and explanations (Units 5 and 7)
- understanding intent (Units 9 and 11)

One feature of the *Open Mind* reading texts is that wherever possible they are taken or adapted from authentic sources, to make the reading experience as realistic as possible. Reading texts are tagged with the source from which they are taken or adapted using one of three labels: *From* (where the text is taken word for word from the source), *Adapted from* (where the text has been adapted from a particular source), or *Information source* (where the text has been written using information from a particular source).

Listening

In *Open Mind Advanced*, training is given in the Listening sections in the development of the following key sub-skills:
- understanding different English accents (Units 2 and 4)
- inferring opinions and facts (Units 6 and 8)
- understanding in difficult situations (Units 10 and 12)

Effective L2 listening is the ability to understand an aural message in another language and respond appropriately. Without the ability to listen effectively, the students will be unable to communicate successfully in the target language. Listening is an essential component of *Open Mind*. For many students, listening can be the most difficult of the four skills and in the classroom it can often seem the most intimidating. Help your students to become better listeners by training them in effective listening strategies.

Speaking

In *Open Mind Advanced*, training is given in the Speaking sections in the development of the following key sub-skills:
- hedging (Unit 1)
- participating in a group discussion (Unit 3)
- summarising a point of view (Unit 5)
- modifying a statement (Unit 7)
- making and responding to invitations (Unit 9)
- softening language for refusals (Unit 11)

Apart from the skills development sections which cover speaking, there are constant opportunities for speaking throughout each unit of *Open Mind*: the students are encouraged to give their own opinions, to discuss their own experiences and to communicate with one another on a variety of topics. A specific speaking stage can always be found in the Grammar section (*Now you do it*), in the Vocabulary section and in the LifeSkills section.

Speaking sections in even units contain an Independent Speaking task, which is similar to the extended speaking task required of students taking the TOEFL exam, as well as being an important part of production as outlined in the Common European Framework. In this task, students take turns to participate in an extended speaking turn for about one and a half minutes.

Writing

In *Open Mind Advanced*, training is given in the Writing sections in the development of the following key sub-skills:
- outlining (Unit 2)
- sentence variety (Unit 4)
- summarising (Unit 6)
- writing a review (Unit 8)
- writing a wiki entry (Unit 10)
- writing an editorial (Unit 12)

Three of the six writing sections in *Open Mind Advanced* deal with a genre of writing rather than with smaller writing sub-skills such as using connectors or writing a topic sentence. It is considered that advanced level students are ready to tackle the broader challenge of genre writing.

2 Integrating and practising skills (skills practice sections – 'off' skills)

These sections (two per unit) provide the students with opportunities to practise skills with a focus on the communicative outcome (e.g. listening to a story in Unit 5; writing a short article in Unit 9). Each section comprises two to three steps and integrates two or more language skills, with a primary skill as the focus. The sections allow students to focus more on the end product, with fluency in mind, and less on the process they go through in order to achieve it. In the activities here, there is a strong emphasis on personalisation – relating the material to students' own experiences.

The unit opener

The first two pages of every *Open Mind* unit are the unit opener. It is an exciting visual opportunity for students to engage with the unit. The first page sets the overall scene visually by means of a striking combination of two photos and also by providing a comprehensive list of language objectives for the unit. This page always features two cogs which indicate the two 'on' skills being developed in the unit and which, through simple questions or tasks, aim to help the students to familiarise themselves with the unit.

The LifeSkills panel at the bottom introduces the life skill of the unit and here again a question helps the students to start thinking about the nature of the life skill.

The second page of the unit opener features photos and provides a quick warm-up to the unit, or can be extended to a much longer and enriching speaking activity. This activity never expects the students to use any vocabulary or grammar in the unit to come. Its key purpose is to create excitement and boost motivation.

CEF-oriented unit objectives.

Introduction to the course ix

Speaking and Writing workshops

The Speaking and Writing workshops are each a page long and come at the end of alternate units. These are intended to provide extra practice and support in the productive skills, as well as expose students to the kinds of writing and speaking they might need to do in exams like IELTS, TOEFL, etc. (Note that extra practice and exam-style questions for reading and listening are provided in the Workbook.)

The structure of both the Speaking and Writing workshops is based on a common concept: the students are first presented with a model, next they analyse it, then they work on their own production and finally they self-assess.

For more independent writing consolidation practice, encourage the students to complete the optional final activity on the SkillsStudio spread in each unit of the Workbook. For more extended speaking practice, use the Independent Speaking feature at the end of Speaking sections in even units.

Step 1
Students are presented with a model conversation or model paragraph, email, etc and a task based on the model. The task focuses on comprehension but it is also an opportunity for the students to start working with the language or structure that will be focused on later.

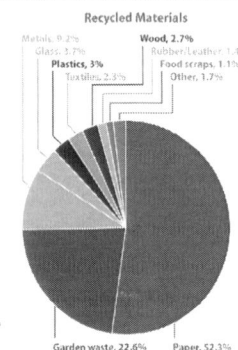

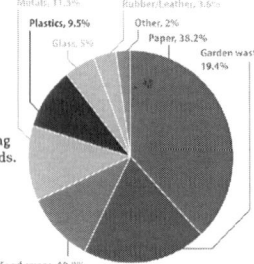

Step 2
This is a task to focus students on the useful language or structure from the model. This is what they will need to employ in the production task later.

Step 3 – Writing
Here students start thinking about their own production. The task helps them prepare in terms of information to include, language to use, ways of structuring and organising their ideas, etc.

Step 4 – Writing
Having prepared for the writing task, students undertake a piece of writing.

Step 4 – Speaking
Having prepared for the speaking task, students engage in a conversation, either in groups, or with a partner.

Step 5
This is a self-assessment feature to get students to analyze and reflect on their production.

Teaching life skills

One of the unique features of *Open Mind* is its focus on life skills. Each unit ends with an inspiring lifeSkills section. This is based on the notion that in today's highly competitive global environment, students of English need other, higher-order skills besides language skills. Life skills include information and research skills, critical thinking and problem-solving skills, self-direction and learning skills, organisation and planning skills and collaboration skills. These skills are highly valued by employers and are essential to the students' continued success, and yet rarely form a part of the students' formal education. The authors firmly believe that it is our responsibility to help the students develop these life skills and, in particular, to prepare them to employ those life skills in English-speaking situations. All the life skills covered in *Open Mind* require a certain amount of collaboration, so pair and group work is an essential component of this section.

The life skills in *Open Mind* feature as parts of three domains: *Self and Society*, *Study and Learning* and *Work and Career*. It is important to understand that the use of these three domains is not meant to function as an organising principle, but rather as a reflection of one of the many ways in which that particular skill can be applied. Life skills are essential in every aspect of our lives and therefore transferable. In every LifeSkills spread in *Open Mind*, the particular life skill to be applied in one of the three domains was carefully chosen.

Each LifeSkills section is introduced by a three-step summary of the approach that will be applied through the different activities in the section. These steps are applicable to the skill in general and can be applied in other situations, beyond the English classroom.

Each LifeSkills section is linked to the general unit topic in which it appears, and the language and skills presented in the previous pages of the unit help to prepare the students for this section.

A three-step summary of the approach that will be applied through the different activities in the section.

The chosen domain for the spread is highlighted, but all three domains are mentioned as a reminder of the transferability of the skill.

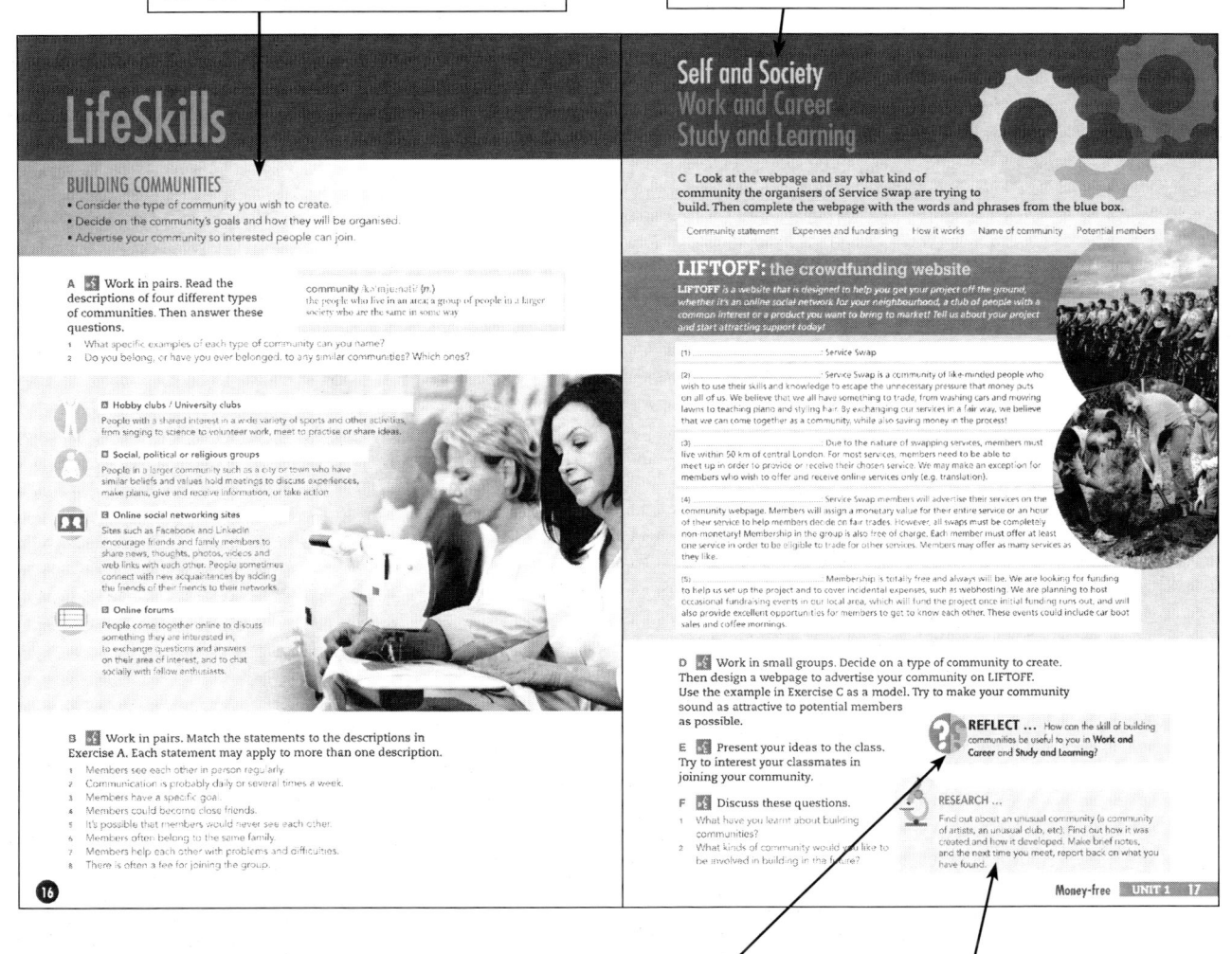

The *Reflect* question gets students to think about how the featured skill can be applied to the other two domains.

The *Research* task encourages students to apply the skill they have learnt, or find out more about it, via a short research project.

Introduction to the course xi

Language wrap-up

Each unit has a Language wrap-up that enables the students to assess their grasp of the new vocabulary and grammar items presented in the unit.

The Language wrap-up exercises can be done in class or assigned as homework. If given as homework, tell the students not to look at the sections of the unit that are being tested in the wrap-up tasks before they do the exercises.

If you use the Language wrap-up in class, you might wish to set a time limit of 10–15 minutes for each task. Again, encourage the students to do the tasks without looking back at the relevant sections of the unit. Motivate them to focus on the tasks individually, as pair or group work could lead to stronger students dominating and would not give accurate feedback on what individual students have learnt.

It is a good idea to go over the answers with the whole class. This can lead to some discussion of the answers that might be useful for students.

Make sure the students read the can-do statements in the score boxes and write their score out of 10 or 12 for both the Vocabulary and Grammar sections. If they have a score lower than 8 (out of 10) or 10 (out of 12), encourage them to read the appropriate sections of the unit again for homework, and then do the exercise or exercises again at home.

> **8–10 correct:** I can talk about consumerism and sustainability and describe used items.
> **0–7 correct:** Look again at the Vocabulary sections on pages 10, 11 and 13.   SCORE: /10

> **8–10 correct:** I can place adverb phrases in a sentence and use negative questions.
> **0–7 correct:** Look again at the Grammar sections on pages 12 and 14.   SCORE: /10

To aid retention and ensure a long-lasting learning outcome, it is crucial to recycle language points from previous sections and units regularly. For example, to recycle grammar, you can ask the students a few questions at the beginning of each lesson, focusing on the grammar content of the previous lesson (e.g. for past simple, begin the lesson by asking *What did you do last weekend? Where did you go after the lesson yesterday?*). Integrated recycling is also emphasised in the way vocabulary is used – the target vocabulary from each section occurs again over the remainder of each unit, reinforcing use of the items and aiding retention.

In addition, to help you plan sub-skills recycling, the cog symbol is used in the unit plan and again in the appropriate heading within the teaching notes, along with a reference in the Student's Book to where that sub-skill was previously practised.

Teaching students at Advanced Level

Teaching students at Advanced level presents the language teacher with certain challenges, often related to gaps in their previous grammatical knowledge and the existence of different levels within a particular group. At this level it is especially important for the students to be independent learners and to expand their vocabulary, in particular, both inside and outside the classroom – by using the internet to research items, through independent reading and listening and so on. As at previous levels, it is essential that you use English as the language of the classroom, although there may be instances (where possible and appropriate) when you might encourage learners to compare and contrast a particular structure, item of vocabulary, or idiom with the equivalent in their mother tongue. The concept of *false cognates* (words that look or sound similar to words in the students' mother tongue but which have a different meaning in English) can be discussed at this level if applicable and examples are highlighted.

Emphasise the advantages of maximising the amount of active use of English during class time in pair and group work activities. The authors have provided the students with model conversations, prompts, and phrases in the *How to say it* feature to ensure that the students have a range of functional language at hand to carry out a task confidently. Moreover, the course teaches a variety of useful skills to overcome any obstacles and to promote interaction. When checking answers to exercises, you may at times want to let the students first compare their answers in pairs. This is particularly appropriate in exercises that are more open-ended, or where more than one answer is possible for some of the items. The practice of pair checking helps to promote a cooperative learning atmosphere and provides extra speaking opportunities.

When presenting new vocabulary, ensure that the students feel comfortable with the pronunciation and stress of any new words and phrases. Encourage the students to keep a vocabulary notebook and focus on establishing good learning practices. In particular, encourage them to make use of monolingual dictionaries (both hard copies and online versions) and highlight the importance of using these as a means of enhancing independent learning through checking meaning, collocations, pronunciation and word stress.

Open Mind Workbook

The *Open Mind* Workbook is an ideal source of additional activities to engage the students in further practice of the Student's Book material. The Workbook follows a format similar to that of the Student's Book and reflects its section organisation. The dynamic and modern design makes the book appealing and easy to navigate through.

Each Workbook unit can be viewed as consisting of two parts: the first four pages help students to practise and consolidate the unit's grammar, vocabulary and the two target sub-skills.

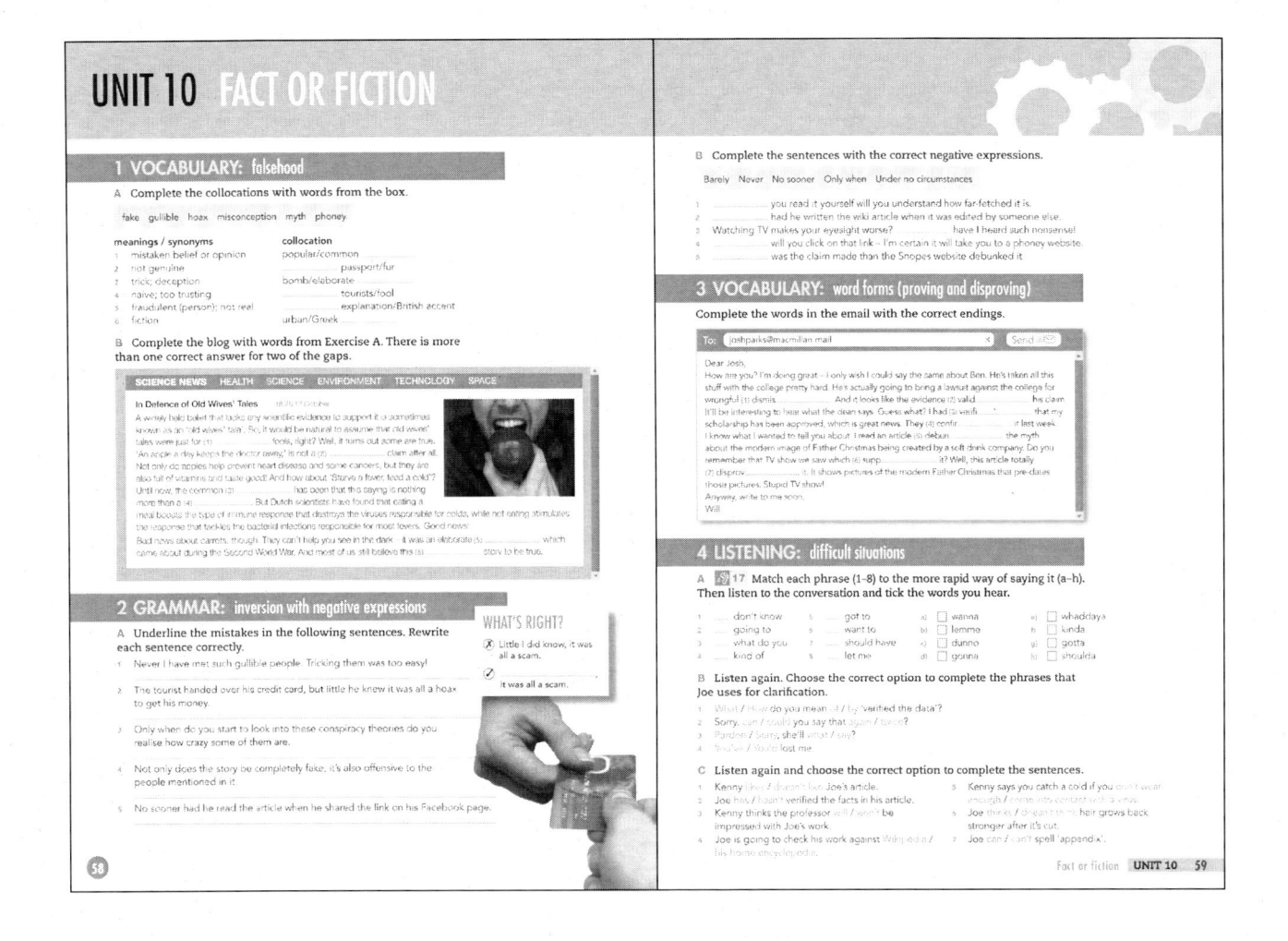

Introduction to the course

The last two pages of each Workbook unit contain the *SkillsStudio*. This spread provides students with an extended reading or listening text as well as tasks similar to the ones they might find in an exam.

Comprehension questions follow each text, and the spread ends with an optional free writing task that requires the student to select and synthesise relevant information from the reading or listening.

The Workbook is accompanied by its own audio CD with the tracks for the listening tasks. The listening activities are signposted by an audio icon, and the audioscripts appear at the end of the Workbook. The answer key for the Workbook activities (including possible answers) can be found on pp. 134–142 of this Teacher's Book or within the Workbook itself if students have purchased the 'with key' version.

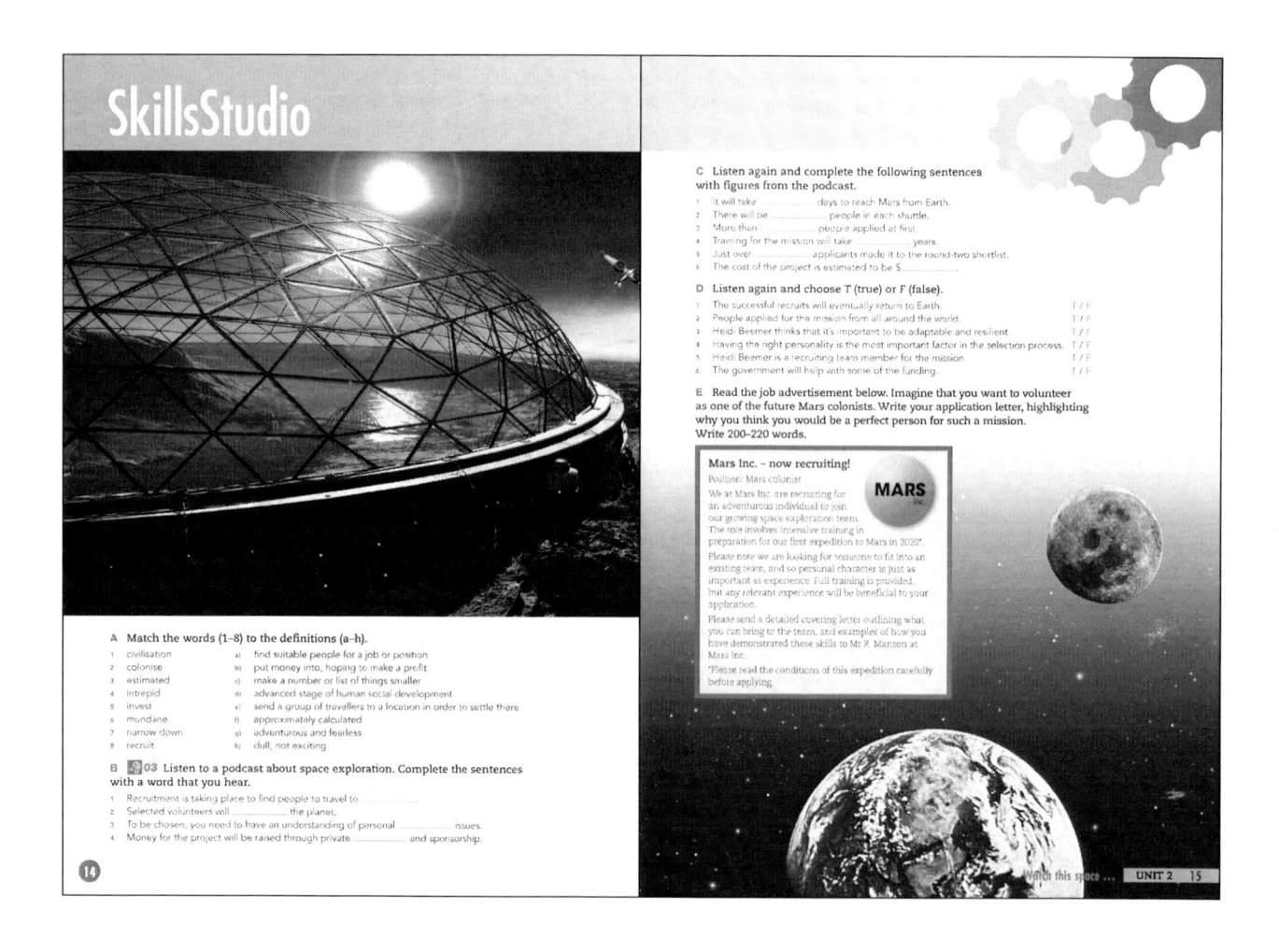

Open Mind Teacher's Book

The Teacher's Book offers carefully planned, well-paced, and insightful procedural notes to help you prepare, present and follow up on the unit material in an appropriate way for the students, teaching circumstances and course requirements.

Along with the procedural notes, the Teacher's Book supplies a complete answer key (including possible answers) and includes the audioscripts for the listening tasks in the Student's Book.

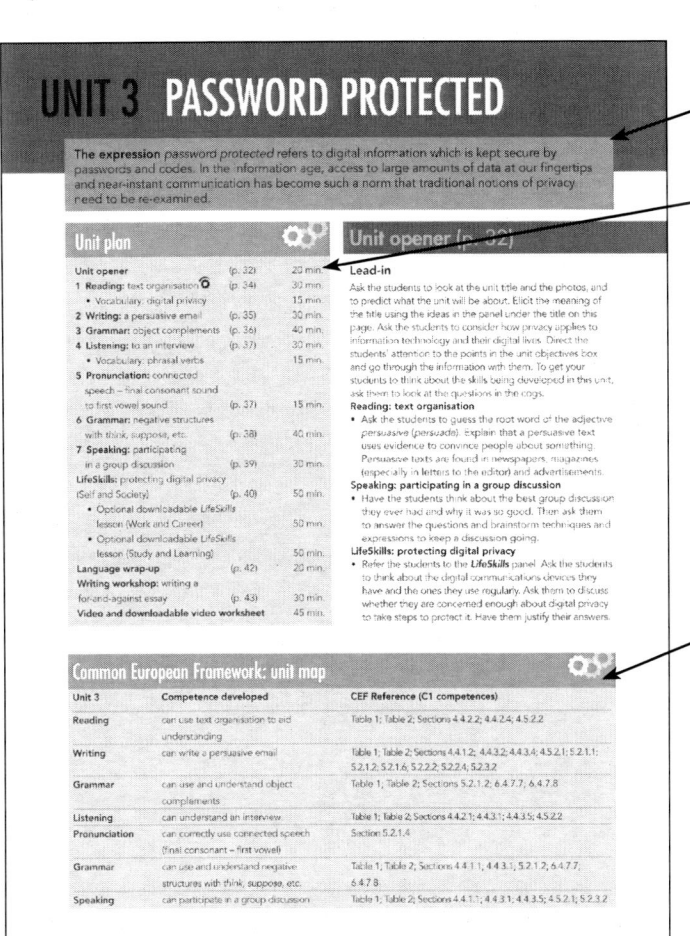

> The course features exciting and authentic phrases as unit titles. The unit title feature offers an insight into the meaning of the phrases and serves as a mini culture note to explain the collocation.

> The information in the unit plan outlines the target language and objectives by section. It also offers suggested timings.

> The Common European Framework of Reference for Languages (CEFR) is an influential document produced by the Council of Europe. Since its publication, it has had a major impact on the work of teachers, teacher trainers, examiners and course designers, both within Europe and in other parts of the world. It describes the linguistic competences language learners possess at different levels of achievement. It does this by describing the things a person with a given language level can do. It covers six main levels of ability: A1, A2, B1, B2, C1 and C2. Students completing *Open Mind Advanced* should reach the level of ability of C1, as described by the CEFR performance descriptors.
> The CEFR unit map lists the sections in the unit and, for each section, a can-do statement is provided. These are based on the type of can-do statements found in the CEFR and describe the ability the students should acquire on successfully completing the section. In the map, reference is provided to the relevant sections of the CEFR. These are either the sections where the CEFR specifically mentions the competence being developed in the Student's Book, or sections where the CEFR mentions competences that rely on the competence being developed in the Student's Book. The complete text of the CEFR is available for download from the Council of Europe website (http://www.coe.int/t/dg4/linguistic/source/framework_en.pdf).

Features of the Teacher's Book

The Teacher's Book authors have developed an array of teacher-friendly features that support, build on and/or extend the material in the Student's Book.

Lead-in This feature provides you with optional activities that help you start your lesson or introduce a particular section of the Student's Book. Typically, the Lead-in does not require any additional preparation.

Alternative This instruction presents you with alternative approaches to the Student's Book material. It addresses different learning styles, provides challenging alternatives for high achievers and facilitates the presentation of activities for students who may need more support.

Culture note Here you can find background information that may be of interest to your students and that will help you with the presentation of the section material. It may provide more information about a person, event or place mentioned in the Student's Book. It may also focus on what people in the English-speaking world do or say in a particular situation.

Extra The optional *Extra* activities equip you with ideas for additional classroom practice and homework. The activities always focus on and extend the language point of the section in which they appear. They are ideal for fast finishers. Extra reading comprehension or grammar items are often provided in case you want to exploit a reading text or a grammar point further with your class.

Introduction to the course

Open Mind Digital

Flexible digital resources are a central part of the *Open Mind* approach to language teaching. The range of online and downloadable components and resources can be tailored to each class's needs and facilities, allowing for flipped and blended approaches as well as more traditional teaching styles.

For students, the Online Workbook and self-study video worksheets and video on the Student's Resource Centre consolidate classroom learning and promote autonomy and awareness.

For teachers, *Open Mind*'s digital components provide tools to save you time and add to the class experience, together with a variety of testing options that range from a placement test to customisable unit and mid-course tests and an end-of-course test.

Teacher's and Student's Resource Centres

The online Resource Centres for teachers and students are bursting with materials to support the course, as well as audio and video. Some features are available to both students and teachers, while others can only be accessed through the Teacher's Resource Centre. See the lists at the end of this page for a complete overview.

Video

Each Student's Book unit is accompanied by a new video (see screenshot below) which provides students with engaging material and further language input. Videos feature authentic footage and a range of genres, including reportage, animated presentations and interviews with real people to provide fascinating lead-ins or jumping-off points for each unit of the course.

All videos are accompanied by downloadable worksheets. These worksheets offer a variety of tasks and activities that build on the students' prior knowledge, generate interest in the topic, check the students' comprehension and practise grammar and/or vocabulary. Each worksheet presents tasks to be done before, during and after watching, and comes with teacher's notes and answer keys where appropriate.

Example from Open Mind Upper Intermediate video

Extra LifeSkills support

The Teacher's Resource Centre includes twenty-four LifeSkills lesson plans – two for every LifeSkills double-page spread in the Student's Book. Each LifeSkills section in the Student's Book presents a skill (for example, 'Evaluating explanations') through one domain (for example, *Study and Learning*), while the extra LifeSkills lesson plans will present this same skill through the two other domains (for example, *Self and Society* and *Work and Career*).

Besides offering alternatives to the Student's Book material, the aim of these extra LifeSkills lessons is to show learners how they can apply the same life skill from the Student's Book to other contexts, thereby further developing these competencies and empowering the students.

Tests

All the tests you need for placement, progress, and achievement purposes are on the Teacher's Resource Centre. These are available both in ready-to-print PDF versions and customisable Word versions, and comprise:
- *Open Mind* course placement test, with instructions on delivering this
- Unit tests: these test the grammar, vocabulary and skills covered in each unit of the Student's Book
- Mid-course tests: a ready-made review combining items from the unit tests for the first half of the Student's Book
- End-of-course test: a ready-made end-of-course test with completely new test items covering the full *Open Mind Advanced* language syllabus

Student's Resource Centre – the complete package

The following features are all accessible to your *Open Mind* students:
- Student's Book and Workbook audio files
- *Open Mind* video files
- *Open Mind* video self-study worksheets and answer key
- CEFR checklists
- Word lists and translated word lists

Teacher's Resource Centre – the complete package

The Teacher's Resource Centre includes everything on the Student's Resource Centre, as well as:
- *Open Mind* video class worksheets with teacher's notes and answer keys
- Extra unit opener lessons
- Extra LifeSkills lessons
- Communicative wrap-up lessons
- Tests
- Placement test

Online Workbook

The Online Workbook provides extra skills, grammar and vocabulary practice to support the Student's Book. It contains interactive activities, audio for listening practice, video and supporting activities and automatic marking – so students can instantly check answers and try again as many times as they want.

The Online Workbook is also linked to an LMS (learning management system) gradebook, which means you can see students' marks for each activity, as well as the amount of time (and number of times) it has taken them to complete each task. The Online Workbook is ideal for self-study, but you may wish to consider using it for reviewing students' work in open class via a projector or an interactive whiteboard.

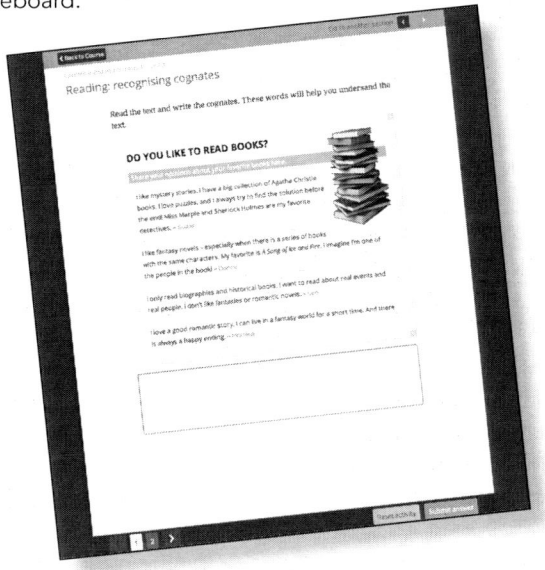

Example from Open Mind *Elementary Online Workbook*

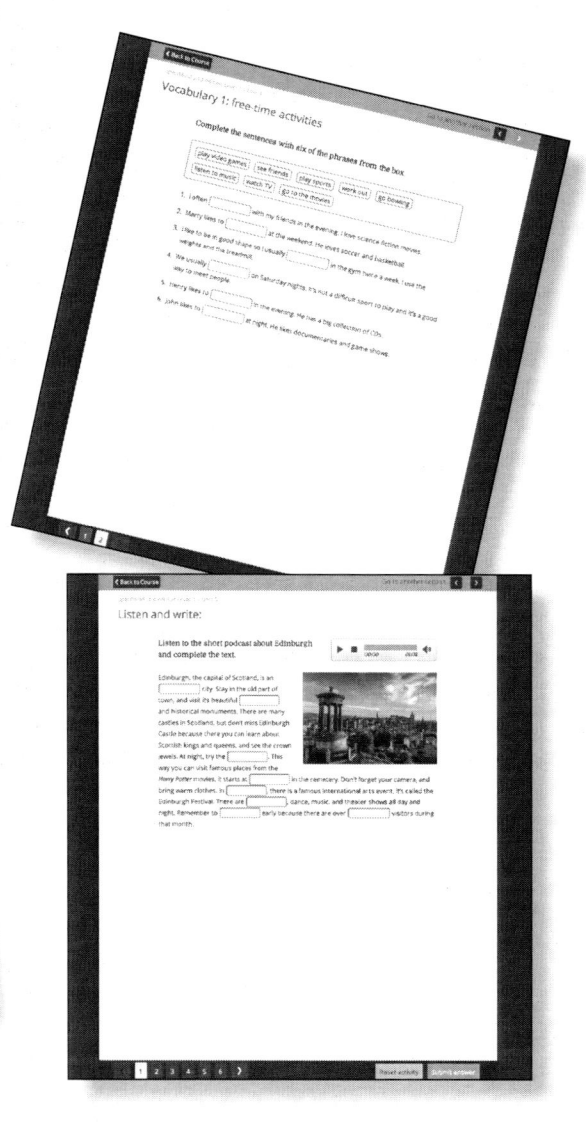

Presentation kit

The Presentation kit is a digital version of the Student's Book designed for enhanced classroom presentation. It features all the content of the print Student's Book with embedded video, class audio, full answer keys and simple interactive whiteboard tools.

Access is easy. The Presentation kit can be downloaded onto your interactive whiteboard or laptop for use with a projector – no disks are required. It's ideal for work in open class as an alternative to 'eyes down' work, as well as for checking and reviewing students' work.

Example from Open Mind *Beginner Presentation kit*

Introduction to the course xvii

Digital Student's Book

Accessed through the course website **www.macmillanopenmind.com**, this is a digital version of the Open Mind Student's Book which offers a fully-interactive learning experience for your students. Once set up, content can be accessed offline.

Audio, video and interactive versions of the activities are embedded in the pages for easy reference. Completed activities will be automatically marked and scores will be synced to the teacher Score Report when online.

In addition, the Digital Student's Book has a selection of user-friendly annotation options such as highlighting, text boxes and writing tools. There is also a note-taking function which allows the user to add notes to activities for their own reference or add links for further study.

The Open Mind Digital Student's Book creates a content-rich, flexible and interactive learning environment for your students and enables you to monitor their progress effectively and ensure they make full use of all that Open Mind has to offer.

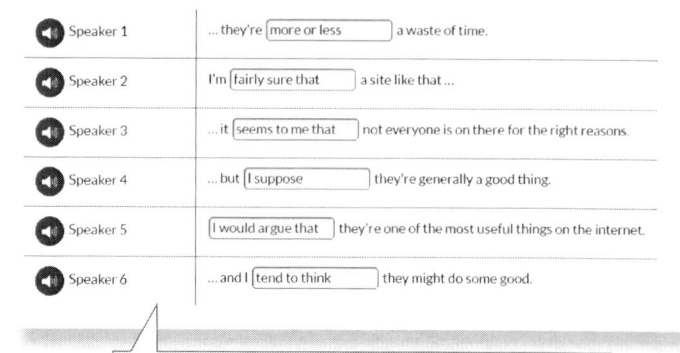

Interactive content with automatic marking.

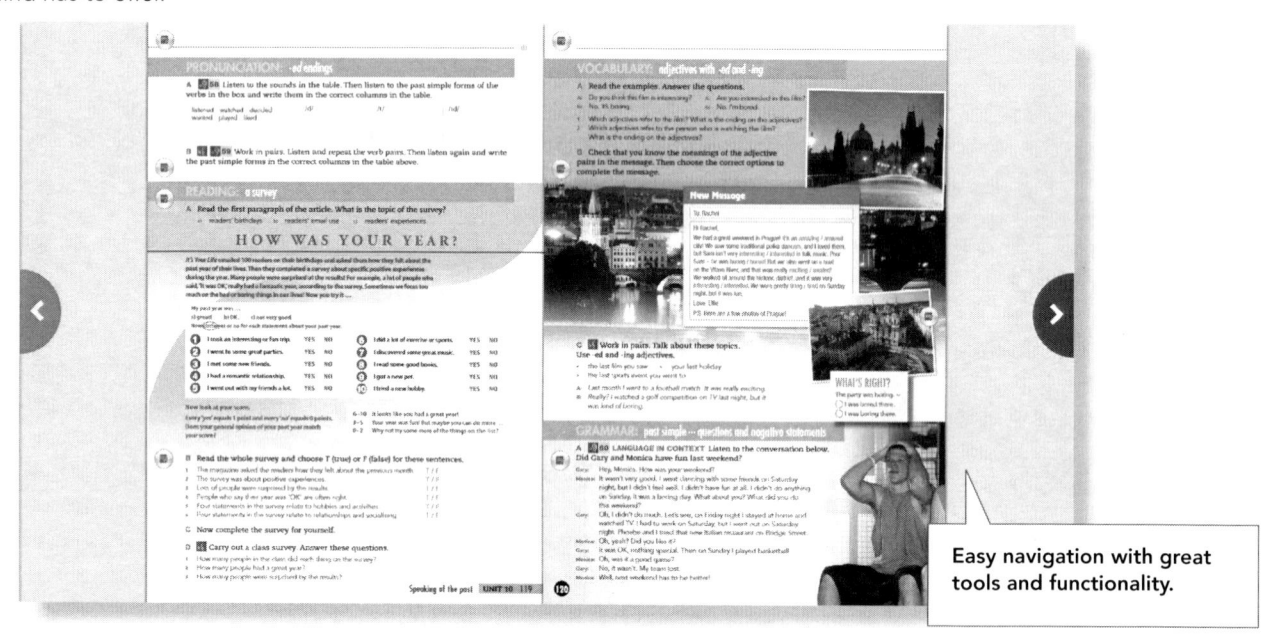

Easy navigation with great tools and functionality.

The videos provide additional and relevant content.

KAGAN STRUCTURES: A MIRACLE OF ACTIVE ENGAGEMENT*

Dr Spencer Kagan and Miguel Kagan
Kagan Publishing & Professional Development
www.KaganOnline.com

Kagan Structures are instructional strategies designed to promote cooperation and communication in the classroom, boost students' confidence and retain their interest in classroom interaction. The Structures work in all teaching contexts – regardless of subject, age group and number of students in class – and are a particularly powerful tool for teaching a foreign language.

In this article, we contrast a conventional classroom lesson and its environment to a classroom where Kagan Structures are brought in. We discuss the benefits of the Structures and explain why this alternative approach to classroom organisation works much better and has a long-term learning effect. Then, we present three of our favourite Kagan Structures that are particularly suitable for the language-learning context, and we offer you an overview and the support to apply them in your daily teaching routines.

For an in-depth presentation of the Structures and our approach to cooperative learning, you can read *Kagan Cooperative Learning* (2009).

Traditional instructional strategies vs Kagan's cooperative structures

Let's compare a typical, traditional English lesson with an English lesson using Kagan Structures. For example, we might want to teach listening for the main idea, or general comprehension.

In a traditional classroom, the teacher may have the class listen to a listening text, then do a whole-class question-and-answer session. During the question-and-answer session, the teacher usually asks questions, then has students raise their hands to volunteer answers. Alternatively, the teacher may ask a question and nominate a student to respond. Finally, the teacher may assign a comprehension activity for individual work and have the students complete it individually. Sound familiar?

Traditional learning is either whole-class, with the teacher leading the class, or independent practice work. As we'll see below, traditional learning lacks a high level of active engagement, creates a more intimidating learning environment and often fails to establish an effective communicative context for natural language acquisition.

Cooperative learning offers a powerful alternative for language teaching – interaction! Many teachers believe they are doing cooperative learning by introducing pair and group work. However, unstructured pair and group work lacks the basic principles of effective cooperative learning and therefore does not produce the gains of true cooperative learning. There is a vast difference between Kagan Structures and conventional pair or group work. Kagan Structures carefully engineer student interaction to maximise cooperation, communication and active engagement by all.

The teacher who is fluent with a number of Kagan Structures would teach the same lesson quite differently. She would likely still provide some direct instruction, but skip the whole-class question-and-answer session and not do the individual exercise. Instead, she would choose a Kagan Structure that will involve everyone, and encourage sharing and cooperation. On the subject of listening for the main idea, the teacher might have the students do *RallyRead* – students work in pairs and take turns to read part of a reading text, switching after an assigned amount of text or time. Partner A reads for a specified period while Partner B listens actively. Partner A asks questions to check Partner B's general comprehension of the passage. Or *Timed Pair Share* could be used to practise listening for the main idea. Pairs take turns to talk about a topic for a specified period of time. Their partner must listen attentively.

> *Kagan Structures carefully engineer student interaction to maximise cooperation, communication and active engagement by all.*

Choosing a cooperative learning structure over traditional methods creates a dramatic positive difference in English language learning. We now know that there are many styles of learning and multiple intelligences. What works for some may not work well for everyone. Therefore, we need a variety of strategies to reach and teach our students with different learning styles and intelligences. If we always use lectures and independent exercises, we may inadvertently create barriers to English learning for many students. If, instead, we use a variety of structures as we teach, we engage the different learning styles and students' multiple intelligences. The variety creates greater novelty, increases motivation and maintains attention. Kagan Structures also create greater engagement, lower anxiety and promote natural language acquisition. Let's see how.

---

* The Publishers would like to thank Dr Spencer Kagan and Miguel Kagan of Kagan Publishing & Professional Development for developing this article for *Open Mind*. Ownership of the copyright remains with the authors.

Cooperative learning increases engagement for everyone

One attribute that sets cooperative structures apart from traditional instruction is that structures don't call for voluntary participation. In the traditional classroom, the teacher asks students a question, and only those who know the answer, or who are daring enough to respond, raise their hands. The rest of the class can opt out.

When students have the option of non-participation, many don't participate. This is especially true for shy students, lower achievers and early language learners. The result: they don't learn as much or as quickly.

With Kagan Structures, participation is not voluntary. Participation is required by the Structure. In *RallyRead*, students take turns to read a text. With *Timed Pair Share*, students must talk for equal amounts of time. In the traditional classroom, the structure does not require participation from every student. It is the same when *RallyRead* is used for pair work. If pair work is not structured properly, one student can simply do the work, while the other student watches, or even tunes out. In contrast, the Structures hold every student individually accountable for participating. There is a direct connection between student participation, engagement, communication and subsequent language learning.

> *There is a direct connection between student participation, engagement, communication and subsequent language learning.*

In the traditional classroom, when one student answers at a time, the ratio of active engagement is quite low. What's more, the rest of the class sits quietly and there is very little involvement. During our cooperative learning practice, the class is divided into pairs, and at least half of the class is generating language at any time and the other half is directly receiving comprehensible input and practising active listening. This radically increases the opportunity to decode and produce language.

Cooperative learning lowers anxiety

Learning and using a foreign language can be stressful. In the traditional English classroom, the teacher quizzes students in front of the entire class. Students may not know the correct answer, may be apprehensive about speaking in public or may be self-conscious about their accent. In global surveys, public speaking ranks as people's greatest fear, beating fear of death, spiders, flying and confined spaces. Whole-class settings for language learning are often perceived as threatening situations. We know from both language learning theory and brain research that stress negatively impacts on attitudes, learning and memory.

With *RallyRead* and *Timed Pair Share*, students are working with just one other student. Most Structures encourage pair work or work in teams of four.

Students who would experience anxiety in a whole-class setting feel more comfortable speaking English in a more intimate setting. Cooperative groups are less intimidating than whole-class settings. This is especially true in cooperative classrooms in which the teacher uses team building to establish trust and encourage support among teammates.

Cooperative learning promotes natural language acquisition

There's a big difference between learning about a language and actually acquiring the language. Too many language courses teach students about the language. Not enough courses allow students to actually use the language in a functional way. In our example of the traditional classroom, students learn about listening for the main idea. They learn to correctly complete a comprehension exercise. But are they really learning effective language use? Results say no.

In the real world, we don't complete exercises on our comprehension of something. But we often do need to understand the main idea of what's being said in many situations.

When the situation of language acquisition (exercise work) is too different from the situation of performance (listening for the main idea), a transference gap is created. *RallyRead* sidesteps the transference gap: the situation of acquisition (listening for the main idea) matches the future situation of performance (listening for the main idea). Many Kagan Structures naturally develop fluency by sidestepping the transference gap.

Too often, language courses fail to build functional fluency. Students learn how to conjugate verbs, memorise vocabulary and learn grammar rules, but too often miss out on the opportunity to use language frequently in a functional way. With the Structures, students not only learn about language, but they actually implement it to accomplish a goal. Natural language acquisition among infants is based on frequent social interaction. Cooperative structures provide the social setting for language use and offer students many more opportunities to receive input, interact in the target language and practise oral production of the language.

Many Structures for many language-teaching objectives

Developing English fluency consists of four major interrelated language objectives: we want to build oral comprehension skills, so students can understand what they hear; we want to build oral fluency skills, so students can communicate with others; we want to build writing skills, so students can express themselves clearly and correctly; we want to build reading skills, so students can read with comprehension and accuracy.

To accomplish these four language goals – reading, writing, speaking and listening – we need an array of teaching tools. That's exactly what Kagan Structures are. Each Structure is a different language-teaching tool designed to develop different skills. Some Structures are more suitable to build listening skills (e.g. *RallyRead*). Others are ideal for practising language skills such as comprehension and fluency (e.g. *Talking Chips*).

A wonderful feature of the Kagan Structures is that they are instructional strategies that can be used repeatedly.

Many Structures simultaneously address multiple objectives that go beyond the four language objectives outlined above.

We have developed over 200 Kagan Structures for promoting interaction in the classroom. Because cooperation and communication are two hallmarks of the Kagan Structures, they are particularly well adapted to English learning. A wonderful feature of the Kagan Structures is that they are instructional strategies that can be used repeatedly. They are not limited to one particular exercise, but are designed as shells so you can slot in any activities and target language. Once you learn some basic Structures, you can integrate them easily into your daily English lessons. For example, you may use *RallyRead* today for reading for the main idea, but you can use it again tomorrow for general reading fluency and comprehension work.

Please refer to the Teacher's Resource Centre for three sample Kagan Structures to experiment with.

About the authors

Dr Spencer Kagan is an internationally acclaimed researcher, public speaker and author of over 100 books, chapters and journal articles. He is a former clinical psychologist and full professor of psychology and education at the University of California. He is the principal author of the single most comprehensive book for educators in each of four fields: cooperative learning, multiple intelligences, classroom discipline and classroom energisers. Dr Kagan developed the concept of structures; his popular brain-based, cooperative learning and multiple intelligences structures like *Numbered Heads Together* and *Timed Pair Share* are used in teacher-training institutes and classrooms worldwide. He has taught workshops and given keynote speeches in over 20 countries, and his books are translated into many languages. Dr Kagan has been featured in leading educational magazines, including *Educational Leadership, Instructor, Learning Magazine,* and *Video Journal*.

Miguel Kagan is Executive Director of Kagan Publishing & Professional Development, an educational organisation that offers publications and workshops on cooperative learning, language learning and active engagement. Miguel, together with Dr Kagan, coauthored a radical revision of the classic book, *Kagan Cooperative Learning*. Miguel has also written, designed and developed a multitude of books, SmartCards, software programs, learning games and electronic devices for Kagan Publishing. He is the editor of *Kagan Online Magazine*, Kagan's e-zine that offers articles, research and tips for educators implementing Kagan Structures.

References

High, Julie (1993). *Second Language Learning Through Cooperative Learning*. San Clemente, CA: Kagan Publishing. This book applies Kagan Cooperative Learning Structures to language learning.

Kagan, Spencer & Kagan, Miguel (2009). *Kagan Cooperative Learning*. San Clemente, CA: Kagan Publishing. This is a recent revision of Dr Kagan's classic book on cooperative learning. It is the most popular and comprehensive book in the field.

Kagan, Miguel (2009). *Match Mine Language Builders*. San Clemente, CA: Kagan Publishing. Based on the Structure *Match Mine*, this book contains 30 ready-made cooperative learning games covering common vocabulary words and concepts.

STUDENT'S BOOK SCOPE AND SEQUENCE

	READING	LISTENING	SPEAKING	WRITING
UNIT 1 **MONEY-FREE**	TEXT ORGANISATION: a feature article	Listening to a radio interview FUNCTION talking about bartering	HEDGING: a university campus survey on the use of freecycling websites	Writing *offer* and *wanted* adverts FUNCTION describing items for sale WRITING WORKSHOP FUNCTION writing a proposal
UNIT 2 **WATCH THIS SPACE ...**	Reading an online article FUNCTION talking about an innovation inspired by science fiction	UNDERSTANDING NATIVE ENGLISH SPEAKERS: short monologues	Talking about the possibility of life on other planets SPEAKING WORKSHOP FUNCTION describing a picture	OUTLINING: writing an essay outline
UNIT 3 **PASSWORD PROTECTED**	✪ TEXT ORGANISATION: an online article	Listening to an interview FUNCTION talking about identity theft	PARTICIPATING IN A GROUP DISCUSSION: a discussion about online privacy	Writing a persuasive email FUNCTION persuading readers to share your view WRITING WORKSHOP FUNCTION writing a far-and-against essay
UNIT 4 **A NEW LOOK AT LEARNING**	Reading a statistics-based argument FUNCTION talking about soft skills	✪ UNDERSTANDING NON-NATIVE ENGLISH SPEAKERS: short conversations	Talking about educational alternatives SPEAKING WORKSHOP FUNCTION expressing and supporting personal preferences	SENTENCE VARIETY: writing a personal essay for a university application
UNIT 5 **ON THE WILD SIDE**	UNDERSTANDING DEFINITIONS: a current affairs magazine article	Listening to a story FUNCTION talking about animal welfare and conservation	SUMMARISING: online comments about keeping wild animals as pets	Writing a letter to a newspaper editor FUNCTION using arguments to support an opinion WRITING WORKSHOP FUNCTION writing a formal email request
UNIT 6 **MORE THAN MACHINES?**	Reading an online news article FUNCTION talking about robots in the workplace	INFERRING OPINIONS: a conversation about artificial intelligence	Talking about automation SPEAKING WORKSHOP FUNCTION comparing and contrasting photographs	SUMMARISING: writing a summary of an online article

PRONUNCIATION	GRAMMAR	VOCABULARY	LIFESKILLS
WORDS: intonation and attitude	**ADVERB PHRASES** **FUNCTION** giving additional information **NEGATIVE QUESTIONS** **FUNCTION** confirming an existing belief	**CONSUMERISM AND SUSTAINABILITY** **FUNCTION** discussing ways to reduce consumption **DESCRIBING USED ITEMS** **FUNCTION** posting adverts on a website	**SELF AND SOCIETY:** Building communities **FUNCTION** creating a new community
WORDS: contrastive stress	**FUTURE PASSIVE** **FUNCTION** talking about inventions of the future **CONDITIONAL CONJUNCTIONS** **FUNCTION** talking about space programmes of the future	**BUSINESS AND INNOVATION** **FUNCTION** talking about how companies launch innovations **NEGATIVE PREFIXES:** *UN-, IN-, IM-* **FUNCTION** talking about space exploration	**STUDY AND LEARNING:** Evaluating explanations **FUNCTION** distinguishing between correlation and causation
WORDS: connected speech — final consonant sound to first vowel sound	**OBJECT COMPLEMENTS** **FUNCTION** talking about data security **NEGATIVE STRUCTURES WITH** *THINK, SUPPOSE,* ETC **FUNCTION** giving opinions on online privacy	**DIGITAL PRIVACY** **FUNCTION** talking about online privacy issues **PHRASAL VERBS** **FUNCTION** talking about identity theft	**SELF AND SOCIETY:** Protecting digital privacy **FUNCTION** giving advice
SOUNDS: vowel length before final consonant sounds	**RELATIVE PRONOUNS WITH** *-EVER* **FUNCTION** talking about online study **MIXED CONDITIONALS** **FUNCTION** talking about hypothetical situations in education	**VERB COLLOCATIONS** **FUNCTION** talking about higher education **WORDS RELATED TO** *STAND* **FUNCTION** talking about the job market	**STUDY AND LEARNING:** Anticipating cultural differences **FUNCTION** finding information needed in advance
SOUNDS: final consonant clusters	**IMPERSONAL PASSIVE** **FUNCTION** talking about beliefs **PASSIVE MODALS** **FUNCTION** giving opinions on wildlife issues	**ANIMAL RESCUE** **FUNCTION** talking about wildlife conservation **ADVERB–ADJECTIVE COLLOCATIONS** **FUNCTION** talking about wildlife population issues	**SELF AND SOCIETY:** Understanding decision-making styles **FUNCTION** making decisions as a group
SOUNDS: linking words with a /w/ or a /j/ sound	**FUTURE PERFECT** **FUNCTION** making predictions for specific times in the future **FUTURE PERFECT CONTINUOUS** **FUNCTION** predicting ongoing events at specific times in the future	**PHRASES WITH ADJECTIVE + PREPOSITION** **FUNCTION** talking about automation in vehicles **PHRASAL VERBS** **FUNCTION** talking about robots in the workplace	**STUDY AND LEARNING:** Organising an argument **FUNCTION** selecting and organising points to make

Student's Book Scope and sequence

	READING	LISTENING	SPEAKING	WRITING
UNIT 7 **THE CRITICAL CONSUMER**	UNDERSTANDING EXPLANATIONS AND EXAMPLES: a magazine article	Listening to a discussion FUNCTION talking about sustainable shopping	MODIFYING A STATEMENT: a discussion about personal finances	Offering advice FUNCTION thinking of ways to reduce consumption WRITING WORKSHOP FUNCTION interpreting charts
UNIT 8 **ARTISTIC LICENCE**	Reading an article about art FUNCTION talking about graffiti artists	INFERRING FACTUAL INFORMATION: a lecture about Surrealism	Talking about meaning in art SPEAKING WORKSHOP FUNCTION proposing a solution	WRITING A REVIEW: giving information and opinions on an event
UNIT 9 **JUST PLAYING?**	UNDERSTANDING INTENT: a magazine article	Listening to a radio talk show FUNCTION talking about how children's play has changed	MAKING AND RESPONDING TO INVITATIONS: formal and informal conversations inviting people to do things	Writing a short article FUNCTION giving an opinion on a controversial issue WRITING WORKSHOP FUNCTION writing a short article
UNIT 10 **FACT OR FICTION**	Reading a wiki entry FUNCTION talking about popular beliefs	DIFFICULT SITUATIONS: a conversation about viral loops on social media	Talking about popular beliefs SPEAKING WORKSHOP FUNCTION responding with an opinion	WRITING A WIKI ENTRY: writing in collaboration with others
UNIT 11 **MUSIC TO MY EARS**	UNDERSTANDING INTENT: a magazine article	Listening to an informal discussion FUNCTION talking about musical intelligence	SOFTENING LANGUAGE FOR REFUSALS: an informal discussion about downloading music	Posting an opinion FUNCTION writing a response to someone else's opinion WRITING WORKSHOP FUNCTION writing a review
UNIT 12 **DOWN TO EARTH**	Reading a feature article FUNCTIONS talking about man-made environmental changes	DIFFICULT SITUATIONS: a conversation about geology	Talking about a mysterious phenomenon SPEAKING WORKSHOP FUNCTION giving a mini-presentation	WRITING AN EDITORIAL: giving an opinion on a current affairs issue

PRONUNCIATION	GRAMMAR	VOCABULARY	LIFESKILLS
SOUNDS: /ʌ/, /ʊ/ and /u/	REDUCED ADVERB TIME CLAUSES FUNCTION talking about food labelling and health REDUCED ADVERB CAUSE-EFFECT CLAUSES FUNCTION talking about consumption and the environment	ADJECTIVES ENDING IN -ABLE/-IBLE FUNCTION talking about sustainable shopping and consumption MONEY AND FINANCES FUNCTION talking about personal finance	WORK AND CAREER: Evaluating claims FUNCTION identifying and testing claims
WORDS: words ending in -ical	INVERTED CONDITIONALS FUNCTION talking about hypothetical situations in a formal context ADJECTIVE PHRASE + INDIRECT QUESTION FUNCTION talking about non-permanent art	DESCRIBING ART FUNCTION talking about meaning and influences in art NEGATIVE PREFIXES: UN-, NON-, MIS-, IM-, IN- FUNCTION talking about opinions on art	SELF AND SOCIETY: Developing curiosity FUNCTION learning about the importance of curiosity
SOUNDS: assimilation	THE SUBJUNCTIVE FUNCTION talking about requests, orders and recommendations in the workplace ALTERNATIVES TO THE SUBJUNCTIVE FUNCTION talking about brain training	CHILDHOOD DEVELOPMENT FUNCTION talking about how children learn and develop MAKING AND RESPONDING TO INVITATIONS FUNCTION making, accepting and declining invitations	WORK AND CAREER: Recognising contradiction FUNCTION identifying points in an argument that contradict each other
WORDS: thought groups	INVERSION WITH NEGATIVE EXPRESSIONS FUNCTION talking about conspiracy theories ELLIPSIS AND SUBSTITUTION FUNCTION talking about internet scams	FALSEHOOD FUNCTION talking about things that aren't true or real WORD FORMS (PROVING AND DISPROVING) FUNCTION talking about proving and disproving claims	STUDY AND LEARNING: Evaluating internet source reliability FUNCTION checking the reliability of websites
SOUNDS: intonation in cleft sentences	PAST TENSE FOR UNREAL SITUATIONS FUNCTION talking about hypothetical situations related to music CLEFT SENTENCES FUNCTION talking about musicians	IDIOMATIC EXPRESSIONS WITH TAKE FUNCTION talking about perceptions of famous musicians SHARING MUSIC FUNCTION talking about ways of sharing music electronically	SELF AND SOCIETY: Identifying bias FUNCTION recognising views that are not balanced or fair
SOUNDS: stress shifts in parts of speech	PARTICIPLE CLAUSES FUNCTION talking about travel destinations IMPERSONAL PASSIVE IN THE PAST FUNCTION talking about natural disasters	ADVERBIAL MODIFIERS FUNCTION describing an unusual place GEOLOGY FUNCTION talking about geological phenomena	WORK AND CAREER: Maximising your potential FUNCTION assessing and developing hard and soft skills

Student's Book Scope and sequence

GRAMMAR REVIEW AND REFERENCE

Grammar review

This Grammar review has been included to help you establish what your students already know before they start *Open Mind Advanced*. It is designed to be used in the first lesson of the course and has a twofold aim: firstly, as an introductory activity to help you get to know your students; and secondly, as a way to establish the general level of the class. It also provides a useful recap of rubrics and classroom language.

The Grammar review can be used in a variety of different ways. It can be done individually, as a formal diagnostic test, to check that students have been placed at the correct level. A more interactive approach would be to elicit the answer to the first question of each exercise as a class and then have the students complete the rest of the exercise individually.

Answers for the Grammar review can be found on p. 180 of the Student's Book. You can choose to check answers after each exercise or at the end of the review. If you wish, the exercises can be exploited further, and ideas for some of them are given below.

1 (*would, used to, be + always + -ing; be used to / get used to; possessive apostrophe*)
- Check that the students understand that they need to add or change one word in each sentence.
- In item 2, students need to read the second sentence to work out that the answer is not *used to speak* (past habit) but *is used to speaking* (being familiar with something).

2 (past modals of deduction)
- Remind the students that *might*, *may* and *could* can have the same meaning, and that all of them may be possible answers in some of the items.
- Check that students understand the meaning of *vanished* in item 4 (disappeared suddenly).

3 (ways of talking about the future, past perfect vs past perfect continuous, the passive)
- If students are struggling with item 4, remind them that we use the continuous form when we want to emphasise the duration of an activity.
- Follow up: Using item 3 as an example, have the students discuss with a partner what they hope will be happening this time next year.

4 (review of past tenses)
- If the students are struggling, tell them they need to change the verbs in brackets into one of three verb forms: past simple, past continuous or past perfect.

5 (reported speech – modal verbs and past perfect, optional back-shifting)
- Check that the students understand they need to write their answers with and without back-shifting in the items where this is possible (items 2, 3 and 4).
- Check that the students know to continue the sentence stems starting with the verb in brackets.

6 (verb + gerund/infinitive with a change in meaning, gerunds after prepositions)
- If the students are struggling, tell them that gerunds often follow verb and adjective phrases: verb + preposition (+ gerund), adjective + preposition (+ gerund).

7 (expressions of purpose)
- Check that the students understand that more than one answer may be possible.
- Follow up: Ask the students to make sentences using each of the words from the box and their own ideas.

8 (*be used to / get used to*)
- Check that the students understand that they need to use the correct form of the verb in brackets as well as the correct form of either *be used to* or *get used to*.
- Encourage the students to use contractions where possible.

9 (review of conditional forms)
- Check that the students know that it may be possible to use modal verbs other than *will/would* (as in items 5 and 6), and that in such cases, more than one modal verb may be possible.
- Check that the students understand the meaning of *calorie intake* in item 5 (the amount of energy that you get from food and drink).

10 (expressing ability, connectors of contrast, verb + object + infinitive, repeated and double comparatives)
- Check that the students know to use the correct form of the word in brackets.
- If the students are struggling with item 4, tell them that *despite* should go at the beginning of the first clause.

11 (noun clauses as objects)
- Check that the students know that each word is to be used once.
- In item 2, the students need to read the second sentence to know that the answer is *when*.

12 (connectors of contrast, connectors of addition / cause and effect)
- Check that the students understand that they need to identify the one *incorrect* option.
- Follow up: Put the students into small groups and have them discuss item 2. What else has the internet made easier?

Grammar reference

The Grammar reference provides further consolidation of the grammar points covered in each unit. It can be found on pp. 152–165 of the Student's Book, and the answer key on pp. 182–183. For each grammar point, there are clear notes and tables outlining the form and function, as well as two exercises providing further practice. It is designed to be done on a unit-by-unit basis and can either be covered as part of the unit, as a follow-up to each Grammar section, or at the end of the unit in a test format.

UNIT 1 MONEY-FREE

The expression *money-free* means without money. A money-free society is one that functions without money. Other expressions with the suffix *-free* include *lead-free* (paint that does not contain lead), *sugar-free* (food that does not contain sugar) and many additional words such as *duty-free, tax-free, fat-free, gluten-free, toll-free, interest-free, hands-free* and *stress-free*.

Unit plan

Unit opener	(p. 8)	20 min.
1 **Reading:** text organisation	(p. 10)	30 min.
• Vocabulary: consumerism and sustainability		15 min.
2 **Pronunciation:** intonation and attitude	(p. 11)	15 min.
3 **Grammar:** adverb phrases	(p. 12)	40 min.
4 **Writing:** *offer* and *wanted* adverts	(p. 13)	30 min.
• Vocabulary: describing used items		15 min.
5 **Speaking:** hedging	(p. 13)	30 min.
6 **Grammar:** negative questions	(p. 14)	40 min.
7 **Listening:** to a radio interview	(p. 15)	30 min.
LifeSkills: building communities (Self and Society)	(p. 16)	50 min.
• Optional downloadable *LifeSkills* lesson (Work and Career)		50 min.
• Optional downloadable *LifeSkills* lesson (Study and Learning)		50 min.
Language wrap-up	(p. 18)	20 min.
Writing workshop: writing a proposal	(p. 19)	30 min.
Video and downloadable video worksheet		45 min.

Unit opener (p. 8)

Lead-in

Ask the students to look at the unit title and the photos and to predict what the unit will be about. Elicit the meaning of the title using the ideas in the panel under the title on this page. Direct the students' attention to the points in the unit objectives box and go through the information with them. To get your students to think about the skills being developed in this unit, ask them to look at the questions in the cogs.

Reading: text organisation

- Ask the students to think about why the way a text is organised is important. Elicit that how a text is organised helps readers to understand and follow it. Have the students brainstorm elements of a well-organised text: *main idea, paragraph structure, topic sentences, supporting details, examples, conclusion*.

Speaking: hedging

- Ask the students to discuss why it might be important to present opinions less forcefully or directly (*to avoid sounding rude or offending someone, to allow for possible errors*, etc). Explain that this is what *hedging* means. Elicit words and phrases that are used to *hedge*.

LifeSkills: building communities

- Refer the students to the *LifeSkills* panel. Ask them to name communities they belong to in addition to their English class (*family/extended family, school clubs, sports teams, groups*, etc).

Common European Framework: unit map

Unit 1	Competence developed	CEF Reference (C1 competences)
Reading	can use text organisation to aid understanding	Table 1; Table 2; Sections 4.4.2.2; 4.4.2.4; 4.5.2.2
Pronunciation	can correctly use intonation to convey attitude	Section 5.2.1.4
Grammar	can use and understand adverb phrases	Table 1; Table 2; Sections 5.2.1.2; 6.4.7.7; 6.4.7.8
Writing	can write a short advert for an item	Table 1; Table 2; Sections 4.4.1.2; 4.5.2.1; 5.2.1.1; 5.2.1.2; 5.2.1.6; 5.2.3.2
Speaking	can use hedging phrases to express polite opinions	Table 1; Table 2; Sections 4.4.1.1; 4.4.3.1; 4.4.3.5; 4.5.2.1; 5.2.2.2; 5.2.3.2
Grammar	can use and understand negative questions	Table 1; Table 2; Sections 4.4.1.1; 4.4.3.1; 5.2.1.2; 6.4.7.7; 6.4.7.8
Listening	can understand a radio interview	Table 1; Table 2; Sections 4.4.2.1; 4.4.3.1; 4.4.3.5; 4.5.2.2

A

- Direct the students' attention to the instructions and the example conversation.
- Put the students in pairs. Ask them to discuss each of the four photos and decide what message about money they might convey. Then ask them to identify evidence in the photos to show that the set could be used to contrast poverty and wealth. Ask students if they feel that the photos show the merits of a simple life as opposed to a materialistic one, giving reasons for their choices. Explain that *materialism* occurs when people value material objects more than social or spiritual values, and that this theme will be explored in detail in the reading and throughout the unit.
- Explain that some items are *necessities* and some items are *luxuries*. Ask pairs to name one basic item in their lives that they need and one luxury item that they enjoy having even if they don't really need it. What makes each item a luxury item? Is there a basic version of the luxury item that costs less and can be used for the same purpose? Are there possible scenarios that could turn any of their luxury items into a necessity and any of their necessary items into a luxury?

Culture note

In many countries, including the UK, there is a widespread culture of buying used goods, for example through adverts in the newspaper; via auction sites on the internet; or in second-hand shops. Some people even retrieve useful items from rubbish bins, skips or recycling centres, thereby reusing objects and minimising their own participation in what they feel is a wasteful consumer society. In some parts of the world, however, new items are valued highly, while second-hand items are disregarded or considered a sign of not having money or status.

B

- Put the students in pairs to imagine what kind of advertising campaign each photo in Ex. A might be used for. Then have them write a short advertising caption for each photo. Ask the pairs to share their captions with another pair.
- Ask the class to suggest ways in which advertising campaigns convince customers to buy certain items. What techniques do they use to turn a luxury item into a perceived necessity? Prompt the students by eliciting/ suggesting a few ways in which this might happen (e.g. using physically attractive models or celebrities to showcase the items; making items seem fashionable, desirable or even essential for everyday use; connecting a certain image or lifestyle to the product; using peer pressure as a marketing strategy).

Extra: speaking

Have the students work in small groups to discuss the role brand names play in their choice of various products. (Encourage them to think of a range of items, from laundry detergent to jeans to technology.) In each case, ask whether they would value a basic version of an item as much as they would value the brand item. When the groups finish, have a discussion with the whole class, eliciting opinions from all the groups. Focus the students' contributions on why the perceived value would go up or down depending on the brand.

Reading: text organisation (p. 10)

Lead-in

Ask the students to read the information in the skills panel. Then ask them to think about what makes a text well-organised. (*There should be a clear logical and structural link between the paragraphs in a text and between the sentences in each paragraph; information should be arranged logically to establish and support the argument;* etc.) Point out that each paragraph in a text usually consists of a main idea followed by supporting information. The main idea is usually contained in a sentence called the *topic sentence*. The topic sentence is usually (but not always) the first sentence in each paragraph. **Highlight** that the sentences in each paragraph are usually arranged in a logical order, and that this connection is often signalled by linking words. Sometimes the topic sentence is followed by examples and explanations. Sometimes examples are given before the topic sentence, with details following afterwards. Point out that paragraphs in a text are usually arranged in a similar way to sentences in a paragraph: the main idea in each paragraph is connected logically with the main idea in the following paragraph. Words like *so, therefore, for example, however,* etc explain the logical relationship between sentences in a paragraph or between paragraphs in the whole text.

A

- Ask the students to look at the online article and guess what it is about. Elicit responses from the class and ask them to justify their opinions.
- Direct the students' attention to the questions. Give them time to read the article, keeping the questions in mind.
- Discuss the answers with the class. Point out that physical clues often help in identifying the main ideas in a text. For example, the answer to the first question is in a sentence below the title. Point out that noticing the title and summary sentences is a useful strategy to get a quick gist of the text. Also explain that the first sentence in the main text is a *hook* – it attracts the reader's attention with a surprising or interesting statement and makes them want to read the rest of the text.

Answer

Mark Boyle is a person who did not use cash for two-and-a-half years while living in a caravan. He wanted to see the consequences of his actions as a consumer.

Extra: discussion

Put the students in small groups to discuss their opinions on Mark's experiment. Do they think it was worthwhile or pointless? Do they think that they could try a similar experiment? What would they give up, and for how long? When the groups finish, extend the discussion with the whole class, eliciting opinions from various groups and reasons for the opinions. To conclude, take a vote by a show of hands to find out how most students answered the first question.

▶ Workbook p. 4, Section 1

▶ Workbook p. 5, Section 2

B

- Have the students work individually to read the text again and insert the sentences into the correct gaps. Ask them to keep track of the kinds of clues they use to work out where each sentence goes.
- Check answers with the class.

Answers
1 e 2 c 3 b 4 d 5 a

C

- Put the students in pairs to discuss what clues they used to complete Ex. B.
- When they finish, elicit different ways in which each pair used both language and logic to solve the problem of sentence placement in each paragraph and within the text as a whole (*context clues, meaning, specific words, paragraph structure, logical connection between ideas*, etc). Ask the students to be as concise as possible in explaining how they made each decision, and to be prepared to identify specific evidence in the text that contributed to those decisions (e.g. *the last sentence in paragraph 3 mentions bread, and in Ex. B item (d) mentions loaf, so this specific word should refer to the bread mentioned in the previous sentence*).

Answers

1. At this point in the text, the writer is talking about the relationship between the consumer and the thing consumed. Sentence e goes on to give further information about that subject.
2. The writer is talking about things he got for free (a caravan, a place to park it). He then contrasts this with something he had to pay for in sentence c. To show this contrast, he uses the emphatic form: *The one thing I did buy …*
3. The writer is listing aspects of his life and things he used in place of things he would have normally bought. Sentence b continues the list.
4. At this point in the text, the writer is contrasting buying bread with making your own bread. Sentence d goes on to give further information about that subject.
5. The writer is talking about the response to his experiment. Sentence a talks about one aspect of people's response.

D

- Have the students work individually to match the words and definitions in Ex. D. Circulate and give help as needed.
- Put the students in pairs to compare answers.

Answers
1 b 2 h 3 d 4 a 5 f 6 c 7 g 8 e

E

- Ask the students to read the questions and check they understand the vocabulary.
- Put the students in small groups to discuss the questions. Set a time limit for the discussion.
- To conclude, extend the discussion with the whole class.

Alternative

Assign one question to each group for their discussion, or ask each group to choose one question they want to discuss. Then have each group report the highlights of their discussion to the class.

Pronunciation: intonation and attitude (p. 11)

A 1.01

- See the Student's Book page for the **audioscript**.
- Write the sentence that students are about to hear on the board. (*You're really good at saving money.*) Ask several students to read it in different ways. For example, ask one student to read the sentence using a tone of surprise. Explain that tone can bring differences in meaning to a sentence. Ask the students to provide some context for the way they read the statement. Direct the students' attention to the instructions. Ask the students to listen carefully to the audio of the same sentence read in three different ways.
- Play the audio. Ask the students to practise repeating the different intonations as closely as they can. Elicit what each of the different intonations might mean, and ask the students to say why.
- Explain/elicit the following possible contexts for each sentence on the audio. First sentence: A friend has just spent a lot of money on clothes at a shop and is telling you about the discounts she received and how much money she thinks she has saved. You think she has spent too much money, and you respond in an ironic/sarcastic tone: *Yes, you're really good at saving money*. Second sentence: You know your friend typically asks you to lend him money at the end of the week before he gets paid. He tells you he is good at managing and saving money. You respond in a doubtful, questioning tone: *You're really good at saving money*. Third sentence: You are amazed at how much money your friend has saved on monthly expenses, and you say in surprise, *You're really good at saving money*.

- Explain that every statement has a literal meaning. In this case, the speaker states that the listener is good at saving money. **Highlight** that intonation can change the literal meaning of the sentence to make it imply different things, like doubt, sarcasm or surprise. The use of intonation can change the literal meaning of the statement into a statement with a very different meaning. So, *how* someone says something can actually change *what* they say.

B 1.02

- See the Student's Book page for the **audioscript**.
- Write the two sentences on the board and direct the students' attention to them. Have the students listen to the audio. Ask the students to practise saying each sentence three times, in a doubtful, surprised and sarcastic way.
- Put the students in pairs and direct their attention to the instructions. In each pair, have one student choose one way to say each sentence and have the other guess which attitude the speaker is showing from the intonation. Then have them exchange roles. Circulate and help as needed. Then check their responses as a class.

Grammar: adverb phrases (p. 12)

Lead-in
Ask the students what they would do with an item that was still functional but that they no longer needed or used often (*an old but working TV set, shoes that have gone out of fashion, etc*). Elicit several answers.

A
- Direct the students' attention to the instructions and the article. Make sure they understand how to identify the main idea in a text by skimming for important points.
- Have the students read the text quickly to find the answer. Wait until all the students finish, but elicit the answer from the student who finished first.
- Direct the students' attention to the title of the article. Explain that, in this case, *want* is used in a way that means *to want for something*, or *to lack something*. The title could be paraphrased as *Don't waste anything, and you won't lack anything (with Freecycle)*.

Answer
The purpose of Freecycle is to help people to get rid of things they no longer need or want and find items they need or want that other people don't want any more.

Culture note
Freecycle groups exist worldwide. There are over 5,000 groups in more than 85 countries, with over seven million members signed up. Freecycle's official slogan is 'Changing the world one gift at a time'.

NOTICE!
- Direct the students' attention to the **Notice!** box.
- Ask them to find the two phrases, and elicit the answers.

Answers
Last week; by signing up online

B

Form
- Ask the students to read the text again, this time carefully.
- Focus the students' attention on the five different types of adverbs in the grammar table. **Highlight** the fact that each type of adverb answers a different question *When? How often? Where? How?* and *Why?)*. Have them look back at Ex. A and find the adverb phrases that complete the sentences.
- Check answers with the class.

Answers
1 Last week 2 every day 3 out of landfills
4 By distributing items to people who want them
5 by signing up online
6 to give away and get things in their local communities

Function
- Have the students read the instructions and fill in the gaps with the question words from the box.

Answers
1 when 2 how often 3 where 4 how 5 why

C
- Direct the students' attention to the adverb phrases in the box. Ask them to decide what kind of information each adverb phrase provides and write the question words in the gaps in the box. Then have the students complete the sentences by writing one of the phrases in each gap.
- After checking the answers, elicit the type of adverb used in each of the gaps: (1) manner, (2) purpose, (3) frequency, (4) place, (5) time, (6) manner.

Answers
a when b how c how often d how e why f where

1 for free 2 for space reasons 3 Every now and then
4 in their wardrobes 5 at your convenience
6 by giving your unwanted item away

Alternative
Have the students cover the box of adverb phrases and try to complete the sentences with their own predictions first. This will encourage them to focus on the general meaning of the text. Next have them uncover the box and do the exercise again to see how accurate and appropriate their predictions were.

D

- Put the students in small groups. Have them read the questions and spend some time preparing their thoughts, making notes if they wish. Give the students time to discuss their answers. To wrap up, have a discussion with the whole class, eliciting the most interesting discussion points from each group.

Extra: homework

Put the students in pairs. Ask one of them to find an interesting news article from a newspaper or the internet, and ask the other to find an extract from a piece of fiction. Ask each of them to look through their text and underline the adverb phrases. In the next lesson, have the pairs compare their texts to see which style of writing uses more adverb phrases and which type.

▶ Workbook p. 5, Section 3

Writing: *offer* and *wanted* adverts (p. 13)

Lead-in

Ask the students to think about the items they identified in the previous section that they no longer want and would like to get rid of. Ask volunteers to tell you some of the items and make a list on the board. Then ask the rest of the class if they would like to have any of these used items for free. Leave the list on the board.

A

- Put the students in pairs. Direct their attention to the Freecycle posts and have them briefly discuss which of the two offered items they would prefer, and why.

B

- Ask the students to read the underlined words and phrases in the posts in Ex. A, and ask them to write each one next to the correct definition.
- Check answers by reading each definition aloud and having the students call out the corresponding word or phrase.

Answers

1 second-hand 2 drop it off 3 condition
4 up for grabs 5 in good working order 6 throw in

C

- Tell the students they are going to write two *offer* posts and two *wanted* posts for a freecycling website. Point out that they can use the ideas on the board if they wish. Remind them that the posts should be short and informal. Encourage them to use vocabulary from Ex. B.

- Have the students write their adverts individually on separate pieces of paper. Circulate and help with spelling and grammar as needed. Make sure that the students use vocabulary from Ex. B.
- When the students finish, have them display their posts on a classroom wall. Ask the students to read each other's adverts and find items that they would like to own, or which they have at home and could give away to a classmate. To conclude, invite the class to share their feedback.

▶ Workbook p. 6, Section 4

Speaking: hedging (p. 13)

Lead-in

Ask the students to read the information in the skills panel. Explain that the way in which we express an opinion can come across as impolite if it is worded too strongly. Write the statement *You are wrong* on the board. Explain that this shows that the speaker has no doubt that the other person is wrong, and it leaves no room for a possible mistake or difference of opinion. It is also aggressive in tone. A strong opinion can be expressed politely to show that the speaker is confident about what they say, but still acknowledges that there is reasonable room for error or disagreement. Elicit or suggest some ways to modify *You are wrong* to make it less forceful: *Well, I would disagree, simply because …; You may be right, but I think …; I'm not sure that I agree with you there …; You might have a point, but the way I see it …* Explain that often speakers also use certain words or phrases (e.g. *It seems to me that …*) to make their opinions less forceful even when they are not disagreeing with someone else. They do this to show that they are not totally confident about their opinion, and to show that there is room for disagreement.

A 🎧 1.03

- See p. 121 for the **audioscript**.
- Explain that the students will hear six people expressing their opinions about freecycling. Ask the students to listen for the hedging words and phrases each person uses and to write them in the gaps.
- Play the audio once, and give the students time to write. Play the audio again if necessary. Then elicit the answers from the class. Ask the students to think about how the way an opinion is expressed affects the way it is received.

Answers

1 more or less 2 fairly sure that 3 seems to me that
4 I suppose 5 I would argue that 6 tend to think

B

- Put the students in pairs to discuss the questions.
- If they choose, they can first try expressing their opinions very forcefully. Then have them practise using different hedging phrases to soften these opinions.

▶ Workbook pp. 6–7, Section 5

Money-free UNIT 1

Grammar: negative questions (p. 14)

Lead-in
Invite the students to imagine a world without money (i.e. no cash, cheques, credit cards, ATMs or banks). Elicit ideas about how their lives would be different.

A 🎧 1.04
- See the Student's Book page for the **audioscript**.
- Ask the students to listen to the audio and identify the answer to the question. Play the audio once. Elicit the answer.

Answer

goods and services

- Give the students time to read through the conversation. Explain that bartering is trading what you have for what you want, without using money. Point out that when we use money to buy things, we are actually using a systematised version of bartering because we are exchanging things for something everyone wants (money). The reason everyone wants money is because it can be used to get almost anything.

NOTICE!
- Direct the students' attention to the **Notice!** box. Have them identify the question and explain what makes it a negative question.
- Explain that a negative question is called a negative question because the verb appears in its negative form. Elicit examples of verbs in their negative forms (*isn't, hasn't, haven't, aren't, don't, can't, won't, wouldn't, shouldn't, couldn't, mustn't*, etc).

Answer

Isn't that a new shirt? It's a negative question because the verb *be* appears in a negative form (*Isn't*).

B
Form
- Have the students read the conversation from Ex. A again, paying attention to the negative questions.
- Have them complete the grammar table with examples from Ex. A. Then ask them to identify and underline the other negative question in the text (*didn't you say …?*).
- Check answers with the class.
- Direct students' attention to the **What's right?** box and ask them to tick the correct dialogue (*1*). Point out that contractions cannot be used in this context.

Answers

1 Didn't I 2 Haven't you 3 Isn't it
Further example: didn't you say

Function
- Direct the students' attention to the statements and have them choose the correct option to complete each explanation. Discuss the answers with the class.
- For numbers 3 and 4, explain that negative questions can be used as one way of hedging or expressing an opinion less forcefully.
- Ask the students to suggest examples of hedging phrases that use negative questions. (*Shouldn't we consider …? Wouldn't that be a problem? Couldn't they try …?* etc.) Make a list on the board.

Answers

1 Yes, it is. 2 hasn't 3 less 4 agree

C
- Ask the students to read the instructions and complete the exercise individually. Then have them compare answers in pairs.
- When the pairs finish, ask them to change their negative questions into positive questions. Elicit what they notice about the effects of this change (*positive questions are a straightforward request for information; negative questions are more complex because they include the speaker's ideas or attitudes together with a request for information*).

Answers

1 Isn't that a new hat?
2 Didn't you find anything interesting on the site?
3 Couldn't you offer your services as a mechanic?
4 Wouldn't it be easier to buy a computer from a shop?
5 Won't bartering become more common in future?

D
- Ask the students to read the instructions. Make sure they understand the task by eliciting some examples of goods (*furniture, electronics, etc*) and services (*car washing, language instruction, babysitting, etc*) they could offer. Put the students in pairs to plan their roleplay and practise it.
- Explain that the roleplay should show how they use negative questions to decide what service they want to offer. (They can also use negative questions to decide which service they want in the first place!)
- When the students finish practising their roleplays, invite several pairs to present their roleplays in front of the class. Invite feedback from the class on how to improve each conversation.

▶ Workbook p. 7, Section 6

Listening: to a radio interview (p. 15)

Lead-in
Review what *services* are with the class. Then ask the students to work in groups to brainstorm three services that could be bartered (*feeding someone's pet while they are away, organising a party, providing cleaning services, custom-made artwork*, etc). Ask the students to consider the factors that make a service more valuable (*skill level, supply and demand, experience, positive reviews from previous customers*, etc).

A
- Ask the students to look at the photos and read the questions. Put the students in pairs to discuss what they would pay for each item or service and what they have or can do that they could trade in return. When the pairs finish, extend the discussion with the whole class.

B 1.05
- See p. 121 for the **audioscript**.
- Explain that the students are going to listen to a radio interview about an organisation called Barterrific. Point out the five topics (a–e) and ask the students to predict the order in which these will be mentioned in the interview.
- Play the audio once and have the students mark the correct order.
- Check answers with the class.

Answers
a 3 b 1 c 5 d 4 e 2

C
- Have the students read the sentences and underline where they think each mistake is. Then play the audio again for them to check their work and make the corrections.
- Check answers with the class.

Answers
1 Bartering as a system is probably as old as owning things.
2 Barterrific bartered land for radio adverts.
3 About 40% of the bartering is for services.
4 Jim Telfer says that hotels have a large markup for their room rates.
5 Monetary systems create pressure and emotional stress.

D
- Put the students in small groups to discuss the questions.
- When the groups finish, extend the discussion with the whole class. Discuss any areas of disagreement for items 2 and 3. Encourage the students to use hedging expressions and polite language when discussing areas of disagreement.

Extra: listening
Write the following questions on the board. Play the audio again and have students write the answers. Check answers with the class.
1 What is Jim's role in Barterrific?
2 How much do people pay to use Barterrific?
3 How did Jim 'pay' the person who designed his website?
4 What two groups of people does Jim mention as having time to trade?
5 In the example Jim mentions, what does the hotel get in return for a room?

Answers
1 He is the person who started the website and he runs its day-to-day business.
2 People don't pay anything to use Barterrific.
3 Jim mowed the lawn for the person who designed his website.
4 students and retired people
5 The hotel gets petrol in return for a room.

Extra: discussion
Write the following statements on the board:
1 I would exchange items but not services on a bartering website.
2 I would never use a bartering website. I would only trade with friends and family.
3 I would like to try a bartering website and see if I like it.
4 I/My friends have used a bartering website and have had good/bad experiences.

Ask the students to read the four statements and choose the one that most closely matches their own opinion about bartering websites. Put the students in groups with others who share the same opinion. Give the groups time to discuss why they feel this way about bartering websites and to prepare their argument to present to the class. When they finish, ask each group to choose a spokesperson to present their argument to the class. To conclude, ask for a show of hands to see if any of the students changed their opinion as a result of the discussion.

Extra: homework
Have the students choose either item 2 or 3 and write their answers to the questions in a short paragraph. Have them share their answers with a partner in the next lesson.

Money-free UNIT 1 **7**

LifeSkills: building communities (p. 16)

Step 1: Consider the type of community you wish to create. (Ex. A, Ex. B, Ex. C)
Step 2: Decide on the community's goals and how they will be organised. (Ex. D)
Step 3: Advertise your community so interested people can join. (Ex. E)

Lead-in
Read the target skill aloud and invite the students to tell you what they think *building communities* means. Elicit how they think communities are usually built, and what they think the most important factors are when it comes to building a community. Then **highlight** the three-step strategy to develop the skill of building communities. Focus the students' attention on the dictionary entry for *community*. Point out that this definition has evolved in recent years (see *Culture note*).

Culture note
Thirty years ago, the word *neighbourhood* was a close synonym for *community* because most communities were geographical in nature (see the first part of the dictionary definition provided). However, as information and communication technology has shaped our world, the word *community* has taken on a new meaning: the positive feeling that you belong to a group (see the second part of the definition) even though the nearest member to you might be in the next town, country or continent.

A
- Put the students in pairs and give them time to read the descriptions of four different types of communities.
- Direct the students' attention to the two questions. Have them brainstorm with their partners and write their answers in note form, ready to provide feedback.
- Discuss the answers with the whole class, eliciting the students' personal examples of community membership. Consider sharing one or two of your own. Point out that these communities can overlap in some ways. For example, there are online forums focused on political or social viewpoints, or hobbies and interests.

Alternative
Have the students close their books while you read aloud the four different types of communities. Ask the students to name examples of each type of community and what brings people in each community together. Then put the students in small groups to read the descriptions and discuss the questions. Invite one person from each group to share the group's ideas with the whole class.

B
- Have the students stay in the same pairs as in Ex. A. Ask them to read the statements and work together to match them to the community descriptions in Ex. A. Point out that each statement may fit more than one description, and that the answers are fairly subjective.
- Then ask the students to discuss their answers with another pair before sharing them with the class.

Answers
1 A, B 2 C, D 3 B 4 A, B, C, D 5 C, D
6 C 7 B, D 8 A

C
- Explain to the students that the webpage text is an example of an online application form for creating a club or a community. Direct the students' attention to the phrases in the box, and make sure they understand the words and phrases. Define *community statement* as a brief description of the community, its viewpoints and its goals. Define *expenses* as how much money is spent and *funding* as how much money they (could) have. Point out that a *fundraising event* (or a *fundraiser*) is an event organised to obtain money for the community.
- Elicit the kind of community the organisers of Service Swap are trying to build (*one where members can save money by exchanging services*). Then have the students read the text and write the phrases from the box in the relevant gaps as headings. Check answers with the class.

Answers
The organisers are trying to build a community free from the pressure of money.
1 Name of community
2 Community statement
3 Potential members
4 How it works
5 Expenses and fundraising

D
- Put the students in small groups. Give them time to discuss the type of community they would like to create and think of a name, write a community statement, and decide how the community will work. They should also decide on ways to attract members and organise funding. Their community should be as interesting, relevant and appealing as possible.
- Ask each group to use these decisions to design a webpage to advertise their community on LIFTOFF. Have them use the application form in Ex. C as a model. Circulate and give help as needed.

E
- When the groups are ready, have each group introduce and describe their community to the whole class.
- Encourage the other students to ask questions and make suggestions on how to improve each group's community. When all the groups have finished, ask the students to decide which community they would like to join. (They can rank three top choices if they prefer.)
- Ask for a show of hands to find out which communities the students would like to join.

F

- Discuss the questions with the whole class. Ask the students to discuss what they learnt about community building in this lesson. (Some useful phrases: *I've learnt that …, One important thing …, One factor …, We should think about …*, etc.) Ask how what they learnt about building different communities can be useful in the domain of **Self and Society**.
- Ask the students to think about what they still need to work on in order to improve their skill of building communities. Have them make notes.
- In small groups, ask the students to discuss what kinds of communities they would like to be involved in building in the future. Then ask them to think about why those communities might be important to them and possibly to others who join them.

REFLECT

- Ask the students to read the **Reflect** question.
- Give them time to think about different situations in the domains of **Work and Career** and **Study and Learning**, where the skill of *building communities* would be useful.
- Elicit the following ideas: *to form a new club, to organise a study group, to lobby for changes to the way something is run, to organise charity events, to work on team projects, to build effective teams in the workplace, to raise awareness about an issue or a problem at school/work*, etc.

RESEARCH

- Explain the task and make sure the students understand what they have to do.
- Have the students discuss some unusual communities they know about (*groups that follow old TV shows/films, people who re-enact historical events, people who do unusual sports activities*, etc). Tell the students to begin their research online and interview community members if possible.
- Ask the students to share the results of their research with the whole class. Have them take turns presenting their example of an unusual community and relevant information about how it developed. Encourage the class to ask questions or make comments. Ask presenters to discuss any challenges they had in completing the research task and how they handled them.

Language wrap-up (p. 18)

There are several approaches that you can use for the Language wrap-up exercises:
- in class as a test
- in class as a review
- as homework

Class test

- Ask the students to do the exercises in test conditions and give a time limit (e.g. 20 minutes).
- Check answers with the class and deal with typical errors or problems.

Class review

- If you decide to do the exercises in class, you can approach the Language wrap-up as a two-step review. First, ask the students to do the Vocabulary section individually. When they finish, ask them to check their answers carefully, and then put them in pairs to compare answers and discuss any differences.
- You can then apply the same procedure to the Grammar section.
- Self- and peer-correction are two excellent ways of developing learner independence and creating a cooperative learning environment.

Homework

- If you give the exercises for homework, you can ask the students to do them in test conditions, i.e. without referring to the language they covered in the unit, their notes, the Grammar reference section, dictionaries, etc.
- Give them a time limit (e.g. 20 minutes).
- Check answers with the class in the next lesson and deal with typical errors or problems.
- The scoring system has been designed to give the students an idea of the progress they are making. Each section has a total score of 10 or 12, depending on the complexity of the language covered and the nature of the exercises. Whichever approach you take to the Language wrap-up, after checking the answers to each section, ask the students to write their score. If they have a score lower than 8 (out of 10) or 10 (out of 12), direct them to the appropriate sections of the unit and encourage them to read them again for homework. After that, ask the students to complete the exercise(s) again at home.

Alternatives

- With any of the approaches above, you can give help by looking at the exercises with the students before they start and discussing how they should go about them. For example, if they have to fill in the gaps in a text, encourage them to read through the whole text first to get an idea of the general meaning of it. If they have to choose the correct option to complete a sentence, encourage them to make sure they read the whole sentence first to understand the context.
- You can also use the Language wrap-up to review the material in the unit with the class and work on the exercises together as a class activity. In this case, you can ask the students, for example, to look back at the appropriate Grammar section in the unit and review the main points to clarify any misunderstandings before they begin an exercise. Similarly, you can ask the students to first work in pairs to check the meanings of words to be used in fill-in-the-gaps exercises in the Vocabulary section.
- Note that the more assistance you give the students, the higher the score you should expect them to get when they do the exercises.

1 Vocabulary

A

- Ask the students to read through the text before they fill in the gaps. Remind them that one word in the box is not used. Also point out that they may need to change the form of the words in the box to make the sentence grammatically correct.

B
- Have the students complete Ex. B and remind them that, this time, every word in the box must be used.

Extra: vocabulary practice
Ask the students to write sentences that are true for them for each of the following vocabulary words or phrases: *consume, in good working order, second-hand, condition.* (*My bike is in a bad* condition, *so I want to buy a new one*, etc.) Have them share their sentences with a partner.

2 Grammar
A
- Explain Ex. A to the class. Point out that the students should first work on using the prompts to write complete sentences. Then have them identify the adverb phrase in the sentence and write which question it answers.

B
- Have the students read the instructions for Ex. B. Explain that they have to change the verb into its negative form. Remind them that they may have to add one or two words to make their negative question fit grammatically into the sentence.

Writing workshop: writing a proposal (p. 19)

Lead-in
Ask the students to look at the photo and say where they think this place is (*in a university*) and what purpose it serves (*student union or café, gathering place for students*). Ask them what improvements might need to be made to this building. Explain to the students that in this workshop they are going to practise writing a proposal for making improvements to a building.

A
- Direct the students' attention to the instructions. Explain that a proposal is a written argument that puts forward a plan to achieve a goal or to solve a problem. It is usually organised by describing a problem or a related set of problems and suggesting solutions. Solutions should be practical and workable ideas for achieving the goals of the proposal. It is important that the proposal explains clearly and concisely how the problem can be solved. A proposal is usually written in a relatively formal way.
- Ask the students to read the proposal and answer the question in Ex. A. Give the students time to read. Then check the answer with the class.

Answer
The writer suggests using freecycling websites to obtain furniture and using the services of students to improve the decor.

B
- Have the students read the instructions. Explain the vocabulary in Ex. B if necessary, (*headings* (section titles), *a formal tone* (avoid colloquialisms and slang), *persuasive language* (convince the reader that the proposal will work), *outlines* (explains briefly), *consequence* (result), etc).
- Have the students work individually to read the proposal again and check whether the writer has covered points 1–4. Ask the students to identify each point by underlining the relevant part of the proposal.
- Check answers with the class.

Answer
Points 1, 2 and 3 are covered.

C
- Read the instructions to the students and explain the task. Make sure they understand that they will be writing a proposal to improve the student library at their university.
- Ask the students to look at question 1 and make notes on two aspects of the building that they would choose to improve. Encourage them to choose from the choices given or use their own ideas. Then have them tick or write their final choices in the space provided.
- Ask the students to brainstorm practical strategies to improve the two aspects of the building that they chose and decide on a final plan. Have them make notes individually first, and then have them discuss their strategies in small groups to receive feedback from others about whether their strategies seem workable and/or inexpensive. If group members don't think particular strategies are workable, ask them to brainstorm other ways to make the overall plan work.

D
- Ask the students to plan an outline of their proposal. Ask them to refer to the sample proposal for guidelines on how to present the plan, describe the problem(s) and suggest solutions. Ask them to include pros and cons of each solution and show how the pros outweigh the cons.
- Give the students time to draft their proposals.
- When the students finish, put them in pairs to revise their work. Then ask each student to post their proposal on the classroom wall and invite others to comment.

Alternative
Have the students compile all the proposals into a booklet to submit to the student council at their university.

How are you doing?
- Ask the students to read the statements and tick the ones they believe are true.
- Ask them to discuss their proposal with another student in the class and identify things they could improve on next time.

▶ Workbook pp. 8–9, SkillsStudio

UNIT 2 WATCH THIS SPACE …

The expression *watch this space* is often used to say that there will soon be an exciting change in a situation. Throughout the space age (the period of history from the 1950s to the present) scientists have been keenly observing space and sending messages in the hope of finding intelligent life on other planets. Their work has led to many technological innovations that have changed the way we live.

Unit plan

Unit opener	(p. 20)	20 min.
1 Reading: an online article	(p. 22)	30 min.
• Vocabulary: business and innovation		15 min.
2 Grammar: future passive	(p. 23)	40 min.
3 Listening: understanding native English speakers	(p. 24)	30 min.
• Vocabulary: negative prefixes: *un-, im-, in-*		15 min.
4 Grammar: conditional conjunctions	(p. 25)	40 min.
5 Pronunciation: contrastive stress	(p. 26)	15 min.
6 Speaking: talking about the possibility of life on other planets	(p. 26)	30 min.
7 Writing: outlining	(p. 27)	30 min.
LifeSkills: evaluating explanations (Study and Learning)	(p. 28)	50 min.
• Optional downloadable *LifeSkills* lesson (Self and Society)		50 min.
• Optional downloadable *LifeSkills* lesson (Work and Career)		50 min.
Language wrap-up	(p. 30)	20 min.
Speaking workshop: describing a picture	(p. 31)	30 min.
Video and downloadable video worksheet		45 min.

Unit opener (p. 20)

Lead-in
Ask the students to look at the unit title and the photos and to predict what the unit will be about. Elicit the meaning of the title using the ideas in the panel under the title on this page. Ask the students what they know about major events in the space age and the kind of exploration that humans have done. Direct the students' attention to the points in the unit objectives box and go through the information with them. To get your students to think about the skills being developed in this unit, ask them to look at the questions in the cogs.

Listening: understanding native English speakers
- Elicit answers to the questions. Ask volunteers to share experiences in which they had difficulty understanding an English speaker and explain why. Have the class agree on three countries or regions where English is more difficult to understand and three countries or regions where English is easier to understand.

Writing: outlining
- Ask for volunteers to answer the questions. Lead a brief class discussion on different ways to organise ideas for writing (*lists, graphic organisers, outlines*, etc).

LifeSkills: evaluating explanations
- Refer the students to the **LifeSkills** panel. Ask how they make choices about who and what to believe and what qualities make a source of information credible.

Common European Framework: unit map

Unit 2	Competence developed	CEF Reference (C1 competences)
Reading	can understand an online article	Table 1; Table 2; Sections 4.4.2.2; 4.4.2.4; 4.4.3.4; 4.5.2.2
Grammar	can use and understand the future passive	Table 1; Table 2; Sections 5.2.1.2; 6.4.7.7; 6.4.7.8
Listening	can understand native English speakers	Table 1; Table 2; Sections 4.4.2.1; 4.4.3.1; 4.4.3.5; 4.5.2.2; 5.2.2.5
Grammar	can use and understand conditional conjunctions	Table 1; Table 2; Sections 5.2.1.2; 6.4.7.7; 6.4.7.8
Pronunciation	can use contrastive stress	Section 5.2.1.4
Speaking	can talk about the possibility of life on other planets	Table 1; Table 2; Sections 4.4.1.1; 4.4.3.1; 4.4.3.5; 4.5.2.1; 5.2.1.1; 5.2.1.2; 5.2.3.2
Writing	can write an outline	Table 1; Table 2; Sections 4.4.1.2; 4.4.1.3; 4.5.2.1; 5.2.1.6

A

- Write some high numbers in digits on the board, including hundreds, thousands, hundreds of thousands, millions, hundreds of millions and billions. Elicit how to say them correctly. Find examples from the internet or other sources to help the students picture how large these numbers are. (*A million miles is 40 trips around the Earth*, etc.)
- Direct the students' attention to the instructions. Read the eight statements about the universe to the class. Divide the board into columns with headings for various large place values – thousands to billions. Take two or three examples from the statements about the universe (except for items 5 and 8) and have the students estimate the place-value column in which the answer belongs.
- Ask the students to individually guess the numbers to complete the eight statements. When they finish, have them check their answers on p. 30. Then have the students compare answers in pairs to see whose guesses were closest.
- Write the correct answers from the answer key on the board, and check them with the whole class. Model saying the numbers and ask the students to listen and repeat. Then point to the numbers on the board in random order and ask a different student to say each number. Write similar numbers on the board and have the students practise saying them.
- Write the date *1969* on the board and have the students practise saying it. Next, write *1,969* and have them practise saying it. Then quickly point to the two numbers and have the students practise saying them. Repeat with *1949/1,948* and *2017/2,017*.

Culture note

Here are some important dates in the story of space exploration:
1957 The USSR launches the first satellite, called *Sputnik*, into space in October and soon after, the first satellite with a living creature – a dog – in it.
1963 Yuri Gagarin of the USSR becomes the first person in space, with a 108-minute flight that orbited the Earth.
1967 The US *Apollo 11* spacecraft lands on the moon and crew members walk on the moon.
1973 The USSR space probe *Mars 2* orbits around Mars and maps it.
1986 Construction begins on the USSR's MIR space station, which was the first consistently inhabited space station.
2000 The first permanent crew moves into the International Space Station, where crews from various nations continue to live and do research.
2013 The US space probe *Voyager I* exits the solar system after thirty-six years of travelling, becoming the first human-made object to reach interstellar space.

B

- Ask the students to read the two statements. By a show of hands, divide the class into two sides: those who agree with the first statement and those who agree with the second statement. Lead a class debate, encouraging volunteers on each side to say why they agree with the statement they chose and why they disagree with the opposite statement. List all the ideas on the board.

- Briefly evaluate the key points of each side's explanation. Invite volunteers to summarise their personal explanation in one sentence.

Alternative

Have each side choose one or two leaders to speak for the entire team. Then conduct a formal debate, in which the leader of each side speaks for their side and against the other side's arguments.

Culture note

Sci-fi is short for science fiction, as is the abbreviation *SF*. In English, it is common to shorten or abbreviate popular names and titles, such as *PM* for Prime Minister and *prof* for university professor.

Reading: an online article (p. 22)

Lead-in

Write the words *science fiction* on the board. Ask the students what images come to their minds when they read these words. Ask them to name examples of famous science fiction books, films and TV shows from the past (*Star Trek, The Twilight Zone, Planet of the Apes, Star Wars, Inception, Jurassic Park, E.T., Back to the Future, The Matrix, Planet of the Apes, The Day the Earth Stood Still*, etc). Elicit examples of things the students found interesting in these futuristic visions of life. Ask if they think they will someday come true.

A

- Ask the students to imagine life without mobile phones and computers. Elicit what students think the main advantages and disadvantages would be. Discuss the ideas as a class.
- Direct the students' attention to the article and the first photo. Ask if any of them have seen *Star Trek*. Explain that it was a popular television series that was later made into a series of films. If you can, play a short clip from it (search YouTube). Elicit conversation about other science fiction TV shows or films the students may know. Ask for examples of futuristic gadgets/tools from these programmes.
- Direct the students' attention to the title of the article. Ask the students to speculate how *Star Trek* might have inspired mobile phones. Write two or three of their answers on the board.
- Have the students read the question. Then give them time to read the article with the question in mind.
- When the students finish reading, put them in pairs to create a short answer (one or two sentences) to the question.
- Elicit answers from several pairs. Write some of their answers on the board. Ask the students which answers they think are the best, and why.

Answer

The connection between space, science fiction and mobile phones is that the inventor of the mobile phone was inspired by a device used in the science-fiction TV series *Star Trek*, which was set in space.

Extra: vocabulary

Make three columns on the board, with the headings *space*, *science fiction* and *mobile phones*. Ask the students to write the headings on a piece of paper, scan the article for key words that belong under each heading and write them in the table. Then have the students call out answers and write them on the board.

B

- Make sure the students understand the difference between a noun (person, place, or thing) and a verb (an action or *being* word).
- Direct the students' attention to the vocabulary exercise. Elicit/explain that *n* stands for *noun* and *v* stands for *verb*. Model how to change a verb to its base form (the infinitive without *to*). Write examples on the board (*inspired* → *inspire*, etc).
- Ask the students to complete the exercise individually. Have them scan the article for the underlined words and match them to their definitions.
- Put the students in pairs to compare answers and discuss differences.
- Check answers with the class. Make sure the students have used the base form of the verb when necessary.

Answers

1 inspire 2 public relations 3 lobby 4 prototype 5 giant
6 gain a lead 7 infrastructure 8 press conference 9 rival
10 launch

Culture note

Star Trek was a popular US television series about a future ship that explores space. It was shown originally in the 1960s, and was followed by a series of television sequels – *The Next Generation*, *Deep Space Nine*, *Voyager* and *Enterprise* – as well as 12 films and many books, comic books and games.

Alternative

Have the students cover the article in Ex. A and work in pairs. Ask them to read the definitions in Ex. B and predict the words. When they finish, have them check the underlined words in the article and compare the actual answers with their predictions.

Extra: vocabulary

Read the following definitions to the students one at a time, with the paragraph number. Ask the students to read the article silently and raise their hands when they find a word or phrase with the same meaning. Invite one of the students to say the word.

1 to move ahead of someone or something – paragraph 1 (leapfrog)
2 easy to carry – paragraph 1 (portable)
3 reporters – paragraph 2 (journalists)
4 demonstrate to be true – paragraph 2 (prove)
5 stared in amazement – paragraph 3 (gaped)
6 produced in order to be sold on the market – paragraph 4 (commercial)
7 gave a sign of something to come in the future – paragraph 5 (foreshadowed)

C

- Ask the students to read the questions. Allow them time to make notes for their discussion.
- Put the students in small groups to discuss the questions. Circulate and help as needed.
- Have the groups share their answers with the class.

Extra: speaking

Have each group choose one future prototype from their answer to item 3. Instruct them to imagine they are going to launch this product and design an advertisement for it. Then have the groups take turns presenting their product. Have the class vote on the best presentation.

▶ Workbook p. 10, Section 1

Grammar: future passive (p. 23)

Lead-in

Ask the students to look at the picture and tell you what it is (*a robot soldier from the science fiction film* Avatar). Elicit what the purpose of this robot might be (*to fight wars to protect society*). Ask the students if they think this might someday come true on Earth.

A

- Direct the students' attention to the text and ask them what they think it will be about.
- Ask the students to read the three possibilities for the main idea. Then have them read the text and decide which sentence best describes the main idea. Take a class vote on the best choice (c).
- Ask the students to find examples in the text that support answer (c) as the main idea (*force fields for British tanks, combat robots for the USA*).
- Ask the students to explain why answers (a) and (b) are not the main idea (*(a) is contradicted by examples in the text, (b) could be true, but it is opposite to what the text describes*).

Watch this space ... **UNIT 2**

NOTICE!

- Direct the students' attention to the **Notice!** box.
- Have them underline all the examples of the passive in the text, and underline all the modal verbs twice. Ask them which of the passive phrases refer to future possibilities.
- Check answers with the class.

Answers

1 and 2
have been created
Could … be invented
will be activated
will be spent
may be developed

3
Could some of those things actually be invented and *may be developed* refer to future possibilities.
Will be activated and *will be spent* are more definite predictions.

B

Form

- Direct the students' attention to the rule and have them choose the correct option (a), using the text in Ex. A for help. Ask them to name the past participle in the future passive examples in the text (*invented, activated, spent, developed*).
- Ask the students to find an example of the passive with *by* in the text. Make sure they understand that *by* is used when we want to identify the person/thing doing the action.
- Direct the students' attention to the **What's right?** box and ask them to tick the correct sentence (2). Ask a volunteer to say what is wrong in the incorrect sentence (*there is no be*, and the verb *use is in the base form, not the past participle form*).

C

- Have the students work individually to rewrite the sentences using the future passive. Circulate and give help as needed.
- Put the students in pairs. Have them discuss each pair of sentences and decide which form works best – the active, the passive, or both forms equally well – and why.
- When the pairs finish, discuss the answers with the class.

Possible answers

1 Personal spaceships will be invented in the next century. (Passive is better because *they* is vague and doesn't add anything to the meaning.)
2 A lot could be learnt from future science-fiction films. (Active and passive are equally appropriate, as the speaker might want to include the word *we* as a way to suggest that everyone could learn from the films.)
3 Astronauts won't/will not be sent to Mars in my lifetime. (Passive is better here, as *they* isn't a specific subject and so isn't necessary.)
4 Astronauts might be trained (by NASA) at a lunar base. (Active might be better here, as the information about who will train the astronauts is important/interesting.)
5 Do you think other planets will ever be colonised? (Passive is better here because it isn't necessary to say that people would colonise other planets; that is understood.)

D

- Put the students in groups and have them brainstorm a list of things they think will happen in space within the next 50 years. Encourage the students to use *will* for definite predictions and *might, could* or *may* for possibilities that are less likely to happen. Direct their attention to the example sentence and its use of future passive.
- Circulate and help as needed.
- To conclude, have the groups share their ideas with the class.

▶ Workbook pp. 10–11, Section 2

Listening: understanding native English speakers (p. 24)

Lead-in

Ask the students to read the information in the skills panel. Ask them to name the different kinds of English accents they are familiar with (*American, Canadian, British, Indian, Australian,* etc). Explain that the difference in English accents often revolves around pronunciation of specific sounds and syllable stress. Write the word *car* on the board. Pronounce it the American way (/kɑr/) and the British way /kɑː(r)/. Next, write the word *magazine* on the board and pronounce it first in the American way with the stress on the first syllable (/ˈmæɡəˌziːn/) and then in the British way with the stress on the last syllable (/ˌmæɡəˈziːn/). Ask the students for other examples of pronunciation differences they have encountered. Point out that Spanish is pronounced differently in Spain, Mexico, Colombia and Argentina, etc.

A 🎧 1.06

- See p. 122 for the **audioscript.**
- Have the students read the instructions. Discuss what a book launch is (*an event to celebrate the publication of a new book, at which the author gives information about it to the public*).
- Explain that the students are going to listen to statements from six people at the book launch and that they will hear three different accents. Ask the students to listen and see if they can match the two people to the same accent.

14

- Play the audio once and ask the students just to listen. Play the audio again and have the students mark the answers.
- Check answers with the class. Ask the students which match was the easiest and which was the most difficult. Ask them to explain why.

Answers

Speaker 1 – Speaker 5
Speaker 2 – Speaker 4
Speaker 3 – Speaker 6

B

- Direct the students' attention to the three maps. Ask the students to explain the connection to Ex. A (*All the speakers come from these three countries.*).
- Explain that you are going to play the audio again. This time, the students should try to match each speaker to one of the countries – the US, Australia or India.
- Play the audio. Check answers with the class.
- Ask the students to identify any specific words, phrases or pronunciation that helped them identify a speaker's country.
- Ask students which of the six speakers was easiest to understand and why, and which was most difficult to understand and why.

Answers

1 India – Speakers 3 and 6
2 USA – Speakers 1 and 5
3 Australia – Speakers 2 and 4

C 1.07

- See p. 122 for the **audioscript.**
- Explain that the students are now going to listen to a Question and Answer, or Q & A, session after the book launch. This time the students should listen for each speaker's opinion about space exploration and the main reason for their opinion. Remind the students to list only one reason per speaker.
- Play the audio. Encourage the students to take notes as they listen.
- Play the audio again and have the students review their answers.
- Check answers with the whole class.
- Ask the students to identify specific words that gave clues to the speaker's opinion.
- Ask the students which speaker was easiest to understand and why, and which was most difficult to understand and why.

Answers

Speaker 1: Against: We should spend money on solving problems on Earth.
Speaker 2: For: We need natural resources from other planets.
Speaker 3: For: The space programme creates jobs.
Speaker 4: Against: We should concentrate on caring for our own planet.
Speaker 5: For: The space programme gives us useful inventions.
Speaker 6: Against: We should spend money on improving life for people on Earth.

D

- Explain that the speakers in Ex. C used several words starting with *un-*, *im-* and *in-*. These are prefixes, and they change the meaning of the root word. Elicit from the students that these three prefixes make words negative (*impossible = not possible*). Instruct them to choose the correct prefix to attach to each of the words in the box, and to write the new word in the appropriate column. Suggest that students use dictionaries for help if they need to.
- Check answers with the class.
- **Highlight** that *in-* changes to *im-* before words beginning with *p*. Point out that *im-* is also used before adjectives beginning with *m* (*immoral, immature*, etc). *In-* can also change to *ir-* in words such as *irresponsible* and *irregular*, and to *il-* in *illegal* and *illogical*. Tell the students that the prefix *un-*, in contrast, never changes in form.
- Put the students in pairs. Have them work together to add other examples of words beginning with *un-*, *im-* and *in-* to the table.
- Ask the pairs to share one new word from each column with the class. Make sure they have used the proper prefix for each adjective.

Answers

im: immeasurable, impatient, imperfect, impractical, improbable
in: inaccurate, incapable, insignificant
un: unacceptable, unavailable, unaware, unbelievable, uncertain

E

- Explain to the students they will work in groups to discuss whether space exploration should continue. Give the students time to organise their arguments and make notes. Encourage them to use as many *un-*, *in-* and *im-* words as they can.
- Put the students in small groups. Circulate and help as needed.
- To conclude, ask the groups share their decisions with the class and justify them.

▶ Workbook p. 11, Section 3

▶ Workbook p. 12, Section 4

Grammar: conditional conjunctions (p. 25)

Lead-in

Write the following on the board: *rain, umbrella*. Ask the students how they might form a sentence using these two words to describe a situation in which they are not sure that it is going to rain. Elicit/provide responses such as *If it rains, I will carry an umbrella*, or *In case it rains, I will carry an umbrella*. Explain that words such as *if* and *in case* are conditional conjunctions. Ask students to define a conditional conjunction (*a conjunction that describes a condition – something that may or may not happen*).

A

- Direct the students' attention to the blog entry and the question. Ask the students to read the blog with the question in mind.
- Elicit answers to the question. Ask the students to note where in the blog entry the answer is found (*in the first sentence*). Explain that in English writing, the main idea of a paragraph is often expressed in the opening sentence.

Answer

The writer believes that there might be intelligent life on other planets, but we have to be careful because it might be dangerous to us.

NOTICE!

- Direct the students' attention to the *Notice!* box. Have the students read the three sentences and choose the one with a different meaning.
- Elicit the answer to the question (b). Ask the students how sentence (b) differs from sentences (a) and (c). Point out that *unless* and *if ... not* are two different ways to express the same meaning. The meaning is that if the action in the *unless* or *if ... not* clause is not done (we protect ourselves), the situation – often an unfavourable one – described in the other clause may occur (we might be putting the human race in danger).

B
Function

- Ask the students to read the blog entry again and complete the exercise on their own.
- Check answers with the class.

Answers

a 4 b 2, 5 c 3 d 1, 6

Form

- Elicit the correct option (a) to complete the rule. Ask the students to provide examples from the blog entry.
- Ask the students if they can think of other examples. Write their suggestions on the board.
- Direct the students' attention to the *What's right?* box and ask them to tick the correct sentences (*2 and 3*). Ask the students why the first sentence is incorrect. Elicit/explain that it doesn't make sense because *if we don't* does not mean the same as *unless we don't*, and we don't use the negative form of the verb with *unless*.

C

- Have the students complete the exercise individually. Remind them that they can only use words or phrases from the answers in Ex. B.
- Check answers with the class.

Answers

1 unless 2 (just) in case 3 provided that, as long as
4 (just) in case 5 since 6 provided that / as long as

D

- Direct the students' attention to the instructions and the prompts. Make sure they understand that they can use these expressions to help them formulate their ideas about space programmes in the future. Elicit some examples.
- Put the students in small groups to discuss their ideas, using the prompts to help them.
- Circulate and help as needed. Emphasise that there are no right or wrong answers.
- To conclude, ask the groups to share ideas with the class.

Extra: grammar practice

Write the following sentences on the board. Tell the students to rewrite the sentences using the correct conditional conjunction. Check answers with the class.

1 I won't believe in the existence of aliens (*unless, in case*) I see them with my own eyes.
2 We should continue to send signals into space (*just in case, provided that*) there are creatures that can receive and understand them.
3 (*Since, Unless*) I don't believe in life on other planets, I think space exploration is a waste of money.
4 (*In case, As long as*) there is life on other planets, I think it is important to explore space.
5 (*Provided that, In case*) governments continue to pay for space programmes, we will continue to learn more and more about the universe.
6 The International Space Station will continue (*as long as, just in case*) nations cooperate and provide money for the programme.

Answers

1 unless 2 just in case 3 Since 4 In case 5 Provided that 6 as long as

▶ Workbook pp. 12–13, Section 5

Pronunciation: contrastive stress (p. 26)

Lead-in

Write the following sentence on the board: *I am going to the shop.* Read the sentence three times. Each time you read it, stress a different word: *I, am, shop*. After each reading, ask the class how stressing the chosen word changes the meaning of the sentence. Elicit that stressing *I* emphasises who is going, stressing *am* confirms your intent and stressing *shop* emphasises where you are going. Explain that in English, it is important to pay attention not only to the words that are said, but also the way they are said.

A 🔊 1.08

- See the Student's Book page for the **audioscript**.
- Direct the students' attention to the sentences and ask them to underline one word in each sentence so that the meaning is the same as the phrases in italics.

- Play the audio once or twice and check the answers. Answer any questions students may have about the differences in meaning between the different readings of the sentence.

Answers

1 I think there may be life on other planets in our galaxy.
2 I think there may be life on other planets in <u>our</u> galaxy.
3 I think there <u>may</u> be life on other planets in our galaxy.
4 <u>I</u> think there may be life on other planets in our galaxy.
5 I think there may be life on other <u>planets</u> in our galaxy.

B

- Put the students in pairs and have them take turns reading the sentences according to the directions. Ask them to pay attention to the stressed words. Circulate and help as needed.
- Model that placing stress when talking can be subtle; a word or phrase does not have to be shouted.

Speaking: talking about the possibility of life on other planets (p. 26)

Lead-in
Direct the students' attention to the blog entry and its title. Write the letters UFO on the board and ask the students if they know what the letters stand for. Elicit the answer *Unidentified Flying Object*. By a show of hands, ask how many students believe that UFOs exist. Lead a brief class discussion or debate about the existence of UFOs. Invite the students to share any stories they know about UFOs.

A

- Ask the students to read the blog entry silently and make notes according to the instructions. Circulate and help as needed.
- Ask volunteers to offer the three reasons and to cite the sentences in the text that support their response.
- Work with the class to form a sentence that summarises the author's belief. (*The writer thinks there is no life on other planets because our technology has not detected it, there is no solid proof that UFOs exist, and we know of no other planet like Earth that is capable of supporting life, etc.*)

Answers

1 If there were other intelligent life, our technology would have detected it.
2 There is no real proof that aliens or UFOs exist.
3 We haven't found other planets capable of supporting life.

B 🔊 **1.09**

- See p. 122 for the **audioscript.**
- Explain that the students are going to listen to a speaker with an opposing opinion to the one in the blog entry. Ask them to take notes according to the instructions.

- Check answers with the class and form a sentence summarising the speaker's belief, as in Ex. A.

Answers

1 With the large number of planets and other bodies in the universe, it is probable that at least one other would have life on it.
2 There is evidence that some other planets have some of the same conditions as Earth.
3 There are so many reports of UFOs that at least some must be true.

C

- Direct the students' attention to the instructions. Give them time to organise their thoughts and make notes if they wish.
- Ask for volunteers to share their opinions in one or two sentences. (*I agree with Dr Fisher because his arguments are more convincing than the blog writer's. I think that this argument is a strong one: there are so many planets and so it seems probable that some could have conditions that support life*, etc.)

D

- Put the students in pairs. Ask them to read and follow the instructions.
- Remind them that when taking notes they should write key words and not complete sentences. They should also use abbreviations, such as UFO, rather than full names.
- When the pairs finish, give each student one minute to report to the class what their partner believes. Encourage the students to summarise their partner's opinion in one sentence.

Writing: outlining (p. 27)

Lead-in
Ask the students to read the information in the skills panel. Explain that an outline is like a road map for a journey. Before we begin a trip, we outline our route on the map. Following the route keeps us from getting lost or wandering off course. Explain that the trip might look easy on the map, but when we're on the road things happen that might throw us off course: road works, missing a motorway exit, etc. When this happens, we need to look at the map again to keep us on track.

A

- Explain that the students are going to read an essay question and then two different outlines for an essay that answers the question. As they read, they should decide which outline is better.
- Direct the students' attention to the box and remind them to keep these questions in mind as they read.
- When they finish reading, discuss with the whole class which outline is better and why.

Answer

Outline 1 is better. It is clearly organised so that each point relates to the topic of the section.
Problems with outline 2:
Introduction: The history of the space programme isn't related to the general topic about whether countries should have space programmes. It's better to have a general statement that there are pros and cons, as in outline 1, if the essay is going to contain both pros and cons.
Paragraph 2: The first point is simply a statement of how much money is spent on the US space programme every year. It is not an argument against the space programme.
Paragraph 3: The first point is an argument against, not for, space programmes. The third point is just an opinion, not an argument for the programmes.
Conclusion: This seems to be just a statement of the writer's opinion rather than a strong conclusion that shows *why* the writer is in favour of space programmes.

Culture note

The United States, Russia, the European Union, China, Canada and India currently have programmes to send humans into space. In addition, the United States, Russia, Canada, Japan and the European Union all participate in the International Space Station. The United States spends about $17 billion a year on NASA (National Aeronautics and Space Administration), which manages its space programme. This is about one-half of one percent of the US national budget.

B
- Put the students in pairs. Explain that they are going to work together to create an outline for the essay question in Ex. B.
- Encourage the students to make a list before they compose their outline. Suggest that they divide a paper into two columns with the headings *probable* and *improbable*, and then list supporting arguments under each heading. Remind them that clear thinking = clear writing.
- Circulate and help as needed.

C
- Put each pair of students together with another pair. Direct their attention to the instructions.
- Have the pairs revise their outlines, incorporating suggestions from the other student pair.
- Post the outlines in the classroom, or pass them around so that all students can read them. Have the students vote on which outline they think is best. Elicit volunteers to explain why.
- To conclude, have a class discussion in which students explain why they think intelligent life on other planets is probable or improbable. List their reasons on the board.

Extra: homework

Ask the students to write an answer to either (a) the essay question in Ex. A using the first outline, or (b) the essay question in Ex. B using the outline they prepared. In the next lesson, have the students share their ideas with their partner from Ex. B and see how their ideas compare.

▶ **Workbook p. 13, Section 6**

LifeSkills: evaluating explanations (p. 28)

Step 1: Understand the difference between correlation and causation. (Ex. A, Ex. B)
Step 2: Read facts presented by the media and advertisers carefully to see if they are implying that one thing causes another. (Ex. C, Ex. D)
Step 3: Evaluate explanations of the facts to decide whether claims of causation are accurate or inaccurate. (Ex. D, Ex. E)

Lead-in

Read the target skill aloud and invite the students to tell you what they think *evaluating explanations* means. Explain that in this lesson they will learn how to evaluate explanations in the media and advertising. Then **highlight** the three-step strategy to develop the skill of evaluating explanations. Ask the students why it is important to evaluate the information they receive. Encourage the students to share examples of misleading or untrue explanations (especially in advertisements) they have encountered.

A
- Direct the students' attention to the magazine article and give them time to read it silently. Ask them to pay attention to the words *correlation* and *causation*.
- Ask the students to close their books. Choose volunteers to explain the difference between *correlation* and *causation* in their own words.
- Ask the students for other examples of correlation and causation they can think of. Make two columns on the board, marked *correlation* and *causation*. Write their examples under the appropriate heading.

Possible answer

Correlation is when things happen together. Causation is when things happen together because one thing causes another.

Extra: group practice

Ask the students to write one example of causation and one example of correlation on separate strips of paper. Put the students into groups of four. Have the members of each group mix their papers together. Ask a student to pick a paper, read the example, and tell whether it shows causation or correlation. Encourage group members to discuss whether this answer is correct. When all agree, have the groups repeat this with another student and example.

B

- Explain that the students are going to consider three claims and some possible explanations for those claims. Ask them to decide whether or not they find each explanation convincing.
- Direct the students' attention to the *How to say it* box, and encourage them to use these expressions as they discuss the explanations.
- Ask the students to read the instructions, and then the first claim and its explanation. Ask if they find this explanation convincing and why or why not. Ask them to consider whether there is causation or just correlation.
- Encourage the students to voice their opinions. Ask for other possible explanations for this claim.
- Repeat this procedure for the second and third claims and explanations. Take a class vote on the most convincing explanation.

Answers

Claim 1: People who play basketball are often taller than average because taller people have an advantage in playing the game. They can jump higher, and so it is easier for them to make more baskets and score more points.
Claim 2: Children with bigger hands write better because they are usually older, and so their language (and fine motor) skills are more developed.
Claim 3: Watching violent films does not necessarily mean the films make watchers violent. Millions of people have seen violent films, but very few people commit violent crimes.

C

- Explain that the students are going to read an online article and decide whether they agree or disagree with the writer, and why.
- Give the students time to read the article silently.
- Ask volunteers to explain in one sentence why they agree or disagree with the writer. (*I disagree with the writer because I find his argument unconvincing; I agree with the writer because his arguments make perfect sense*, etc.)

D

- Put the students in pairs and direct their attention to the instructions.
- Encourage them again to use expressions from the *How to say it* box on the previous page. Tell them to come up with at least one other possible explanation for each key fact, even if they find the writer's explanations convincing.
- Circulate and help as needed.

Possible answers

Key fact 1: We haven't heard anything.
Explanation: There's nothing to hear because there's no one out there.
Alternative explanations: We might have been looking and listening in the wrong places; there might be intelligent civilisations which are not sending signals into space; we might not be looking for the right kind of signal.
Key fact 2: We haven't yet found a planet capable of sustaining life.
Explanation: They don't exist; the Earth is unique.
Alternative explanations: We don't have strong enough equipment to detect similar planets; we might not be looking for them in the right places; intelligent life might be able to develop on planets very different from Earth.

E

- Explain to the students that they are going to share their ideas with the class.
- Allow each pair of students to explain how convincing they found the explanations in the article and to present their alternative explanations.
- As a class, decide which pair has the most convincing explanation(s), and why.

F

- Direct the students' attention to the questions. Lead a class discussion about the skill of evaluating explanations learnt in this lesson and how it can be useful to them in the domain of **Study and Learning.**
- Make a list of reasons for item 2 on the board, with the headings *believe* and *disbelieve*.
- Point out that if you believe there is causation, it is important to consider as many explanations as possible, and not just accept the first (or only) reason given.

REFLECT

- Ask the students to read the *Reflect* question.
- Give them time to think about different situations in the domains of **Work and Career** and **Self and Society** where the skill of *evaluating explanations* would be useful.
- Elicit the following responses: choosing the best proposal or determining the cause of a problem at work; reading an opinion article; deciding which candidate or issue to vote for, etc.

RESEARCH

- Explain the task and make sure the students understand what they have to do.
- Discuss possible ideas to replace the *X* in the examples with the class. Then have the class think of other possible *cause* statements for each category and say them. List them on the board.
- Ask the students to choose a topic that interests them and write it in the form of a statement similar to the ones in the bullet points (e.g. *lack of exercise causes heart disease*). Ask them to find articles on the topic to check if there is really causation.

- Give the students a deadline to do research on the topic and come to a conclusion on the issue of causation vs correlation. Have the students present their findings/conclusions to the class.
- Ask the class to give their reactions to the presentations and express their ideas about whether one thing is caused by the other.

Language wrap-up (p. 30)

For notes on how to approach the exercises in the Language wrap-up section, please refer to page 9.

1 Vocabulary
- Ask the students to read through the text before they fill in the gaps with the words from the box. You could suggest that they do the ones they are sure about first.

Extra: vocabulary practice
Divide the class into two to four teams. Call out a word that can be made negative by adding *in-*, *im-* or *un-*. You can use words from this unit, and/or search online or in dictionaries for more. The first team to respond with the correct prefix earns a point. After a few words, change the game: call out a prefix, and the first team to respond with an appropriate word that could take that prefix wins a point.

2 Grammar
- Ask the students to circle the correct option in the pair of choices in each sentence.
- Encourage them to read each sentence aloud to themselves, once with each option. If they are unsure, tell them to choose the option that sounds the best to them.

Speaking workshop: describing a picture (p. 31)

Lead-in
Explain to the students that, in this workshop, they are going to practise describing a picture using an outline.

A 🎧 1.10
- See p. 123 for the **audioscript**.
- Tell the students that they will listen to a speaker describing a picture of a space colony. Ask the students to explain what a space colony is (*a place where people would live somewhere in space in the future*). Ask the students to describe space colonies that they have seen depicted in films or on science programmes.
- Explain that they will listen to the audio several times. The first time, they should number the main points in the order they hear them, from 1–5.
- Read the list of main points to the class, and make sure they understand all the vocabulary (i.e. *round, oval*). Elicit other shape adjectives (*circular, square, rectangular, triangular*, etc) and draw the shapes on the board.
- Play the audio once, but do not check answers with the class.

Answers
4 Details about the types of buildings
2 The shape of the colony (round, oval, etc)
5 The speaker's opinions of life in a space colony
1 Information printed on the picture
3 Details about transport

B
- Direct the students' attention to the sentences and the phrases in the box.
- Explain that they will listen to the audio again and fill in the gap in each sentence with a phrase from the box.
- Play the audio again.
- Put the students in pairs to compare their answers to both Ex. A and Ex. B, discussing any differences.
- Play the audio one more time, and then check answers with the class.

Answers
1 says that **2** shape of **3** look like **4** similar to **5** type of
6 appears to be **7** as long as

C
- Direct the students' attention to the illustration of a space colony. Tell them this is what an artist thinks such a colony might look like in the future.
- Explain that they will prepare a short talk describing the colony in the illustration. The first step is to make an outline. Point out that we make outlines for talks as well as for written texts. Ask the students to explain why making an outline is important for any kind of writing or presentation. Refer them to the skills panel on page 27.
- Direct the students' attention to the outline in the box. Instruct the students to follow the format listed in the box for their talk.
- Remind them that an outline should contain notes, not complete sentences.
- Give them time to work on their outlines individually. Circulate and help as needed.

D
- Put the students in pairs for their speaking task.
- Ask them to use their outlines to talk to their partner about the illustration.
- Explain that they will have only one-and-a-half minutes for their talk, and their goal is to include all the points in their outline in that time. Have their partners time the speech.
- When the students finish, allow time for their partners to give them feedback. Ask if they included all the points in their outline. If not, have them analyse why.
- If there is enough time, have each partner practise speaking again.

How are you doing?
- Ask the students to read the statements and tick the ones they believe are true.
- Ask them to discuss their talk with their partner and identify things they could improve next time.

▶ Workbook pp. 14–15, SkillsStudio

UNIT 3 PASSWORD PROTECTED

The expression *password protected* refers to digital information which is kept secure by passwords and codes. In the information age, access to large amounts of data at our fingertips and near-instant communication has become such a norm that traditional notions of privacy need to be re-examined.

Unit plan

Unit opener	(p. 32)	20 min.
1 **Reading:** text organisation	(p. 34)	30 min.
• Vocabulary: digital privacy		15 min.
2 **Writing:** a persuasive email	(p. 35)	30 min.
3 **Grammar:** object complements	(p. 36)	40 min.
4 **Listening:** to an interview	(p. 37)	30 min.
• Vocabulary: phrasal verbs		15 min.
5 **Pronunciation:** connected speech – final consonant sound to first vowel sound	(p. 37)	15 min.
6 **Grammar:** negative structures with *think, suppose*, etc.	(p. 38)	40 min.
7 **Speaking:** participating in a group discussion	(p. 39)	30 min.
LifeSkills: protecting digital privacy (Self and Society)	(p. 40)	50 min.
• Optional downloadable *LifeSkills* lesson (Work and Career)		50 min.
• Optional downloadable *LifeSkills* lesson (Study and Learning)		50 min.
Language wrap-up	(p. 42)	20 min.
Writing workshop: writing a for-and-against essay	(p. 43)	30 min.
Video and downloadable video worksheet		45 min.

Unit opener (p. 32)

Lead-in
Ask the students to look at the unit title and the photos, and to predict what the unit will be about. Elicit the meaning of the title using the ideas in the panel under the title on this page. Ask the students to consider how privacy applies to information technology and their digital lives. Direct the students' attention to the points in the unit objectives box and go through the information with them. To get your students to think about the skills being developed in this unit, ask them to look at the questions in the cogs.

Reading: text organisation
- Ask the students to guess the root word of the adjective *persuasive* (*persuade*). Explain that a persuasive text uses evidence to convince people about something. Persuasive texts are found in newspapers, magazines (especially in letters to the editor) and advertisements.

Speaking: participating in a group discussion
- Have the students think about the best group discussion they ever had and why it was so good. Then ask them to answer the questions and brainstorm techniques and expressions to keep a discussion going.

LifeSkills: protecting digital privacy
- Refer the students to the *LifeSkills* panel. Ask the students to think about the digital communications devices they have and the ones they use regularly. Ask them to discuss whether they are concerned enough about digital privacy to take steps to protect it. Have them justify their answers.

Common European Framework: unit map

Unit 3	Competence developed	CEF Reference (C1 competences)
Reading	can use text organisation to aid understanding	Table 1; Table 2; Sections 4.4.2.2; 4.4.2.4; 4.5.2.2
Writing	can write a persuasive email	Table 1; Table 2; Sections 4.4.1.2; 4.4.3.2; 4.4.3.4; 4.5.2.1; 5.2.1.1; 5.2.1.2; 5.2.1.6; 5.2.2.2; 5.2.2.4; 5.2.3.2
Grammar	can use and understand object complements	Table 1; Table 2; Sections 5.2.1.2; 6.4.7.7; 6.4.7.8
Listening	can understand an interview	Table 1; Table 2; Sections 4.4.2.1; 4.4.3.1; 4.4.3.5; 4.5.2.2
Pronunciation	can correctly use connected speech (final consonant – first vowel)	Section 5.2.1.4
Grammar	can use and understand negative structures with *think, suppose*, etc.	Table 1; Table 2; Sections 4.4.1.1; 4.4.3.1; 5.2.1.2; 6.4.7.7; 6.4.7.8
Speaking	can participate in a group discussion	Table 1; Table 2; Sections 4.4.1.1; 4.4.3.1; 4.4.3.5; 4.5.2.1; 5.2.3.2

A

- Direct the students' attention to the survey and elicit what it is designed to do (*measure different people's attitudes toward digital privacy*). Make sure the students understand that they should circle 1 if a statement doesn't describe them at all, and 5 if it describes them accurately.
- Ask the students to respond to the survey statements by circling the ratings that apply to them.
- Have the students compare answers in pairs and discuss their responses. Encourage them to find out why their answers varied by asking follow-up questions designed to draw out more detail. For example, for item 3 they could ask: *Why are you unwilling to allow others to use your electronic devices? Do you make any exceptions for family members or best friends?*

Culture note

As more and more people use computers and electronic communication in their day-to-day activities, the issue of digital security has moved to the forefront of society. *Digital security* refers to the protection of a person's electronic data and files. The most common method of security is the use of unique usernames, passwords, and PINs. Data encryption is also used effectively to maintain the confidentiality of data transferred across the internet. Credit and debit cards use secure chips that are embedded in the card to identify the account holder. Many countries now issue biometric passports that contain a digitalised photograph and personal information stored on a microchip for viewing by officials in airports and at border crossings.

Extra: speaking

For each student, select someone who is sitting far away from them in the classroom and tell them this is their Prediction Partner. Have each student complete the survey again, this time guessing their Prediction Partner's opinions. Encourage them to use previous knowledge of their partner, if possible, to guess how they would respond to each statement. Then ask each pair to sit together and check their predictions. Prompt them to form direct questions from the statements in the survey and use them to compare the predictions with each other's real responses. (**A:** *Do you use social media a lot? I put 5 for you – very important.* **B:** *No, it's more like a 2 or a 1. I don't like posting information about my daily life on Facebook. What about you?* etc.) To conclude, have a discussion with the whole class, eliciting which statements were hardest to predict each other's responses to.

B

- Put each pair with another pair. Direct the students' attention to the questions. Ask them to discuss the questions, and come up with some answers.
- Invite each group in turn to share their ideas with the rest of the class. Encourage the class to ask additional questions.
- Have a discussion with the whole class in which the students give opinions on whether they think that the people in their class give out personal information too readily, or if they are too cautious in giving out information. Discuss areas of disagreement.

Reading: text organisation (p. 34, p. 10 ⊙)

Lead-in

Ask the students to read the information in the skills panel. Remind them of other types of text structure, such as factual texts, which contain main ideas, details and examples, and news articles, where the most important information is contained in the headline and the first paragraph. Make sure they understand which type of text they are going to read here (*persuasive*) and the text structure they will focus on (*cause-effect*).

A

- Direct the students' attention to the two questions. Ask the class to brainstorm what they think the term *cyber threat* means. Elicit as many answers as possible (*any threat that can damage or hack into computer systems, theft of personal information or money through the internet,* etc).
- Point out that the word *cyber* is used to refer to anything related to computers and information technology.
- Encourage the class to suggest as many examples of cyber threats as they can (*hacking, computer viruses, credit card theft, identity theft, fraud,* etc).
- Write the term *Big Brother* on the board and elicit what this means to the students (see *Culture note*). Ask the students how they would feel if they lived under an ever-watchful eye. Would they choose to change their behaviour as a result? **Highlight** the title of the article and ask in what ways we may be under surveillance in our daily lives (*supervision by authority figures in school or at work, internet tracking of websites we visit, speed cameras, security cameras,* etc).

Culture note

Fear of Big Brother, a fictional government surveillance system, first gripped the world in 1949, when George Orwell's novel *Nineteen Eighty-Four* featured the slogan *Big Brother is watching you*. Recently the name Big Brother has been used for an internationally franchised TV game show in which contestants live in a house equipped with cameras and microphones in every room. Everything they say and do is closely observed by others. Themes of surveillance and control have recently become popular in young adult fiction. Two bestselling series are *The Hunger Games* by Suzanne Collins, and *Divergent* by Veronica Roth, both of which have become popular films.

B

- Ask the students to look at the photo, and elicit what it shows (*an image that symbolises data theft*). How does the photo set expectations of what we are about to read?
- Ask the students to read the questions. Then have them read the text to determine their responses to the questions. Encourage them to think about how the information in the article is structured to persuade the reader to share the author's opinion. Put the students in groups to share their answers. Then check answers to questions 1 and 2 with the class.

Answers

1 People need to be more aware of the amount of data that is collected about them, and they need to demand to know how it is used.
2 Examples of how data is collected (mobile phones, credit cards), an explanation of the types of crimes that cyber criminals commit, and a reminder of how our personal information is shared and used.

- Lead a discussion with the whole class on the third question. Elicit the author's specific concerns (*people's increasing loss of control over their private information, the risks of misuse of this private information*). Ask the students if they think that these concerns are valid. Ask if the text has made them aware of a problem that they were previously unaware of. Ask if they share the author's concerns or if they feel that the text is exaggerating the problem. Point out that, by considering these questions, they are evaluating whether the text was persuasive enough to convince them to share the author's concerns.

Extra: grammar review

Review the passive voice (*be* + past participle; the subject is not the agent, or doer, of the action). Ask the students to underline examples in this article (*data is collected, it will be shared, information ... could be used,* etc). Ask them why they think the passive voice is used throughout this article (*because it is the effect of these actions that is important, not the agent; we may not be sure who the agent is in some cases,* etc).

C

- Point out that the table shows the paragraph structure of the article in Ex. A. **Highlight** the three body paragraphs: each paragraph clearly describes one cause and one or more effect.
- Ask the students to complete the table by scanning the text in Ex. A. Then elicit the answers from individual students and encourage the rest of the class to say why they agree or disagree.

Answers

2 **Effects:** internet scams, blackmail
3 **Effect:** Information collected for one purpose can be used for a different purpose.
4 **Cause:** doing nothing about the situation; **Effect:** Companies and governments will demand more and more information until every aspect of our lives is recorded.

D

- Direct the students' attention to the words and phrases in the box and explain that they were used in context in Ex. A. Ask the students to read the sentences and complete them. Encourage them to scan for the target words in the text to work out the meaning from context if necessary.
- Ask different students to share their answers with the class.

Answers

1 invade your privacy 2 compile 3 leave, open to
4 information age 5 monitor 6 Identity theft 7 hack
8 blackmail 9 scam 10 database

E

- Put the students in pairs. Have them read the three statements, decide whether they agree or disagree, and explain why.
- Ask each pair of students to join another pair. Encourage them to discuss and justify their opinions about the statements.

▶ Workbook p. 16, Section 1

▶ Workbook p. 17, Section 2

Writing: a persuasive email (p. 35)

Lead-in

Ask the students at what age they think children or young adults should be free to buy what they want without their parents' permission. Ask them at what age they think parents should allow young people to get credit cards.

A 1.11

- See p. 123 for the **audioscript**.
- Direct the students' attention to the notice and ask them to read it carefully. Elicit who wrote it (*campus administration*) and why (*to find out what students think about the new law allowing parents to monitor their underage children's online credit card purchases*). Ask the students to identify an argument *for* the proposal and an argument *against* it.

- Ask the students to make notes as they listen to two students discussing the notice. Explain that they should listen for points *in favour of* (or *for*) the proposal and points *against* the proposal. Play the audio once and check progress. Play the audio again if necessary. Then check answers with the class.

Answers

In favour of: Parents supporting their children at university have a right to know what their money is being spent on. Parents end up paying if their children make mistakes.
Against: It is an invasion of privacy. Young people have to learn how to manage money. It will make people feel that their parents don't trust them.

B

- Ask the students to think about their own responses to the suggested law. Then ask them to write an outline for an email to the website explaining their view.
- Encourage them to extend, add to, or disagree with the opinions they have heard. Remind them to think about the target audience for their email (*other students who use the university website*) and adjust their email accordingly. Circulate and help as needed.

Extra: homework

Ask the students to review their drafts at home and write a final version of their persuasive emails. In the next lesson, display the emails on the classroom walls, and invite the students to read and comment on their classmates' work.

Grammar: object complements (p. 36)

Lead-in

Direct the students' attention to the photo. Elicit the name of the item shown (*a paper shredder*) and the verb for destroying documents in this way (*to shred*). Ask the students if any of them has a shredder at home, and if so, what types of things they use it for.

A

- Direct the students' attention to the text and the questions. Have them read the text quickly.
- Elicit what advice the writer gives. Ask those students who said they had a shredder whether or not they routinely shred documents with personal information. Ask the other students if they do anything else to destroy their personal documents.

Answer

We should keep our private information secret/secure; we should always shred documents before we throw them away.

NOTICE!

- Direct the students' attention to the **Notice!** box.
- Have them circle the direct objects in the text.
- Elicit the answer to the question.

Answer

A direct object comes after a verb.

B

Form

- Ask the students to read the text in Ex. A again, paying attention to the direct objects.
- Then ask the students to read the explanation and study the table, which gives examples of adjective/noun object complements.
- Point out that the direct object can either be a noun (e.g. *the situation*) or an object pronoun (*him, it*, etc).
- Ask the students to look again at the text in Ex. A and underline the six examples of object complements. To check answers, invite different students to give their examples to the class.
- Direct the students' attention to the **What's right?** box and ask them to tick the correct sentence (*1*). Have them underline the one word that is different in the correct sentence (*yourself*). Elicit what part of speech this is (*reflexive pronoun*) and why it is needed (*the subject and the object of the sentence refer to the same person*).

Answers

consider <u>our personal information secure</u>
don't see <u>identity theft as a problem</u>
don't keep <u>your data secret</u>
find <u>it very easy</u>
make <u>your life very hard</u>
prove <u>yourself an innocent victim</u>

Alternative

Have the students circle the adjective in each example in row one of the grammar table (*dangerous, unacceptable, private*) and the noun in each example in row two (*priority, criminal, thief*). Tell the students to study the sentences and identify the verbs in the grammar table that can take either an adjective or a noun as an object complement (*consider, make, call, prove*).

C

- Direct the students' attention to the instructions and ask them to do item 1. When they finish, elicit the answer to make sure everyone understands the structure and the exercise.
- Have the students complete the rest of the sentences individually. Invite different students to share their answers with the class.

Answers

1 Do you consider identity theft (to be) very common?
2 You can't just call yourself a police officer!
3 Do you see invasion of privacy as a major problem?
4 It's not always easy to prove that an ID is fake.
5 The press describes her as a great leader.
6 Did you find the article interesting?

D

- Direct the students' attention to the instructions and the sentence stems. Give them time to think individually about how to complete them with their own ideas.
- Then put the students in pairs to discuss their ideas. Circulate and help as needed.
- To check answers, ask each pair to share one or two of their ideas with the class. Correct language as necessary.

Extra: grammar practice

Write the following items on the board. Ask the students to put the words in order to make sentences with object complements. Check answers with the class.
1 see / cyber security / as / important / an / issue / I
2 effective / IT departments / consider / many / antivirus software / this
3 government / proved / the / those / hackers / guilty / identity theft / of
4 their / people / personal information / keep / don't / private / many
5 nervous / thought / me / identify theft / a / victim / makes / the / of / being / very / of

Answers

1 I see cyber security as an important issue.
2 Many IT departments consider this antivirus software effective.
3 The government proved those hackers guilty of identity theft.
4 Many people don't keep their personal information private.
5 The thought of being a victim of identity theft makes me very nervous.

▶ Workbook p. 17, Section 3

Listening: to an interview (p. 37)

Lead-in

Documentaries and talk shows present and discuss people's real-life experiences in a way that creates sympathy and interest in the audience. These programmes can help raise public awareness about many types of cyber crime. Ask the students to discuss any such shows that they have seen or heard.

A

- Ask the students to read the instructions and the question. Have them read the description of the radio programme and predict what they think happened after Justine became a victim of identity theft (e.g. *The thieves stole money from her and/or ran up debts in her name. She may have got into trouble with the bank/police*).

B 1.12

- See p. 123 for the **audioscript**.
- Explain that the students will hear the interview with Justine. Ask them to read the five sentences and circle T or F for each statement as they listen.
- Play the audio once and check progress. Play the audio again if necessary.
- Check answers with the class.

Answers
1 F 2 F 3 T 4 F 5 T

C

- Ask the students to read the verbs and prepositions and listen for these phrasal verbs in the conversation. Play the audio again.
- Have the students complete the eight phrasal verbs that they heard in the interview with the correct prepositions. Play the audio again if necessary. Encourage the use of dictionaries.
- Check answers with the whole class.

Answers

1 call on 2 take out 3 run up 4 end up 5 get hold of
6 get out of 7 clear up 8 go through

D

- Read the instructions to the class and explain the task. Encourage the students to read all the sentences before completing them. Remind them that they may have to change the form of the phrasal verb.
- Put the students in pairs to discuss what each phrasal verb means, based on the context. Then have them think of another example sentence using each phrasal verb.
- Discuss the answers with the whole class. Elicit the meanings of the phrasal verbs and write them on the board. Have each pair give example sentences from their discussion. Ask the class if these example sentences used the phrasal verb appropriately.

Password protected UNIT 3 25

Answers

1 get hold of
2 ran up
3 take out, cleared up
4 calling on
5 get out of
6 go through
7 end up

Suggestions for how to explain meanings:
get hold of – get or obtain
run up – accumulate or increase (debt or bills)
take out – apply for and get (a credit card, loan, etc)
clear up – solve (a problem, mystery or misunderstanding)
call on – ask (someone to do something)
get out of – avoid (doing something)
go through – experience (something unpleasant or difficult)
end up – be in a certain situation, after a series of events

▶ Workbook p. 18, Section 4

Pronunciation: connected speech – final consonant sound to first vowel sound (p. 37)

A 1.13

- See the Student's Book page for the **audioscript**.
- Direct the students' attention to the instructions and the pronunciation table for the phrasal verbs.
- Play the audio once and ask the students to tell you what happens to the final consonant sound of the first word in each case (it links to the next vowel sound).
- Play the audio again and pause it after each phrasal verb for the students to repeat. Model and correct as necessary.

B 1.14

- See the Student's Book page for the **audioscript**.
- Ask the students to read the sentences and underline the words they think might be linked together in connected speech. Have them check whether the first word ends in a consonant sound and the second word begins with a vowel sound. Remind them that more than two words might be linked together.
- Play the audio once. Have the students work in pairs to practise pronouncing the sentences. Play the audio again, and encourage them to check their pronunciation.

Extra: homework

Have students write their own sentences with at least five of the phrasal verbs in Ex. A. In the next lesson, have them read their sentences to a partner, who checks for correct pronunciation and correct use of the phrasal verbs.

Grammar: negative structures with *think, suppose*, etc. (p. 38)

Lead-in

Ask the students if they think their attitudes toward digital privacy have changed recently. Ask them about their friends' attitudes compared with their own.

A 1.15

- See the Student's Book page for the **audioscript**.
- Have the students read the question. Ask them to listen to the conversation to find the difference between Roberta and Susan's attitudes toward privacy.
- Play the audio and have students listen and read along. Then invite a student to give the answer. Ask the rest of the class if they agree and/or if they would like to add anything to the answer.

Answer

Susan shares a lot of personal information on social networking sites, while Roberta doesn't like to give out a lot of personal information online, but prefers to keep it private.

NOTICE!

- Direct the students' attention to the **Notice!** box.
- Have them find and circle the six different opinion verbs in the conversation. Ask them which verbs also have meanings apart from feelings or opinions.

Answer

Verbs with other meanings apart from feelings or opinions are *think, feel, expect, guess, suppose, imagine*.

B

Form & Function

- Ask the students to read the conversation again, paying attention to the opinion verbs.
- Direct the students' attention to the underlined sentence in the conversation and ask them to complete the rule. Elicit the answer from a volunteer. **Highlight** that it is the first verb, rather than the second verb, that is made negative. Reinforce the structure *I don't feel that everybody needs …* instead of *I feel that everybody doesn't need …*
- Ask the students to complete both tables with examples from the conversation and check answers with the class.
- After checking the answers, point out the fact that *suppose* has two different forms in the second table because it can form the negative in two ways (*I suppose not./I don't suppose so.*). Also explain that *feel* is an exception and cannot be used in negative short answers, either with *so* or *not*.

Answers

1 I don't feel that everyone needs to know …
2 I didn't think there was anyone who wasn't on Facebook!
3 I guess I shouldn't post about everything …
4 I don't suppose many people actually think about …
5 I don't expect I'm the only person …
6 I don't imagine so.
7 I guess not.

Alternative

Have the students cover the conversation in Ex. A. Ask them to read the information about negative structures in the grammar tables and predict the correct form of the negative for item 1. Then have them check their answer by looking back at the conversation. Repeat this process for items 2 to 7.

C

- Explain that negative short answers are most likely to be used in conversation. Direct the students' attention to the four mini-conversations, and ask them to complete the responses using the prompts in brackets. Remind them to refer to the grammar table in Ex. B if necessary.
- Check answers with the class.

Answers

1 … suspect not. I hope (that) identity theft doesn't/won't increase.
2 … don't think so. I don't believe (that) opinions stay …
3 … hope not. I don't imagine (that) people will give up …
4 … guess not. I don't feel (that) it helps …

Extra: grammar practice

Put the students in small groups. Ask them to take turns asking the questions in Ex. C, going quickly around the group. Have those answering respond using short answers with other verbs from the grammar table (*guess, suspect, assume, think, imagine, suppose*). Encourage the students to add their own questions to the activity.

D

- Put the students in pairs. Have them ask each other the questions in Ex. C and answer them with their own opinions. Encourage the students to listen carefully to their partner's responses and to ask follow-up questions to prompt their partner to explain their opinion fully.
- To conclude, invite the students to report to the whole class the most interesting or unusual opinions they discussed.

▶ Workbook pp. 18–19, Section 5

Speaking: participating in a group discussion (p. 39)

Lead-in

Ask the students to list the features of a good group discussion (*a clear purpose to the discussion, previous knowledge of the topic, feeling comfortable, good guidance*, etc). Elicit their best and worst experiences of participating in group discussions. Ask them to identify examples of helpful and unhelpful types of behaviour during group discussions. Write the most important factors on the board. Ask the students to read the information in the skills panel. Elicit the four reasons for using specific phrases to manage a discussion (*to keep the discussion moving, to interrupt politely, to focus on relevant points, to invite contributions*, etc).

A 🎧 1.16

- See p. 124 for the **audioscript**.
- Explain that the students are going to listen to a group discussing privacy. Ask them to put a tick next to any of the five points they hear mentioned. Play the audio once. Then invite volunteers to share their answers with the class.

Answers

Points mentioned:
1 I don't want anyone to invade my privacy.
2 I share more information online than my parents.
4 Different cultures view privacy differently.
5 Opinions about privacy depend on people's experiences.

B

- Explain that the students are going to listen to the discussion again. Tell them that this time they are going to listen specifically for phrases that the people use to manage the discussion. Tell them to listen to the audio to complete the discussion-management phrases. **Highlight** that the discussion-management phrases are categorised into three main functions: *starting, finishing and keeping the discussion moving, interrupting politely* and *inviting contributions*.
- Play the audio once, and have the students fill in the gaps. Put them in pairs to compare their answers. Play the audio again if necessary. Check answers with the class.

Answers

Starting, finishing and keeping the discussion moving:
1 begin
2 move on
3 So
Interrupting politely:
4 Sorry
Inviting contributions:
5 add

Password protected UNIT 3 27

Alternative

Put the students in groups and write the three discussion-management categories on the board. Ask the class to suggest phrases that could be used to perform each function and write them on the board. Play the audio, and have the students listen for the phrases given or additional phrases to add to each category. Have them write down the phrases they hear. Finally, have them check their discussion-management phrases against those in the Student's Book and complete the ones given there.

C

- Put the students in small groups to discuss the three points. Remind them to use the phrases in Ex. B to manage the discussion. Have three volunteers read the model conversation between Students A, B, and C to demonstrate how the conversation might begin.
- Circulate and help as needed while the groups are working. Prompt them to use relevant phrases as the discussion progresses (e.g. if somebody seems to be dominating or monopolising the discussion, point out the *interrupting politely* phrases to another group member). Encourage the students to discuss all three points.
- To conclude, extend the discussion to the whole class. Ask each group to share an interesting or unexpected conclusion from their discussion.

Extra: homework

Have the students listen to a radio interview or watch a TV interview in English and identify the discussion-management phrases used by the interviewer. Ask them to make notes and present a brief report in the next class.

▶ Workbook p. 19, Section 6

LifeSkills: protecting digital privacy (p. 40)

Step 1: Understand the potential threats to digital privacy. (Ex. A, Ex. B, Ex. C)
Step 2: Think about practical steps to take to increase digital security. (Ex. B, Ex. C, Ex. D, Ex. E)
Step 3: Institute digital security measures in your everyday online routines. (Ex. E)

Lead-in

Read the target skill aloud and invite the students to tell you what they think *protecting digital privacy* means. Ask the students if they or anyone they know has had any negative experiences related to digital privacy issues. To start, you could recount an experience of your own, real or invented, (*your credit card information was stolen when you made an online purchase, and the thief ran up a large amount of credit card debt.*) Then **highlight** the three-step strategy to develop the skill of *protecting digital privacy*.

A

- Have the students read the instructions and then make a list of all the online services and accounts they use regularly. Refer them to the pieces of information in Ex. A and ask them to tick the boxes of items that an identity thief could potentially find online. Ask them to consider all the information about themselves that they have put online or that can be found online in other places.

B

- Put the students in pairs. Ask them to compare their answers to Ex. A, and then use these to imagine what might happen if any online information got into the wrong hands. Refer them to the example of attracting spam to their email address, and then have them make a list of their own ideas. Allow time for discussion before inviting the pairs to share their lists with the class.

C

- Ask the students to stay in their pairs from Ex. B, and read the instructions. Have them decide on their roles: Student A and Student B. Ask them both to read the whole article, with Student A reading the paragraphs Your Software and Your Browser more carefully, and Student B focusing more on the paragraphs Your Email, Secure Payments and Privacy Policies.
- Circulate while they read and help with any vocabulary required (keystroke: *a single action of pressing a key on a keyboard*; to disable: *to stop a machine or system from working properly*; to configure: *to arrange the parts of something, especially computer software, so that it works in the way you want it to*; padlock: *a portable lock that has a D-shaped bar on top that moves when you open the lock with a key, typically fixed to bicycles and suitcases for security*).
- Have the students cover the text and paraphrase the basic advice in their paragraphs to their partner. They can elaborate on the information or add their own examples and anecdotes if they wish.

Possible answers

Software and browsers:
You should use good anti-virus, anti-spyware and firewall software to protect your computer from viruses that let hackers get hold of your personal information. You should also configure your browser so that it doesn't allow websites, adverts, or anything else that you don't want.

Email, secure payments and privacy policies
You should have different email addresses for your personal mail and for online shopping. That way, you won't get spam in your personal email. When you buy something online, look for the padlock symbol because it means that it's a secure site. Make sure that websites have a privacy policy. They have to explain how they will use your data. It's better not to use a site if it doesn't have a privacy policy.

Extra: note-taking

As one partner paraphrases the advice in their paragraphs, have the other student take notes. Then ask them to change roles (speaker/listener). Then have the students compare their notes with the original text and look for any differences or omissions. Ask the students to provide feedback to their partner about what they noticed.

D

- Put the students in groups and ask them to read the online forum question. Elicit what advice the person wants (*tips on making up effective passwords*). Have them discuss what advice to give the writer and to note the key points. Encourage them to bring their personal knowledge and experience to this task.
- Direct the students' attention to the examples in the **How to say it** box, and encourage them to use the expressions in their discussion.
- Allow time for the discussion. Then invite each group to tell you one of their tips while you write it on the board. Continue until there are no more original ideas remaining. At the end, have students vote on the best idea presented.

> **Possible answers**
>
> Change passwords on a regular basis. Change your passwords at least every 90 days to reduce the chance that a computer criminal can gain access to your computer or online accounts. Don't use the same password across multiple sites.

E

- Rearrange the groups so that different students are working together. Ask them to review the entire lesson and decide which three pieces of advice they would give to a friend who was concerned about online privacy. Encourage the students to think about frequency of the problem occurring, seriousness of the consequences and ease of prevention when prioritising advice.
- Allow time for the discussion and then ask the groups to share their ideas with the class. Choose one or two students to oversee the creation of a class list of advice. If possible, have the students present their combined advice in a printed list of tips and notes or on a webpage.

F

- Discuss the questions with the whole class. Ask the students to say what they feel are the most useful points they learnt from this skill and how the information they obtained might be useful in the domain of **Self and Society**, either now or in the future.
- Have the students work in pairs to discuss the two questions and share any changes that they personally intend to make to their online habits to safeguard their privacy. Extend the discussion with the whole class, and make a list of answers to item 2 on the board.

REFLECT

- Ask the students to read the **Reflect** question.
- Elicit ways to protect digital privacy (*changing passwords to professional email accounts regularly, avoiding talking about colleagues or confidential work on social media sites, protecting company data from theft by following company procedures for data handling, not saving essays or assignments on school computers, etc*).
- Give the students time to think about different situations in the domains of **Work and Career** and **Study and Learning** where the skill of knowing how to *protect digital privacy* would be useful.

- Elicit the following ideas: *handling confidential material at work, working on class projects in which students are exchanging documents or chatting in forums, applying for jobs posted online in public forums*, etc.

RESEARCH

- Explain the task and make sure the students understand what they have to do.
- Suggest some websites that list common types of cyber crimes, such as *Norton* and *Computer Weekly*. Also suggest that, as an alternative, students talk with people they know who have been victims of cyber crimes.
- Ask the students to take turns presenting their example of an internet scam or another example of cyber crime to the whole class. Have them explain where they found the information and how they came to know about it. Encourage the class to ask questions and make comments after each presentation.

Language wrap-up (p. 42)

For notes on how to approach the exercises in the Language wrap-up section, please refer to page 9.

1 Vocabulary

- Ask the students to read the whole paragraph for general understanding before filling in the gaps with the words or phrases from the box. Remind them that each gap is worth one point.
- Check answers with the class.

2 Grammar

A

- Ask the students to read the question-answer pairs or statements first. Have them silently recall the grammar rule for forming negative structures with these verbs. Then ask them to complete the exercise by choosing the correct option for each item. After checking answers with the class, remind the students of the grammar rule if necessary.

B

- Have the students look at the mixed-up words in each sentence. Point out that the sentences are not complete and that they will need to add other words to each sentence to make it grammatically correct. Then have them complete the exercise by writing out each sentence as fully as possible. Accept all viable options for each sentence as long as all the given words are used in a logical way and are in keeping with the theme of the unit.
- Check the answers with the class. Point out that all the sentences can be written with object complements. Have the students identify the object complements in their completed sentences.

Writing workshop: writing a for-and-against essay (p. 43)

Lead-in
Explain to the students that in this workshop they are going to practise writing an essay that argues both *for* and *against* an issue.

A
- Explain the instructions to the students. Then focus the students' attention on the two parts of the essay question. The first part asks the writer to express a clear opinion that is either *for* social media (i.e. to argue that social media has primarily positive effects on society) or *against* it (i.e. to argue that social media has primarily negative effects on society). The second part of the question asks the reader to give reasons for this opinion.
- Ask the students to read the essay and decide whether the writer is *for* or *against* social media.

Answer
The writer seems to be against social media. The writer emphasises that the use of social media has many disadvantages, such as spending more time communicating with electronic devices than in person, putting a lot of personal information in cyberspace and doing fewer physical activities.

B
- Ask the students to read the essay again, paying attention to how it is structured.
- Have the students work individually to identify the topic sentence in Paragraph 1. (*However, the fact that many people use social media does not mean that it is a positive development for society.*) Remind the students that a topic sentence contains the main idea of the paragraph.
- Ask them next to identify the topic sentence in Paragraph 2. (*Of course, there are good arguments in favour of social media.*) Then have the students note how many points the writer gives in favour of social media. ((1) *People can find old friends.* (2) *It is easy to stay in touch with family and friends.* (3) *You can stay close to family and friends by sharing photos and videos.*)
- Elicit ideas from the class about why arguments *in favour of* social media are in an essay which is *against* it. Explain that this makes the overall argument seem objective: the writer is aware of the benefits of social media, but is still against it for what he or she considers more important reasons. Have the students identify the topic sentence in Paragraph 3. (*However, there are a number of problems with social media.*) Point out that the topic sentence in this paragraph is in line with the writer's main argument. Ask the students to identify each point that highlights a negative aspect of using social media. ((1) *People spend more time communicating with electronic devices than in person.* (2) *People put an enormous amount of information online, which can lead to data theft or blackmail.* (3) *People spend less time doing physical activities, which contributes to obesity.*)
- Then ask the students to identify the general statement of the writer's opinion in Paragraph 4. (*To summarise, although using social media allows us to communicate easily, it has many disadvantages.*)
- Discuss with the class whether the writer's essay was persuasive or convincing enough to discourage the students from using social media.

Answers
The main idea of the whole essay: Social media is an important part of people's lives, but it may not be a positive development for society.
Paragraph 2:
Topic sentence: Of course, there are good arguments in favour of social media. Points that support it: (1) People can find old friends. (2) It is easy to stay in touch with family and friends. (3) You can stay close to family and friends by sharing photos and videos.
Paragraph 3:
Topic sentence: However, there are a number of problems with social media. Points that support it: (1) People spend more time communicating with electronic devices than in person. (2) People put an enormous amount of information online, which can lead to data theft or blackmail. (3) People spend less time doing physical activities, which contributes to obesity.
Paragraph 4: To summarise, although using social media allows us to communicate easily, it has many disadvantages.

C
- Ask the students to read the essay question first. Explain the question if necessary, and answer any questions the students may have.
- Have the students work individually to make notes on the main idea of the essay and the points they will include in it according to the guidelines in Ex. C. Point out that by doing this, they are actually creating an essay outline which will provide a basic logical structure for the points in their essay.
- Put the students in pairs to compare their notes and offer constructive comments on each other's work. Encourage them to revise their notes based on the feedback they receive.

D
- Encourage the students to use their notes to help them draft their essays. Remind them to write about 250 words. Circulate and help as needed. When the students finish writing, put them in groups of four to review each other's work and offer tips on revision. Remind each group to offer guidance on the quality of the points, the structure of the essay and the language used.
- Ask the students to work individually to revise their essays based on the peer feedback they have received.

How are you doing?
- Ask the students to read the statements and tick the ones they believe are true.
- Ask them to discuss their essay with a partner and identify things they could improve on next time.

▶ Workbook pp. 20–21, SkillsStudio

UNIT 4 A NEW LOOK AT LEARNING

The expression *a new look at learning* refers to the fast-changing pace of formal education in the 21st century. Technological advances have prompted changes in the way information is transmitted, the way classes are taught and the way students learn. Pressed for time and money, many 21st century students are seeking alternative routes towards their university, college and even secondary school qualifications.

Unit plan

Unit opener	(p. 44)	20 min.
1 Speaking: talking about educational alternatives	(p. 46)	30 min.
• Vocabulary: verb collocations		15 min.
2 Grammar: relative pronouns with *-ever*	(p. 47)	40 min.
3 Pronunciation: vowel length before final consonant sounds	(p. 48)	15 min.
4 Listening: understanding non-native English speakers	(p. 48)	30 min.
5 Grammar: mixed conditionals	(p. 49)	40 min.
6 Reading: a statistics-based argument	(p. 50)	30 min.
• Vocabulary: words related to *stand*		15 min.
7 Writing: sentence variety – punctuation with connectors	(p. 51)	30 min.
LifeSkills: anticipating cultural differences (Study and Learning)	(p. 52)	50 min.
• Optional downloadable *LifeSkills* lesson (Self and Society)		50 min.
• Optional downloadable *LifeSkills* lesson (Work and Career)		50 min.
Language wrap-up	(p. 54)	20 min.
Speaking workshop: expressing and supporting personal preferences	(p. 55)	30 min.
Video and downloadable video worksheet		45 min.

Unit opener (p. 44)

Lead-in
Ask the students to look at the unit title and the photos and to predict what the unit will be about. Elicit the meaning of the title. Find photos from different eras of students in classrooms. Ask the students to identify similarities and differences in the photos (*whiteboards vs chalkboards, computers vs overhead projectors*, etc). Invite the students to discuss how a classroom might look when their children are in school. Direct the students' attention to the points in the unit objectives box and the questions in the cogs.

Listening: understanding non-native English speakers
- Elicit answers to the question. List the responses on the board. Ask the class to rank the top three challenges to listening to a conversation between non-native speakers (*pronunciation, accents, grammar mistakes,* etc).

Writing: sentence variety – punctuation with connectors
- Invite the students to answer the questions. Explain/elicit that a series of long sentences can be hard to follow, while a series of short sentences can sound repetitive and choppy. If possible, find examples and read them to the class.

LifeSkills: anticipating cultural differences
- Refer the students to the **LifeSkills** panel. Elicit answers to the three questions on preparing for a trip. Ask students if they like to get factual information before travelling to a place or prefer to get personal impressions from other people. Discuss the reasons for the choices.

Common European Framework: unit map

Unit 4	Competence developed	CEF Reference (C1 competences)
Speaking	can talk about educational alternatives	Table 1; Table 2; Sections 4.4.1.1; 4.4.3.1; 4.4.3.5; 4.5.2.1; 5.2.1.1; 5.2.1.2; 5.2.3.2
Grammar	can use and understand relative pronouns ending in *-ever* (*whatever, whoever,* etc)	Table 1; Table 2; Sections 5.2.1.2; 6.4.7.7; 6.4.7.8
Pronunciation	can correctly pronounce vowels of different length before final consonants	Section 5.2.1.4
Listening	can understand non-native speakers of English	Table 1; Table 2; Sections 4.4.2.1; 4.4.3.1; 4.4.3.5; 4.5.2.2; 5.2.2.5
Grammar	can use and understand mixed conditionals	Table 1; Table 2; Sections 5.2.1.2; 6.4.7.7; 6.4.7.8
Reading	can read and understand a statistics-based argument	Table 1; Table 2; Sections 4.4.2.2; 4.4.2.4; 4.5.2.2
Writing	can use the correct punctuation with connectors	Table 1; Table 2; Sections 4.4.1.2; 4.5.2.1; 5.2.1.5; 5.2.1.6

A new look at learning UNIT 4

A

- Put the students into pairs, and direct their attention to the photos and accompanying statements/quotes. Refer them to the four areas listed in the box (*technology, education, soft skills, globalisation*) and ask them to decide which area each statement/quote best relates to. Encourage them to focus only on the strongest connections, even though a statement/quote might relate to more than one area.

Culture note

A great deal of emphasis is now placed by employers on hiring people with *soft skills*. These are skills that do not depend on specific knowledge or education, but rather on qualities such as being able to communicate effectively, to work in or lead a team and to have a positive, flexible attitude.

- When finished, put two pairs of students together to discuss and explain their answers. Circulate and monitor, assisting where needed.
- Ask students if they know of any other statements or quotations that would apply to one or more of these four areas. If so, list the statements/quotes on the board, and ask the class to suggest which area they best relate to.

B

- Have the pairs from Ex. A remain together in groups of four. Ask the groups to discuss the two questions. For question 1, encourage the students to think of examples they have seen or read that relate to the statement or quote. For question 2, ask them to consider how the statement/quotes might affect their personal future educational plans. Encourage them to be specific.
- To conclude, ask each group to choose a spokesperson, and then lead a brief discussion with the whole class in which each spokesperson summarises the views of their group.

Speaking: talking about educational alternatives (p. 46)

Lead-in

Ask the students how they learn best. Elicit or suggest a list of learning styles, such as social (*working with other people*) vs independent (*working alone*), visual (*through pictures/images*), verbal (*through speaking and reading*), aural (*through listening/sound/music*) and physical or kinesthetic (*through touching, feeling, moving*). Write the names of the learning styles discussed on the board. Ask for volunteers to share personal examples of something they have learnt (in or out of school) using one of these styles.

A

- Direct students' attention to the online article. Explain that they are going to read about virtual degree programmes and try to discern the author's opinion about these programmes. Check to ensure students understand the meaning of *virtual*. Encourage them to look for words and phrases in the article that express the author's viewpoint.

- Give the students time to read the article, and then put them into pairs. Instruct them to discuss with their partner whether the author favours or opposes virtual degree programmes, and why. Circulate and monitor, assisting where needed.

Answer

The author is in favour of virtual degree programmes for several reasons. First, they are cheaper than normal tuition. Second, they are practical for students who live far from a university. Third, they foster important personal skills such as self-discipline. Fourth, they allow for more individualised teaching, free from the social distractions of campus life. Finally, students can try out free online courses before signing up for a degree programme.

- Lead a brief class discussion, encouraging students to cite key words and phrases in the article that support their answer choice.

B

- Direct the students' attention to the six verbs and verb phrases. Elicit or explain the meaning of *collocation* (*words that are typically used together*). Explain that these verbs typically are used together with certain nouns. It sounds unnatural, for example, to say *take* a university degree instead of *get* a university degree or *make* a chance instead of *get* a chance.
- Read aloud one or two of the collocations in the text and ask volunteers to read aloud the rest.
- Have the students look over the article in Ex. A to find more collocations for each verb or verb phrase and complete the exercise individually.
- Check answers with the class. Ask volunteers to read the verb collocation first and then the entire sentence from the article that contains the collocation.

Answers

1 account
2 into debt, a taste, a university education
3 university
4 courses
5 (their) own schedule
6 (social) distractions, (peer) pressure

Extra: verb collocation practice

Write the following words on the board: *take, do, have* and *make*. Explain that these are common verbs used in English in specific collocations – for instance, *take a walk, do homework, have a drink, make money*. Invite students to come up with more collocations for each listed verb, and to use the collocations in a sentence. List correct collocations on the board. Note: Explain that collocations can be different in American English and British English. For example, in Britain they will say *have* a shower, while in America, it is *take* a shower.

C

- Put the students in small groups and have them discuss the three questions. Circulate and help as needed.

- When the groups finish, ask each group to explain one of their answers to the rest of the class.

D 🎧 **1.17**
- See p. 124 for the **audioscript**.
- Tell the students they are going to listen to someone who has a different opinion from the writer in Ex. A. Instruct them to take notes as they listen on how the speaker, Dr George Cowell, disagrees with the author in Ex. A. Play the audio twice, circulating and monitoring as students write notes.
- Check answers with the entire class. Ask for volunteers to summarise Dr Cowell's arguments in one or two sentences. Elicit specific words and phrases from Dr Cowell's interview that express his differences with the author of the online article in Ex. A.

Answer
The speaker says that most young adults lack the maturity, motivation and self-discipline to take online courses. He also says that even though online tuition is much cheaper, most students get important benefits from attending a university, such as increasing their social skills, making new friends and learning to become independent.

E
- Ask the students to review the online article in Ex. A and their notes from Ex. D. Ask them to decide what their own opinion is about online universities.
- Have them write notes for an outline of a two-minute talk to express their opinion. Tell them they may use ideas from Ex. A and Ex. D as well as their own thoughts.

F
- Put the students in pairs. Ask them to take turns giving their two-minute talk. Have the partners time each other and remind them not to interrupt when their partner is speaking. Circulate and help as needed.
- When the pairs finish, ask each partner to critique the other's speech.

Extra: speaking
Ask the class, by show of hands, which degree is better when searching for a job: an online degree or a traditional degree. Divide the class into two groups and have a debate on the topic.

▶ Workbook p. 22, Section 1

Grammar: relative pronouns with -ever (p. 47)

Lead-in
Write *-ever* on the board. Explain that several English pronouns are made by combining a question word (a word typically used to ask questions) with this ending. Elicit examples, such as *whoever, wherever, whatever, whenever, however* and *whichever*. Tell students that *whyever*, though it is a word, is rarely used. Write two or three example sentences on the board, such as *I'll always love you, wherever you are*; *Whatever you do, try your hardest*; and *Whoever wrote this poem is a genius*. Ask the students what role *-ever* words play in sentences. Elicit that they express indefiniteness or uncertainty.

A
- Tell the students they are going to read a discussion thread from an online forum in which students in an online class are introducing themselves. They should decide which students do not feel confident about the class, and why.
- Give the students time to read the text and consider their answers to the question. Ask for volunteers to answer the question. Invite them to cite words from the text that support their reasoning.

Answer
Luc is worried about having enough time to do the work for the class. Agata is having trouble registering.

NOTICE!
- Direct the students' attention to the **Notice!** box.
- Ask the students to underline the *-ever* words in the text. Elicit answers to the question.

Answer
They are formed from a question word plus *-ever*.

B

Function
- Ask the students to read the discussion in Ex. A again, paying attention to the *-ever* words.
- Elicit the correct option (*b*) to complete the rule.

Form
- Direct the students' attention to the table. Ask the students to find examples from Ex. A and write them in the appropriate gaps in the table.
- Check answers with the class.
- Refer students to the *whoever* row in the table. Tell them there is a similar pronoun called *whomever*, which is not on the table. Write *whoever* and *whomever* on the board. Explain that *whoever* is a subject. Write *whoever is ready can go first* on the board. Point out that *he/she* can be substituted for *whoever*: *He/She is ready*. Explain that *whomever* is an object. Write *whomever we hire will succeed* on the board. **Highlight** that *whomever* is the object of *we*. *Him/Her* could be substituted for *whomever*: *We will hire him/her*.
- Direct the students' attention to the **What's right?** box and ask them to tick the correct sentence (*2*). Ask students to explain why the incorrect sentence is wrong. Elicit that *whatever* is a singular noun, and takes a singular verb.

Answers
1 whatever you do
2 Whatever password I try to choose
3 whenever I want
4 however I want

A new look at learning UNIT 4 33

C

- Direct the students' attention to the instructions. Tell the students that these are sentences, but the words are out of order. Ask them to re-order the words so the sentences make sense.
- Check answers with the class.

Answers

1 I can take my tablet with me wherever I go.
2 You can study whatever language you want.
3 Students can study whenever they have time.
4 It's up to you however you choose to study.
5 Whenever I try to log on, I get an error message.

D

- Put the students in groups. Direct their attention to the questions. Encourage them to discuss what they think it would be like to take an online course using relative pronouns with -ever.
- Circulate and help as needed.
- When the students finish, ask each group for one or two ideas and write them on the board. To conclude, compare and discuss the answers with the whole class.

Extra: order of clauses

Point out that many sentences in English can be constructed in more than one way. For example, sentence 1 in Ex. C could be written *I can take my tablet with me wherever I go* or *Wherever I go, I can take my tablet with me*. Both constructions are grammatically correct. Draw the students' attention to the comma after *go* in the second sentence. Note that the comma signals that the -*ever* phrase should be written as a clause at the beginning of the sentence. Have the students find the sentence in Ex. C that has a comma (item 5), and elicit that this sentence should be written with the -*ever* clause at the beginning: *Whenever I log on, I get an error message*. Have the students write pairs of sentences with -*ever* clauses at the beginning and at the end.

Extra: grammar practice

Write the following sentences on the board. Ask the students to write the sentences and fill in the gaps with the correct -*ever* words. Check answers with the class.

1 Online chat help is available to _____ needs it seven days a week.
2 Someone on the chat line can answer _____ question you have.
3 You can get help _____ you want – by online chat, by phone or by email.
4 _____ you live, you can take classes given by this university.
5 You can sign up for English classes _____ you want since new classes start every week.

Answers

1 whoever/whomever 2 whatever 3 however
4 Wherever 5 whenever

Culture note

Whatever is often used in everyday English speech to express the idea of *I don't care* or *I don't have a preference*. For example:
A: *Do you like the blue one or the red one?*
B: *Whatever.*

▶ Workbook pp. 22–23, Section 2

Pronunciation: vowel length before final consonant sounds (p. 48)

Lead-in

Explain that some pairs of English consonant sounds go together because the mouth looks exactly the same when they are pronounced. Make the mouth movements for /p/ and /b/ without voicing the sounds. Ask the students to guess which sounds they are. Then say the sounds aloud. Invite the students to place two fingers over their vocal chords and say /p/ and /b/. Elicit that with /b/, the vocal chords vibrate, or buzz, whereas they don't with /p/. Explain that vibrating sounds like /b/ are called voiced sounds, while non-vibrating sounds like /p/ are voiceless sounds. Have the students experiment with these pairs of consonant sounds to work out the voiceless/voiced sounds: /s/ and /z/; /t/ and /d/; /k/ and /g/; and /tʃ/ and /j/. Elicit that the voiced sounds are /z/, /d/, /g/, and /j/.

A 1.18

- See the Student's Book page for the **audioscript**.
- Direct the students' attention to the instructions.
- Play the audio once. Ask the students which row contains the longer vowel sounds (*the bottom row*), and ask them to listen for this. Encourage them to mouth the words along with the audio. Ask them if they hear the difference between vowel sounds in the top row and bottom row.
- Say each word pair and have the class repeat. Tell the students to try and say the vowel sounds in the words in the bottom line for a slightly longer time.
- Play the audio again and have the students say the words along with the audio.
- Write one of the pairs of words on the board (e.g. *1 late; 2 laid*). Point to the words, pronounce them, and have the students repeat. Then say one of the words and have the students say the number of the word they hear – 1 or 2. Repeat with the other pairs of words.

B 1.19

- See the Student's Book page for the **audioscript**.
- Direct the students' attention to the sentences. Have the students underline the contrasting voiced and voiceless words from Ex. A in the sentences.
- Allow the students enough time to practise saying the sentences to themselves.
- Play the audio. Stop after each sentence and have the students repeat the sentence.

- Say each sentence twice, once correctly, and once switching the length of the vowel sounds, making vowels shorter before voiced consonants and longer before unvoiced consonants. Ask students to identify the correct pronunciation of each sentence by raising their hands when they hear it.

Listening: understanding non-native English speakers (p. 48, p. 24)

Lead-in

Write *perfect English?* on the board. Tell students they are going to practise listening to accents in this lesson, as they did in Unit 2. Ask the students what 'perfect English' is. Draw attention to the information in the skills panel. Ask the students if there are speakers in their own culture who are difficult to understand, and why. Make a list of their reasons, and then compare them with the reasons stated in the skills panel: stress, intonation patterns, unfamiliar sounds. Ask them what strategies they use to understand a difficult speaker in their own culture. Encourage them to apply the same strategies to their English listening.

A 1.20

- See p. 124 for the **audioscript**.
- Tell the students they are going to listen to three conversations between non-native English speakers. They should try to understand the general topic, or gist, of all three, rather than the details. If the word gist is unfamiliar, introduce it as a new vocabulary word.
- Play the audio once, stopping after each conversation to ask the students to summarise the gist of what they heard. Replay the conversations once if necessary.

Answers

1 The downsides of technology for education
2 How working online helps students
3 Pros and cons of a professor's Twitter assignment

B

- Explain that you are going to play the audio again. This time, ask the students to choose the speaker in each conversation who is easiest for them to understand and choose the reason(s) why. They should put a tick in the box next to each reason that applies.
- Play the audio, and have the students make notes for each conversation as they listen.
- Put the students in pairs to compare and discuss their answers.
- Circulate and help as needed.
- Invite a few students to share their answers and reasons with the rest of the class.

C

- Put the students in groups. Explain that they are going to discuss issues related to accents and listening to non-native speakers of English.
- Ask the students to read the questions. Give them time to think and prepare for the discussion, making notes if they wish.
- During the discussion, circulate and help as needed. Encourage the students to try to agree on one answer to each question.
- After the groups finish their discussion, discuss their answers with the class. Ask each group if it was easy to agree on an answer to each question, and why or why not.
- Extend the discussion with the whole class by asking the students how speakers of their own language might sound when speaking English to native and non-native English speakers. What might make it more difficult for other people to understand them – stress, intonation, the pronunciation of particular sounds or something else?

▶ Workbook p. 23, Section 3

Grammar: mixed conditionals (p. 49)

Lead-in

Write the following on the board: *If I didn't use a computer in my studies, I would _____.* Ask students how their school life would be different without computers by completing this sentence. Invite volunteers to give their answers and write them on the board. (e.g. *I would have to type my essays on a typewriter; I would do all my research in the library instead of at home.*) Point out that their answers are conditional sentences. Review that conditional sentences deal with cause/condition and result: *If this, then that.* Ask the students which conditional form this is (*second conditional*). Review the purpose of the second conditional (*to indicate present unreal or hypothetical situations*) and the verb tenses in the clauses (*past tense in if-clause, would + base form of the verb in result clause.*) Next, write the following on the board: *If I hadn't used a computer in my studies, I would have _____.* Ask the students which conditional form this is (*third conditional*) and review its purpose (*to indicate past unreal or hypothetical situations.*) Ask volunteers to finish the sentence using the ideas listed on the board. (*I would have had to type my papers on a typewriter; I would have done all my research in the library instead of at home.*) Review the verb tenses in the two clauses (*past perfect in the if-clause, would + have + past participle in the result clause.*)

A 1.21

- See the Student's Book page for the **audioscript**.
- Direct the students' attention to the conversation and the question. Ask them to listen for the answer to the question.
- Play the audio. Elicit the answer. Make sure the students know the meaning of the word *obsolete* (*no longer useful, out of date*).

A new look at learning UNIT 4

Answer

Technology is changing very quickly. This means that students in technical fields learn things at university that will be out of date by the time they graduate. Yet good technology skills are still important in getting a job.

NOTICE!

- Direct the students' attention to the **Notice!** box.
- Ask the students to underline all the *ifs* in the conversation in Ex. A, and then underline the *if* clauses and circle the result clauses.
- Elicit an answer to the question.

Answer

No. They do not follow the pattern of the second or third conditionals. Some sentences have the past simple in the *if* clause, and *would have* in the result clause. Other sentences have *would* in the result clause and past perfect in the *if* clause.

B
Form & Function

- Have the students read the conversation again, paying attention to the conditional sentences.
- Use the sentences written on the board from the Lead-in to briefly review the forms of the second and third conditional. **Highlight** that both clauses in the second conditional refer to the present, and both clauses in the third conditional refer to the past.
- Direct the students' attention to the grammar table. Read through the information horizontally. Note that the top example is a present situation with a past result, while the bottom example is a past situation with a present result. **Highlight** that this is why they are called mixed conditionals.
- Ask the students to find examples from Ex. A to complete the table and to choose the correct options to complete the rules in the third column. Check answers with the class.
- Direct the students' attention to the **What's right?** box and ask them to tick the correct sentence (*2*). Ask a volunteer to say what is wrong in the incorrect sentence (*the verb* would *is missing*). Ask students to describe the time function in the sentence (*a current situation with a past result*).

Answers

1 had **2** would have got **3** second **4** third
5 hadn't learnt **6** would have **7** third **8** second

C

- Explain that in this exercise, the students will write sentences with mixed conditional clauses. Read the instructions to the class. Point out that their sentences must be mixed conditionals, as in the table in Ex. B.
- Circulate and help as needed.
- Check answers with the class.

Answers

1 If my cousin were good at taking exams, he'd/he would/might/could have passed the university entrance exam.
2 If my sister had studied hard at university, she'd/she would/might/could have a good job now.
3 If the university had offered a degree in Management, I'd/I would/might have applied to study there.
4 If my uncle had kept up with changes in technology, he wouldn't/mightn't have lost his job.
5 If I'd/I had stayed at my old job, I'd/I would/could/might be a department manager there now.
6 If the internet had existed 40 years ago, my dad would/might use it as well as I do.

D

- Put the students in pairs. Direct their attention to the instructions and ask them to think about the topic. Ask them to use sentences with mixed conditionals as they discuss the topic.
- Give the students time to organise their thoughts and make some notes before they begin their discussion.
- Circulate and help as needed.
- When the students finish, ask each pair for one or two ideas and write them on the board. To conclude, compare and discuss the answers with the whole class.

Extra: the chain game

Put the students in small groups and write this phrase on the board: *If I hadn't studied English ...* Tell each group to choose one student to complete the sentence with a result clause. For example, *... I wouldn't be in this class.* The next student to the right must then form a new sentence that begins with the preceding result clause: *If I weren't in this class ...* Explain that the goal of the game is to keep the chain of clauses going as long as possible. The chain is broken when a student cannot think of a new clause to add. Circulate and monitor, praising creativity and modeling correct language.

▶ Workbook p. 24, Section 4

Reading: a statistics-based argument (p. 50)

Lead-in

Read this quotation from Lewis Carroll, the author of *Alice in Wonderland*, to the students as you write it on the board: *If you want to inspire confidence, give plenty of statistics. It does not matter that they should be accurate, or even intelligible, as long as there are enough of them.* Ask the students if they agree or disagree, and why. Invite volunteers to share their opinions with the rest of the class.

A

- Read the heading aloud. Ask students to predict the author's arguments based on the heading.
- Read the questions at the beginning of Ex. A, and have the students read the article silently with the questions in mind.

- Ask the students to find a partner and compare their answers with the questions. Then check answers with the whole class.

Answers
The author's main point is that to be successful in the world of work, workers need to be able to adapt to change. Students at university would benefit from learning how to develop this skill.
The statistics demonstrate how companies have to deal with change and the kinds of skills they look for in employees.

B

- Have the students read the eight words and phrases containing *stand*. Ask them to find and underline these phrases in the article.
- Ask the students to match the words and phrases to their definitions (a–h). Encourage them to deduce the meaning from their context in Ex. A.
- Check the answers with the class. After a student gives an answer, have them read the sentence in Ex. A that contains the *stand* word or clause. Ask the rest of the class if they agree with the answer.
- Once the class agrees on a definition, challenge the students to volunteer a new sentence using the same item with *stand* that they just checked. For example, after checking item 1, a student might say: *From where I stand, I am convinced that a university education is worth the expense. People I know who have a university degree have decent jobs, while people I know who don't have a university degree have trouble finding good jobs.*

Answers
1 c 2 b 3 g 4 f 5 h 6 a 7 d 8 e

C

- Put the students in small groups. Refer them to the discussion questions and ask them to read the questions carefully. Give the students time to think and make notes before they begin their discussion.
- Circulate and help as needed.
- To conclude, ask a different group to share their answer to each question with the whole class. Encourage the rest of the class to add any points they consider important.

Extra: homework
Have the students write a paragraph that presents a statistics-based argument. Tell them they must include two statistics to support their opinion. To get the students started, brainstorm topics/questions related to the article such as *What are the most important qualities employers look for in applicants? What jobs give people the most personal satisfaction?* Suggest that they look for articles on a topic/question that interests them and use the statistics in them to support their position. In the next lesson, put the students in groups and have them read their paragraphs to each other. Ask the students to critique each argument. Which arguments used statistics effectively to support the author's point? Which did not?

▶ Workbook p. 25, Section 5

Writing: sentence variety – punctuation with connectors (p. 51)

Lead-in
Ask the students to read the information in the skills panel. Ask the class to name all the kinds of connectors they know in English. Make a list on the board (*and, but, because, before, although, however, therefore,* etc). Ask the students what function connectors serve. Elicit that they combine two ideas. Write the following items on the board and have students write a new sentence combining the two sentences in each item with the given connectors:
1 I had never bargained before. I soon learnt how to do so. (*but* – coordinating conjunction)
2 I like to learn about local customs. I always shop in local markets. (*therefore* – connector)
3 I go abroad to visit another country. I read about local customs. (*before* – connector)

Answers
1 I had never bargained before, but I soon learnt how to do so.
2 I like to learn about local customs; therefore, I always shop in local markets.
3 Before I go abroad to visit another country, I read about local customs.

Have volunteers write the answers on the board. Point out the different punctuation marks needed to combine sentences correctly (**1** comma, **2** semicolon and a comma, **3** comma after a clause at the beginning of a sentence). Explain that the use of these punctuation marks will be a focus of this lesson.

A

- Explain to the students that they are going to read an excerpt from a university application essay. Direct the students' attention to the directions. Have them scan the text first, underlining all the connectors. Then give them time to read the essay on their own.

Answers
where, even though, since, However, so, that is, Because

B

- Direct the students' attention to the exercise. Read the instructions and review the punctuation symbols, then allow the students enough time to complete the exercise. Tell the students to look at the examples they underlined in Ex. A for help. Circulate and monitor, giving help where needed.

A new look at learning UNIT 4 37

- Put the students in pairs or small groups to compare their answers. Circulate and go over the answers with the class. Put the students in pairs if they are not already. Have them work to write an example for each of the three punctuation rules in Ex. B. (**1** I like travelling abroad, but I don't have much time to travel. **2** I like travelling; however, I have very little time for travelling. / I like travelling. However, I have very little time for travelling. / I like travelling. I have very little time for travelling, however. **3** Because I don't get much holiday in my job, I don't travel very often. / I don't travel very often because I don't get much holiday in my job.)

Answers

1 comma **2** comma **3** semicolon, Use **4** Use **5** comma

C

- Direct students' attention to the exercise, and ask them to define a sentence. Elicit that a sentence is 1) a phrase that begins with a capital letter and ends with a full stop, question mark or exclamation mark; 2) usually has a subject and a verb; and 3) expresses a complete thought.
- Tell students that they are going to create complex sentences by linking two or more complete thoughts together in one sentence. Read the instructions, and then allow enough time for them to complete the exercise. Circulate and monitor, assisting where needed.
- Put students in pairs or small groups to compare their answers. Circulate, and choose example answers to have students write on the board. Analyse each example sentence with the whole class. Emphasise that there are two complete thoughts – two sentences – on either side of each connector. Choose two or three of the sentences on the board, and ask for volunteers to label the subject and verb for each complete thought.

Possible answers

1 Cross-country running is a compelling activity for me, because it is one of the purest forms of effort. / Because it is one of the purest forms of effort, cross-country running is a compelling activity for me.
2 I train hard all year; however, I truly learnt what 'trying hard' meant when our team took part in the Snowdon International Mountain Race.
3 Although I wasn't a top runner on the team, I decided to take the challenge. / I decided to take the challenge, although I wasn't a top runner on the team.
4 Sometimes I felt like quitting, but my teammates encouraged me.
5 When we were almost at the top, all my teammates quit and walked. / All my teammates quit and walked when we were almost at the top.
6 I didn't quit because I didn't want to let myself down. / Because I didn't want to let myself down, I didn't quit.

▶ Workbook p. 25, Section 6

LifeSkills: anticipating cultural differences (p. 52)

Step 1: Consider what information you need to know. (Ex. A)
Step 2: Consider possible difficulties caused by cultural differences. (Ex. B)
Step 3: Work out how and where to get the information you need. (Ex. C)

Lead-in
Write *breakfast* on the board. Ask students to shout out the first word or words that come to their mind, and write them under *breakfast*. Then write these words next to the students' list: *cereal, toast, tea, orange juice, coffee*. Tell the students this is what a typical British citizen might have said. How is their list different and similar? Read the target skill aloud and invite the students to tell you what they think *anticipating cultural differences* means. Ask the students in which types of situations it would be appropriate to consider cultural differences. **Highlight** that this skill could apply not only to travelling abroad, but also to receiving foreign visitors in your own country and being sensitive to their cultural concerns. Ask students for examples of any awkward situations they know that were caused by cultural differences. Then **highlight** the three-step strategy to develop the skill of anticipating cultural differences.

Culture note
Cameroon is a country in Central Africa with a population of approximately 20 million people. Cameroon shares its borders with Nigeria, Chad, Central African Republic, Congo, Gabon and Equatorial Guinea. A small area of the country borders the Atlantic Ocean. The official languages of Cameroon are French and English, but over 200 different ethnic/linguistic groups populate the country. The literacy rate is close to 70% although it is higher among boys than girls as many girls must leave school early due to local customs. Health conditions are poor and there are few doctors. Nearly 70% of the population are farmers. Cocoa and coffee are the leading agricultural exports.

A

- Direct the students' attention to the text and photo. Read the instructions to the class. Ask the students where Cameroon is (*in Africa*). Have a student find it on a world map or a globe. Ask the students to imagine what life is like there. What does the landscape look like? What about the people? Elicit some suggestions.
- Give the students time to read the information on the website and think about what other information they would like to find out.
- Direct the students' attention to the chart and the sample questions. Ask them to work individually to make a list of other questions they would have.
- When they finish, ask the students for examples of some of their questions.

Possible answers

Clothing: Are there any clothing restrictions or things I can't wear? *Food*: Is there any food not eaten, or not eaten on certain days? *Time*: What time do people normally start and finish work? *Gifts*: When is gift-giving appropriate *Making friends*: What kind of social activities do people normally participate in? *Other*: What are some important religious customs and traditions? What are some polite language forms and gestures? etc.

B

- Explain that the students are going to read a blog entry written by a former intern. Direct their attention to the blog and the photo. Ask the students what they think the photo has to do with the text.
- Have the students read the text. Then put them in pairs to discuss the four questions.
- Check answers with the class.

Possible answers

1 He expected his trip to begin at the stated time, without delays.
2 Not understanding Cameroonians' attitudes towards time and social relationships
3 Probably his culture values punctuality, and social relationships are expected to give way to demands of a set schedule.
4 He could have searched for information on common differences between Cameroon and his country; expected frustrations for people from his country and suggestions for overcoming them; he could have researched those points of his own culture that people from Cameroon would find most different. Reading about experiences from other people from his own country who had visited or lived or worked in Cameroon before could have shown him some of these points.

C

- Put the students in pairs and direct their attention to the instructions and the list of sources. Ask the students to think about what type of information they would get from each source on the list.
- Have the students refer back to the questions they wrote in Ex. A. Ask them which of the sources in this exercise would have answers to those questions. Ask the pairs to work together to discuss each question from Ex. A, and decide where to look for the answer on the list.
- Discuss the students' questions and their ideas as a class.

Possible answers

- The website of the internship organisation: Factual information about the organisation and the internship requirements (such as dates, cost, transport, housing, food)
- A citizen of Cameroon: Personal opinions about what is special or important about the country.
- A former intern from your own country: Personal opinions on the challenges and benefits of working and living in Cameroon
- A guidebook: Factual information about the country (population, languages, size, weather), main cities, well-known customs and traditions
- A travel agency: Factual information about tourist sites, transport, weather, when to go, costs
- An online blog by a foreign tourist visiting Cameroon: Personal opinions about what to see and do, possible difficulties for foreign travellers
- A news article about current events in Cameroon: News about political, social and sporting events, and cultural exhibitions that involve Cameroon and neighbouring countries
- The Embassy of Cameroon in your own country: Factual information about the country (similar to a guidebook); information about visas and how to apply; necessary inoculations; and any necessary official information for travelling

D

- Put the students in groups and have them read the instructions. Ask the students to imagine that they are hosting a foreign visitor and to think about what information would be most useful for the visitor to know.
- Ask the students to discuss the questions as a group and be ready to share their answers with the class.
- Direct the students' attention to the examples in the *How to say it* box, and encourage them to use the expressions in their discussions. Circulate and help as needed during the group discussions.
- To conclude, encourage each group to share their answers.

REFLECT

- Ask the students to read the **Reflect** question.
- Give them time to think about different situations in the domains of **Work and Career** and **Self and Society** where the skill of *anticipating cultural differences* would be useful. Elicit answers and write them on the board (Work and Career: personal interactions with colleagues and bosses, travelling to foreign countries, hosting foreign business guests. Self and Society: religious customs, making new friends, voting/elections, teachers talking with parents, etc).

RESEARCH

- Explain the task and make sure the students understand what they have to do.
- Give the students time to choose a decision or event, and then ask them to write a list of questions and a list of research sources for finding answers to those questions. Check these before the students begin their research.

A new look at learning UNIT 4

- Have them share their findings in class. Ask them to explain which questions were easiest to answer and why. Ask them if any of their sources did not have the information they were looking for, and if so, where they found the information instead.

Language wrap-up (p. 54)

For notes on how to approach the exercises in the Language wrap-up section, please refer to page 9.

1 Vocabulary
- Ask the students to read through the text before they fill in the gaps with the words from the box. Suggest that they review vocabulary on pages 46 and 50 before they begin. You could suggest that they do the ones they are sure about first.

2 Grammar
A
- Ask the students to fill in the gaps with the correct -ever word.
- Encourage them to focus on the meaning of the -ever word, such as time (*whenever*), place (*wherever*), manner (*however*), a person (*whoever*) and so on.

B
- Ask the students to combine the sentences using the word *if*. Suggest that they look at page 49 for examples of mixed conditionals and focus on the third column of the chart for the forms to use in this exercise.

Speaking workshop: expressing and supporting personal preferences (p. 55)

Lead-in
Ask the students to look at the two photos and describe what is happening in each (*students listening to a lecturer in a lecture hall; student working online*). Ask them which way of learning they prefer. Explain to the students that in this workshop, they are going to practise expressing their personal preferences – what they prefer and explaining why. Brainstorm ways to express preference in English. Elicit: *I would rather/not (I'd rather/not)* and/or: *I prefer to/prefer not to (I'd prefer to/prefer not to)*. Explain that these are the most polite ways to express preference in English, and that it's also common to give a reason or reasons for our preferences: *I'd rather/not, because ...*

A 1.22
See the Student's Book page for the **audioscript.**
- Direct the students' attention to the question in the box. Explain that they will listen to someone answer this question.

- Play the audio, and have the students listen for the speaker's opinion and the reasons she gives. Have them take notes as they listen. Play the audio again if necessary.
- Put the students in pairs to compare their notes. Check answers with the class, writing the reasons on the board.

Answer
She gives three main reasons for preferring to study in a traditional classroom: she's not good with technology; she works better in small groups; she needs direct supervision.

B
- Direct the students' attention to the sentences. Explain that they are going to hear the audio again. This time, they should listen for the phrases that will complete the sentences, and fill in the gaps.
- Play the audio. Then check answers with the class, replaying the pertinent parts of the audio for each answer.

Answers
1 would rather, than in **2** There are three **3** is that **4** For example **5** The second reason **6** Finally **7** isn't for me

Alternative
Have students fill in the gaps before listening again, and then check their answers as they listen.

Extra: expressing preference
Have the students write sentences using these phrases to express their personal preferences: *I'd rather, I'd rather not, I'd prefer, I'd prefer not to*. Invite the students to take turns reading their sentences to the class.

C
- Ask the students to look at the outline. Explain that they are going to present their own answer to the question in Ex. A, and that they will use the outline to prepare their talk.
- Give the students time to prepare their answers and make notes according to the outline. Circulate and help as needed.

D
- Put the students in small groups for their speaking task. Explain they will each have a minute and a half to answer the question in Ex. A. They may use their outline from Ex. C while giving their talk. Ask other students to keep time and to stop the speaker after one-and-a-half minutes, whether or not they have finished.

How are you doing?
- Ask the students to read the statements and tick the ones they believe are true.
- Ask them to discuss their talk with a member of their group and identify things they could improve on next time.

▶ Workbook pp. 26–27, SkillsStudio

UNIT 5 ON THE WILD SIDE

The expression *on the wild side* refers to human behaviour that is beyond, or at the edge of, social acceptability. Animals who live *in the wild* exist in natural habitats, outside of human society. As cities and developed areas grow, many wild animals have decreased in number due to loss of habitat, and some species are in danger of extinction. Protecting these animals and finding ways to ensure their continued survival is an important part of safeguarding the Earth.

Unit plan

Unit opener	(p. 56)	20 min.
1 **Grammar:** impersonal passive	(p. 58)	40 min.
2 **Listening:** to a story	(p. 59)	30 min.
• Vocabulary: animal rescue		15 min.
3 **Grammar:** passive modals	(p. 60)	40 min.
4 **Pronunciation:** final consonant clusters	(p. 61)	15 min.
5 **Speaking:** summarising	(p. 61)	30 min.
6 **Writing:** a letter to a newspaper editor	(p. 62)	30 min.
• Vocabulary: adverb-adjective collocations		15 min.
7 **Reading:** understanding definitions	(p. 63)	30 min.
LifeSkills: understanding decision-making styles (Self and Society)	(p. 64)	50 min.
• Optional downloadable *LifeSkills* lesson (Work and Career)		50 min.
• Optional downloadable *LifeSkills* lesson (Study and Learning)		50 min.
Language wrap-up	(p. 66)	20 min.
Writing workshop: writing a formal email request	(p. 67)	30 min.
Video and downloadable video worksheet		45 min.

Unit opener (p. 56)

Lead-in

Ask the students to look at the unit title and the photos, and to predict what the unit will be about. Elicit the meaning of the title using the ideas in the panel under the title on this page. Elicit the names of any wild animals that the students have seen in their own habitats. Ask them to describe the animals and say where they saw them. Direct the students' attention to the points in the unit objectives box and go through the information with them. To get your students to think about the skills being developed in this unit, ask them to look at the questions in the cogs.

Reading: understanding definitions
- Elicit ideas about why writers often give definitions of words directly in a text. (*It allows the reader to understand what is being said and continue reading. Using a dictionary to find the meaning of a word interrupts the reading process and may cause the reader to lose interest in the text*, etc.)

Speaking: summarising
- Ask the students to think about situations in which they have to give an oral summary. Then elicit answers to the questions (*summarising a talk/lecture/lesson; giving brief progress reports at work; providing background information*; etc). Point out that constructing an effective summary is an important skill for writing as well as for speaking.

LifeSkills: understanding decision-making styles
- Refer the students to the **LifeSkills** panel. Ask them to think about how they function as members of a group. Elicit their preferences in making decisions: do they like making decisions, or do they prefer to have someone else make them? Ask them to discuss the advantages and disadvantages of each approach.

Common European Framework: unit map

Unit 5	Competence developed	CEF Reference (C1 competences)
Grammar	can use and understand impersonal passives	Table 1; Table 2; Sections 5.2.1.2; 6.4.7.7; 6.4.7.8
Listening	can understand a story	Table 1; Table 2; Section 4.4.2.1; Section 4.5.2.2
Grammar	can use and understand passive modals	Table 1; Table 2; Sections 5.2.1.2; 6.4.7.7; 6.4.7.8
Pronunciation	can correctly pronounce and recognise final consonant clusters	Section 5.2.1.4
Speaking	can summarise a text	Table 1; Table 2; Sections 4.4.1.1; 4.4.1.3; 4.4.3.1; 4.4.3.5; 4.4.4.1; 4.5.2.1; 5.2.1.1; 5.2.1.2; 5.2.3.1; 5.2.3.2
Writing	can write a letter to a newspaper expressing an opinion	Table 1; Table 2; Sections 4.4.1.2; 4.4.3.2; 4.4.3.4; 4.5.2.1; 5.2.1.1; 5.2.1.2; 5.2.1.6; 5.2.2.2; 5.2.2.4; 5.2.3.2
Reading	can recognise and understand definitions	Table 1; Table 2; Sections 4.4.2.2; 4.4.2.4; 4.5.2.2

On the wild side UNIT 5 **41**

A

- Read the instructions to the class. Point out that the students will need to decide and explain exactly what connection each of their arrows indicates. Illustrate this by discussing the first example sentence. Explain that the arrow connecting the mosquito to the heron shows that insects *can be eaten* by birds. Then go over the second sentence in the same way. Point out that the arrow connecting the trees to the heron shows that the trees *provide shelter* for birds.
- Have the students look at the sample structures carefully to help them formulate their own sentences. Then ask the students to work individually to study the photos and decide on the connecting arrows they will draw. Remind the students that they should have a logical reason for drawing the arrows.
- Put the students in pairs to compare their ideas about the relationships between the parts of the ecosystem and discuss the reasons for their choices.
- Check answers with the class. Elicit one connection from each pair in turn and continue until they run out of suggestions. Ask different students to give the answer each time and make sure that they justify their connections.

Possible answers

fish – water plant: Fish fertilise the plants.
mosquito – bird: Some birds eat mosquitoes.
mosquito – fish: Fish eat mosquito larvae.
fish – water bird: Water birds eat fish.
fish – water plant: Plants provide shelter/food for fish.
water bird/bird – mosquito: Female mosquitoes feed on blood, including birds'.
mosquito – lake (background photo): Mosquitoes lay their eggs in standing water.
tree – lake: Tree roots need water.
lake – water bird: Birds drink water.

Culture note

These photographs feature wetlands, areas that are covered with surface water or groundwater. Wetlands provide habitats for fish and wildlife. Wetlands can be placed in four broad categories: marshes, swamps, bogs, and fens. The first photograph shows a wetland habitat which has been greatly affected by human activity. The swamps depicted here were once common in the coastal areas along the Gulf of Mexico. The large trees protected inland areas from storms. As cities such as New Orleans expanded, swamps were drained, and the trees died out. As a result, large storms such as 2005's Hurricane Katrina, caused widespread damage.

B

- Put the students in small groups to discuss how the things in the photos can affect people. Encourage them to be as specific as possible.
- Ask a volunteer from each group to explain how and why the things pictured are important to people. Have them refer to the example given, and accept any plausible answer. Point out that different species depend on each other, and that the students will be learning more about these connections in this unit.

Possible answers

Some kinds of fish are eaten by people. The fish, in turn, eat water plants or other fish, and live in the water.
People eat some kinds of water plants, or parts of them (e.g. water lily roots).
Wetlands are important ecosystems that process salt water and turn it into fresh water. Both people and animals drink fresh water.
Mosquitos can spread diseases to people.
People use trees for fuel/construction.

Extra: discussion

Ask the students to recall the names of some of the wild animals that came up in the discussion earlier. Put the students into small groups and have them make a list of three or four of these animals. Then have them discuss how these animals could be connected. Encourage them to provide logical reasons for their responses. Circulate and help as needed.

Grammar: impersonal passive (p. 58)

Lead-in

Ask the students to look at the photo of the bat and discuss whether it looks more like a bird or a mouse. Encourage them to justify their choice as logically as possible.

A

- First elicit where this article might be found (*nature magazines, newsletters,* etc). Ask the students to read the text individually and decide which opinion about bats is closest to their own.
- Take a quick poll by asking which students have a negative opinion of bats. Ask these students to give their opinions to the class and to explain their reasons. Then ask the students who have a positive opinion of bats to explain their viewpoints.

NOTICE!

- Direct the students' attention to the **Notice!** box.
- Ask the students to underline all the passive verbs they can find in the text and to circle the subjects of those verbs. Then ask them to notice the two ways in which these sentences are constructed.

Answer

One form of the impersonal passive begins with *It ...* and has a *that* clause after the verb. The other form of the impersonal passive begins with the subject of the sentence (e.g. *bats*) followed by the passive (impersonal) verb and the infinitive *to*.

B
Form
- Ask the students to read the text in Ex. A again, paying attention to the passive forms.
- Direct the students' attention to the grammar table. Give the students time to read through it individually. Point out that they have already encountered many of these impersonal passive constructions in texts that they have read.
- Ask the students to refer to the two forms of impersonal passive to guide them as they complete the table with examples from the article in Ex. A.
- Check answers with the class.

Answers

1 Bats are thought to be
2 It is known that
3 It is believed that

Function
- Ask the students to choose the correct option to complete each of the three sentences.
- Check answers with the class. Explain that the impersonal passive makes a sentence more formal in tone. Contrast this with the use of the subject *people* or *everyone* in the active construction of the sentences in the table, which makes it more informal or even colloquial. Then point out that the impersonal passive is less common than the active, especially in spoken English, and that we use it with reporting and opinion verbs.

Answers

1 formal 2 less 3 reporting and opinion verbs

C
- Ask the students to read the active sentences and rewrite them using the two forms of the impersonal passive. Elicit the answers to the first sentence as an example: *In ancient Egypt, it was believed that beetles were lucky; In ancient Egypt, beetles were believed to be lucky.* Have the students refer to the grammar table in Ex. B as they work.
- Check answers by asking individual students to write their sentences on the board. Answer any questions that arise.

Possible answers

1 In ancient Egypt, it was believed that beetles were lucky. / In ancient Egypt, beetles were believed to be lucky.
2 Bulls are thought to represent strength in Greece. / In Greece, it is thought that bulls represent strength.
3 Deer are often shown in Chinese art because they are said to symbolise prosperity. / Deer are often shown in Chinese art because it is said that they symbolise prosperity.
4 Elephants are thought to have a good memory. / It is thought that elephants have a good memory.
5 In some cultures, goldfish are believed to bring good luck to marriages. / In some cultures, it is believed that goldfish bring good luck to marriages.
6 Where I grew up, black cats were thought to be unlucky. / Where I grew up, it was thought that black cats were unlucky.

D
- Write the word *superstition* on the board and elicit the meaning from the class (*a belief or custom that is based on fear instead of knowledge*). Give an example of a superstition involving a kind of animal (*black cats are unlucky, yellow butterflies are lucky*, etc).
- Put the students in small groups and direct their attention to the questions. Ask them to discuss animals that have positive associations in their culture, as well as those that are considered unlucky. Ask them to explain why they think these animals have positive or negative associations. Encourage them to use the impersonal passive as they discuss these issues.
- Allow the students enough time to prepare their thoughts before the discussion and to make notes if they wish.
- Circulate and help as needed. To conclude, extend the discussion with the whole class.

▶ Workbook p. 28, Section 1

Listening: to a story (p. 59)

Lead-in
Direct the students' attention to the photo of the orangutan and elicit what they know about this animal.

Culture note

Orangutans are the only great apes found exclusively in Asia. They are an endangered species native to Malaysia and Indonesia. They are extremely intelligent and spend a lot of their time in trees. Their name comes from the Malay language and means *man of the forest*: *orang* = man; *hutan* = forest.

Borneo is in Asia, near other Indonesian islands like Java and Sumatra, and off the north coast of Australia. Borneo is the third largest island in the world and the largest in Asia. The island belongs to three different countries: the north part to Malaysia and Brunei, and the south part to Indonesia.

A
- Have the students read the synopsis from the radio show guide and guess what the story is about.
- Ask them to say what they think happens in the story, and why. Elicit reasons why orangutans might need a sanctuary (*they are an endangered species, for protection from poachers, loss of habitat*, etc).
- Have the students predict whether the story has a happy ending, and explain why they think so using evidence from the synopsis. (The text says 'this <u>is not just</u> another feel-good animal story with a happy ending ...' which means there is a happy ending to the story.) Point out that the phrase *not just* here implies that while the story ends happily, there are important messages in it to think about.

Possible answer

It is a story about an orangutan that has a happy ending.

On the wild side UNIT 5 43

B

- Have the students read the sentences and match the words and phrases in bold to the definitions. Encourage them to consider the context as they think about the meaning of each sentence. To check the answers, invite individual students to share their responses with the class.

Answers

1 b in captivity 2 c the wild 3 d endangered species
4 e release 5 f smugglers 6 a natural habitat

C 1.23

- See p. 125 for the **audioscript**.
- Ask the students to take notes while listening to the story. Play the audio once and then check progress. If necessary, play the audio again.
- Give the students time to prepare their summaries from the notes they have made. Encourage them to use the words in Ex. B in their summaries.
- Put the students in pairs to retell different parts of the story to each other.

D

- Direct the students' attention to the three questions. Give them time to think about their responses before the discussion. Ask the students to work individually first, writing key words for their answers to each question. Encourage them to use the vocabulary from Ex. B in their notes. Remind them to use their own ideas and knowledge in addition to the information from the story.
- Put the students in pairs to discuss the questions. Give them time for discussion and then invite different pairs to share their ideas with the class.

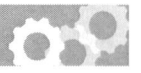

▶ Workbook p. 29, Section 2

Grammar: passive modals (p. 60)

Lead-in

Ask the students to suggest reasons why we might keep animals in zoos (*for educational purposes, to protect endangered species by providing them with a safe place to live and breed*, etc) and why people might be against zoos (*some zoos may not treat the animals well or provide them with a mate, it is cruel to deprive wild animals of their freedom and to keep them in cages for display*, etc).

A 1.24

- See the Student's Book page for the **audioscript**.
- Explain that the students will hear two people talking about a zoo. Ask them to listen and make notes about what the speakers agree and disagree about. Play the audio and have the students listen without looking at the conversation.
- After eliciting the answers from the class, ask the students whom they agree with most: Mark or Lee. Ask them to explain why and to provide further ideas of their own.

Answer

They agree that animals' habitats shouldn't be destroyed. They disagree on whether animals should be kept in zoos.

NOTICE!

- Direct the students' attention to the **Notice!** box.
- Ask them to look at the underlined phrases in the conversation and answer the question.

Answer

the past participle

B

Form & Function

- Ask the students to read the conversation, paying attention to the verb forms with past participles.
- Direct the students' attention to the grammar table and give them time to read it individually. Point out that they have encountered all of these modals in previous exercises. Explain any terms if necessary. Then have them look back at the conversation in Ex. A and identify more sentences with modal verbs.
- Ask the students to complete the table with examples from the conversation. Remind them to carefully review the information about how to use passive modals and to focus on using the tense correctly.
- Check answers with the class.
- Direct the students' attention to the **What's right?** box and ask them to tick the correct sentence (*2*). Point out that in this example, the passive form is the correct form to use because the habitats are not performing the action; they are receivers of the action. Remind the students to use the correct tense.

Answers

1 could be bred
2 can be done
3 would, be released
4 shouldn't be kept
5 ought to be banned
6 can't have been closed
7 may have been saved
8 shouldn't have been allowed

C

- Direct the students' attention to the instructions. Elicit from the students the best way to approach an exercise like this, and why (e.g. *read through the whole text first to get a better idea of the context*).
- Have them read the paragraph individually first.
- Complete item 1 as a class (*ought to visit*). Ask the students *who* is performing the action (*supporters of zoos*), what the object of the verb is (*zoos*) and whether the sentence is active or passive (*active*). Remind them to do this kind of questioning when deciding if a verb should be active or passive.
- Have the students complete the exercise individually. Check answers as a class.

Answers

1 visit 2 realise 3 be kept 4 be used 5 save 6 be given
7 be held 8 be protected 9 have been saved 10 demand

D

- Put the students in groups to discuss the ideas in Ex. C. Give them time to decide if they agree or disagree with the ideas and to make notes. Encourage them to support their opinions with examples.
- Circulate and help as needed.
- When the groups finish, invite volunteers to give their opinions to the class and elicit opposing opinions. Explain that the reasons for opposition can differ as long as they take a clear stand on the issue.
- To conclude, take a vote to see how many people are in favour of zoos and how many disapprove of them. Take another vote to see how many think governments should take more action to protect the well-being of the planet and how many disagree.
- Have the students decide individually if they agree or disagree with the different statements in Ex. C, and why. Then ask them to discuss their opinions in groups. Remind them of ways of agreeing and politely disagreeing if necessary.

▶ Workbook p. 29, Section 3

Pronunciation: final consonant clusters (p. 61)

A 1.25

- See the Student's Book page for the **audioscript**.
- Refer the students to the wordpool. Point out that some of the words have two consonant sounds at the end, and some of them have three consonant sounds at the end. Point out that groups of consonant sounds together are called *consonant clusters*.
- Play the audio and have the students complete the table.

Answers

Two final consonant sounds	Three final consonant sounds
absor**bed**, hi**ves**, len**gth**, pa**ths**, pe**st**, swar**med**, ur**ged**, war**ned**, wat**ched**, wi**dth**	gli**mpse**, insti**ncts**, invo**lved**, ma**sks**, ri**sks**, ta**stes**

B 1.26

- See the Student's Book page for the **audioscript**.
- Ask the students to look at the text and think about how to pronounce the words they have practised. Play the audio and ask them to listen carefully. Put the students in pairs and have them read the text to each other, taking care to pronounce the words with final consonant clusters correctly.

- Remind the students that there should be no unnatural pauses or overemphasis on words ending in consonant clusters when saying the complete sentences. The sentences should sound as smooth and fluent as possible.

Speaking: summarising (p. 61)

Lead-in

Ask the students to read the information in the skills panel. Point out that by now they have read many texts, and in doing so, have had a lot of practice in identifying the main idea. Ask the students what summarising is (*giving a brief and accurate statement of the main points of a text, presentation, report, etc*) and elicit when they might do this orally (*at a meeting, at work, in some study situations, etc*). Ask the students if they can use their own ideas in a summary (*No, but they can express the given ideas in their own words, i.e. paraphrase*).

A

- Direct the students' attention to the text and elicit where they would probably find a text like this (*on an internet forum*).
- Ask the class to read the forum question. Put the students in pairs, and have them decide on their roles: Student A and Student B. Have Student A read Jake509's response and Student B read Diane_Flint's response. Allow enough time for reading. Then ask the class which writer is *for* the sale of wild species as pets and which writer is *against it*.

Answer

Jake is *for*; Diane is *against*.

B

- Ask the students to read their text again and underline the main ideas. Direct the students' attention to the questions. Have them work individually to use the four questions as a guide in preparing their summary. Circulate and help as needed while they are working. Encourage them to make brief notes, and have just 3–5 key words as prompts.

Answer

Jake 509: Pet shops should be allowed to sell wild species to benefit both animals and people.
Diane_Flint: Wild animals should not be sold in pet shops because people can't adequately care for them.

Alternative

Put two Students A and two Students B from Ex. A together to work through the questions. Have them discuss the text and prepare their summary. This will enable them to help each other and develop confidence by practicing before presenting their summary to a new partner in Ex. C.

On the wild side UNIT 5 45

C

- Ask the students to close their books. Put them in pairs with the partners they had in Ex. A, and have them present their summary to their partner. Allow them to use their brief notes and key words on note cards, but not their books.
- When the pairs finish, invite them to discuss both viewpoints and decide which one they agree with. Take a class vote to see if anyone has changed their mind because of something they learnt during their discussion.

Extra: homework

Ask the students to find an online article that interests them and prepare a brief oral summary of it. Remind them to read the article carefully, make notes of the key points, and then decide on the best order to present the points. Encourage them to write a few brief notes or key words on note cards to prompt them as they deliver their summaries. In the next lesson, put the students in groups of four or five and have them present their oral summaries to their classmates. If the students wish, they can bring a printout of the original article to class, without the title, and have the listeners match the corresponding articles to each summary after listening to each presentation in their group.

▶ Workbook p. 30, Section 4

Writing: a letter to a newspaper editor (p. 62)

Lead-in

Explain that *a letter to the editor* is a short piece of writing that expresses an individual's strong feelings about an issue. Letters to the editor are written to convince readers of a specific viewpoint and to encourage discussion about the issue.

A

- Ask the students to read the questions. Write the word *deer* on the board, and divide the space into two columns labelled *for* and *against*.
- Elicit reasons for protecting deer and for getting rid of them and write them on the board. Then discuss with the class which section has a stronger argument. Repeat the process for *mosquitoes* and *wolves*.

Possible answers

1 Deer – *Protect*: The local ecosystem would be disrupted without them. They provide food for animals higher up in the food chain. *Get rid*: – They get into people's gardens and destroy plants. They carry diseases.
2 Mosquitoes – *Protect*: They are important in the aquatic food chain since algae eat their larvae. *Get rid*: They can carry deadly diseases.
3 Wolves – *Protect*: Wolves are predators and, without them, the relationship of animals below them in the food chain would change. *Get rid*: They can be a danger to people.

B

- Ask the students to read the letter to the editor of a newspaper individually. Ask them to think about how to summarise the main argument in one sentence.
- Ask the students what the letter is about (*suburban deer*) and what the writer wants to happen (*a well-organised effort from the townspeople and the local government to address the overpopulation of suburban deer*).
- Point out the conventions of a letter to the editor, which has a formal tone and begins *Dear Sir …* Direct the students' attention to the structure of the letter: how the letter begins (*by stating the reason for the letter*), how it presents the argument (*by explaining (1) the background and cause of the problem; (2) what threats suburban deer pose to people; (3) why current measures to control the deer population are ineffective*) and how the letter ends (*with the writer's opinion on how to address the problem effectively*).
- Ask the students to summarise the main argument of the letter in one sentence. Then check the answer with the class.

Possible answer

The local council needs to help find ways to control the suburban deer population, as it poses health and safety issues for the citizens of our community.

C

- Write the following sentences on the board and ask the students to complete them by filling in the gaps with the words in brackets:
1 The job is __ paid (*well/badly/poorly*).
2 The meat was ___done (*over/well*).
- Ask the students to name the part of speech of the words in brackets in item 1 (*adverbs*). Explain these adverbs can go before the word *paid* to form adverb-adjective collocations. **Highlight** that in item 2, *overdone* uses a prefix (*over-*), and *well done* uses an adverb (*well*).
- Ask the students to work individually to match the adverbs to the adjectives they are commonly used with. Point out that there is no particular rule governing why they go together; English language collocations must be learnt through practice.
- Put the students in pairs to compare answers, and then check answers with the class.

Answers

1 b 2 a 3 c

D

- Ask the students to review the letter in Ex. B and decide which collocations go with each concept. Go over the answers with the whole class.

Answers

1 (not) highly successful   2 well-organised
3 overpopulated
Point out that when a phrasal adjective follows a verb, it is usually unhyphenated, but when it comes before a verb, it usually is hyphenated. (e.g. *A well-trained athlete works hard* vs *That athlete is well trained*.)

E

- Direct the students' attention to the instructions, and ask them to read the guidelines carefully. Clarify if necessary. Then put the students in pairs to select one of the topics and write a letter to the editor.
- Point out that while each pair can divide the writing task in whatever way they prefer, they must first reach an agreement about the content of the argument. Encourage them to write both the topic sentence and the concluding sentence together. Circulate and help as needed.
- Ask the students to display their letters to the editor on the classroom walls. Have them circulate and read their classmates' letters on the same topic. Invite them to say which letter has the most effective argument, and why.

Alternative

Ask each pair of students to pass their letter to a pair near them. They should write comments on the letter and then pass it to a third pair, who should add their own comments to it. Finally, ask the original writers to retrieve their letter and discuss the comments their letter received, as well as any suggested changes. Circulate and help as needed during this process.

▶ Workbook p. 30, Section 5

Reading: understanding definitions (p. 63)

Lead-in

Ask the students to read the information in the skills panel. Explain that a text may often include definitions of key terms to make it easier for readers to understand the main idea or the basic argument of the text without interrupting the reading process to consult a dictionary. These definitions can be given either directly or indirectly in the text. Examples of direct definitions include explanations of what the term means, signalled by punctuation (e.g. in brackets or separated by dashes) or by explicit phrases such as *which means*. Examples of indirect definitions include examples and/or implications suggested by the information in the text.

A

- Put the students in pairs. Ask them to read the questions and discuss them together.
- Have each pair share their responses to items 1 and 2 with the whole class, and encourage them to explain the reasons behind their answers. Elicit the answer to item 3 (*in a current affairs magazine*).

B

- Focus the students' attention on the article and have them read it individually. Then put the students into small groups and have them answer the questions.
- Give the students time for the group discussion. Circulate and help as needed.
- Check answers with the class.

Answers

1 The article discusses the death of millions of bees through colony collapse disorder. It's important because bees are needed to pollinate plants that provide food for us.
2 The article mentions pesticides, mites, loss of habitat and climate change as causes of CCD.
3 The article suggests protecting bees' habitats and reducing or eliminating the use of chemicals that make bees ill.

C

- Ask the students to look at the first sentence of the text and identify the term being defined (*colony collapse disorder*). Then ask them to identify the definition (*the death of millions of bees*), and decide whether the definition is given directly or indirectly (*directly*). Point out that the definition here is an explanation that actually comes before the term itself is introduced.
- Ask the students to look at the example in Ex. C. Point out the term (*colony collapse disorder*), the method of definition used in the article (*known as*) and the actual definition (*the death of millions of bees*), all connected by arrows.
- Ask the students to read the article again to find the six terms and how they are defined. Have them complete the exercise individually before comparing their answers with a partner.
- Check answers with the class.

Answers

1 f, iii 2 d, ii 3 a, v 4 b, iv 5 e, i 6 c, vi

Extra: using definitions

- Write the following on the board:
  1 Africanised bees spread to North America around 1990. (known as) (aggressive variety of honeybee)
  2 An Africanised queen bee can take over the colony of different species of honeybee. (or) (leader of a colony)
  3 In the southwestern part of the USA, Africanised bees are considered to be an invasive species. (that is) (they are a non-native species that harms the local population)
  4 Killer bees are more aggressive than domestic honeybees. (explanation between dashes) (more likely to attack and pursue for longer distances)
  5 In some Latin American countries, Africanised bees are the most common variety used in beekeeping. (such as) (Brazil, Argentina)
- Ask the students to work individually to rewrite each sentence so that it includes a definition for the underlined expression. Remind them to use the expressions in brackets.
- When the students finish, put them in pairs to compare answers. To conclude, discuss the answers with the whole class. Provide explanations as necessary, and demonstrate how to insert the definitions into the sentences on the board if required.

On the wild side UNIT 5

Answers

1 Africanised bees, known as an aggressive variety of honeybee, spread to North America around 1990.
2 An Africanised queen bee, or leader of a colony, can take over the colony of different species of honeybee.
3 In the southwestern part of the USA, Africanised bees are considered to be an invasive species; that is, they are a non-native species that harms the local population.
4 Killer bees are more aggressive – more likely to attack and to pursue for longer distances – than domestic honeybees.
5 In some Latin American countries, such as Brazil and Argentina, Africanised bees are the most common variety used in beekeeping.

▶ Workbook p. 31, Section 6

LifeSkills: understanding decision-making styles (p. 64)

Step 1: Understand the advantages and disadvantages of different decision-making styles. (Ex. A, Ex. B)
Step 2: Determine which decision-making style is most appropriate for a given situation. (Ex. C)
Step 3: Carry out the decision-making process and reflect on whether it went well. (Ex. D, Ex. E)

Lead-in
Read the target skill aloud and invite the students to tell you what they think *understanding decision-making styles* means. Ask the students about the last decision they made in a group and how they made it. Start with an example of your own (e.g. *After some discussion, my family decided to go to Hawaii instead of Florida for a short holiday*). Ask whether the students think group decisions are made differently in different situations (*at home, in sports, in courtrooms, by governments, etc*). Ask in what ways they think the processes are different (*decisions are made by different numbers of people; some decisions take into account a mixture of rules and/or opinions; there may be a hierarchy when it comes to certain decisions, etc.*). Then **highlight** the three-step strategy to develop the skill of *understanding decision-making styles*.

A
- Put the students in pairs. Ask them to read the questions and give them time to think about their responses individually before discussing them with their partners.
- Allow time for pair discussion and then discuss as a class. Elicit key differences when making decisions as part of a group instead of individually. Have the students think about the positive and negative aspects of each difference (*decisions can be easier to make on your own because you don't have to consider other points of view; group decisions can be better decisions because different people can contribute different viewpoints on the same issue; some problems can be foreseen before they occur; etc*).

- Next, ask the students to consider the kinds of difficulties that can arise from making decisions as part of a group. Elicit answers from the whole group and write them down on the board (*it can be very time-consuming to decide something in a group; it may be difficult to channel input from many different people into one course of action; some group members may not feel as if their opinions are valued as much as others; some group members may not want to compromise to reach a decision; some group members may want to make decisions more actively than others; people may not be able to agree on a decision, etc*).

B
- Explain to the students that they are going to learn about four methods for reaching a group decision. Focus the students' attention on the four different decision-making styles in the box, and have them work individually to match them to the descriptions. Then check answers with the class.
- Ask the students to suggest situations where each of these decision-making methods is used (*in a school context, authoritarian: when the principal tells the students they will visit a museum; committee: when a group of student class representatives meet to discuss and decide where to visit; majority rule: the whole class votes on two choices for an outing; consensus: the class discusses and eventually agrees on an outing*).

Answers
1 majority rule 2 committee 3 authoritarian 4 consensus

C
- First, have the students work individually to complete the table by ticking the appropriate columns. Make sure they understand that several columns can be ticked for each style.
- When they finish, put the students in pairs or small groups to compare ideas and discuss any differences.
- While checking answers with the class, invite the students to share with the class any interesting ideas that came up in their discussion.

Answers
a committee, consensus
b authoritarian
c consensus, majority rule
d consensus, majority rule
e authoritarian, committee
f majority rule
g consensus

D
- Have the students read the instructions and the list of situations. Allow time for the students to prepare their thoughts for the discussion, making notes if they wish. Put the students in pairs and have them discuss their ideas for each situation. Point out that there may be more than one suitable answer for each situation. Remind them that they will need to provide a reasonable explanation for their answers.

48

- Give the pairs enough time for the discussion, and then check the answers with the class. Ask the students to say why they have chosen a certain decision-making style for each situation. Ask the rest of the class if they agree or disagree, and elicit viable alternatives.

E
- Put the students into groups of three, five, or seven (an uneven number is necessary for the group decision-making to be authentic). Give them time to read the biology assignment and the three ideas proposed.
- Make sure the students understand the task. Then refer them to the three steps of the process and have them start work.
- Circulate and help as needed.

F
- Have the students remain in the same groups. Direct the students' attention to the questions. Ask them to discuss their decision-making process and share their answers with the class.
- Direct the students' attention to the examples in the *How to say it* box and encourage them to use the expressions in their discussion.
- Give the groups enough time to discuss the questions. Circulate and help as needed.
- To conclude, ask each group in turn to share their experiences. Remind them to use the phrases in the *How to say it* box.

Extra: discussion

Elicit a basic difference between decisions made by an authority and decisions made by consensus or committee. Consensus or committee decisions often involve communities – such as families or groups of local people – and can take a long time. Authoritarian decisions can be made in urgent situations where there is less time for discussion, such as who to evacuate first in a fire. Encourage the students to tell you how and where they think they can apply the strategies they have learnt or practised during this section.

G
- Direct the students' attention to the questions. Give the students time to think about the skill of understanding decision-making styles they learnt in this lesson and how it can be useful to them in the domain of **Self and Society**.
- Ask the students to work in small groups to discuss the two questions. Ask the groups to exchange ideas on the decision-making style that they think works best for doing group assignments, choosing class activities, and organising club activities. Encourage them to give reasons for their choices. Have each group share their responses to item 2 with the whole class.

REFLECT
- Ask the students to read the *Reflect* question.
- Give them some time to think about different situations in the domains of **Work and Career** and **Study and Learning** where the skill of *understanding decision-making styles* would be useful.

- Elicit the following ideas: *selecting a team leader for a project, making budget decisions, deciding how to approach a group project, discussing possible solutions for a problem, assigning various tasks to different people*, etc.

RESEARCH
- Explain the task and make sure that the students understand what they have to do.
- Suggest sources of information on community groups and law-making bodies, such as newspapers and local news websites and interview programmes. Also suggest that the students attend a meeting of local community organisation or governing body, or view one on the internet, if possible.
- Invite the students to present the results of their research to the class, including reactions to any decision-making experiences they observed first-hand. Then have them explain what decision-making style(s) they think were in operation.
- Encourage the class to ask questions and make comments after each presentation.

Language wrap-up (p. 66)

For notes on how to approach the exercises in the Language wrap-up section, please refer to page 9.

1 Vocabulary
- Ask the students to read the whole letter for general understanding and to gain an idea of the context before filling in the gaps with the words or phrases from the box. Remind them that each gap is worth one point.
- When checking answers with the class, point out that *the* must be used before *wild* when it is used as a noun (e.g. animals in the wild), and so *wild* must be the correct answer for item 5, rather than *natural habitat*, which is used with the article *a* or a possessive adjective such as *their*). Also, draw the students' attention to the two hyphenated adverb-adjective collocations: *under-utilised* and *over-estimated*.

2 Grammar
- Make sure the students understand the question. Point out that they will be filling in the gaps with the correct form of the impersonal passive and the verb (in brackets), whereas they will be circling the correct modals.
- Ask the students to read the whole letter first before completing the exercise. Encourage them to say each sentence silently to themselves before deciding on their answers.
- Check answers with the class and explain any items as necessary.

Writing workshop: writing a formal email request (p. 67)

Lead-in
Explain to the students that in this workshop they are going to practise writing a formal email as part of a fundraising campaign.

On the wild side UNIT 5 49

A
- Direct the students' attention to the email and elicit the name of the organisation that has sent it (*Oakdene Wildlife Centre*). Explain that this is a formal email that asks the public for financial donations as part of a campaign to raise money for a charitable organisation.
- Ask them to read the email quickly on their own to find the answer to the question.
- Put the students in pairs to discuss their answers. Then check the answer with the class.

Answer

The money is needed to take care of the birds, to provide educational programmes and for the nature centre.

B
- Ask the students to read the email again, paying attention to what information the email contains and how each paragraph is structured.
- Have them work individually to read the list of features and identify them in the email where possible.
- Put the students in pairs to compare answers and discuss any differences.
- Point out that the email identifies the receiver (or recipient) of the email as a 'Community Supporter'. Although this is not technically a name, it identifies the receiver as a member of a community who helps support it, probably by giving money. Ask the students to think about the psychological effect of the pronouns *you*, *I* and *we* on the receiver and what role these pronouns play in the email. (*It creates a sense of community and makes a request for money seem more personal.*)
- Ask the students to look at the email and discuss whether the explanation of what each donation of £20 or £50 gives each donor functions as a recommendation. (*Yes, it is an indirect recommendation because people are more likely to donate £20 or £50 since they know they will get something specific in return./No, it is only a suggested amount; the letter says that donors can give 'any amount of their choosing'.*)

Answers

The email contains:
2 the sender's name
3 the pronoun *you*
4 the pronouns *I* or *we*
5 an explanation of what the organisation does
8 what the organisation will spend money on
9 a recommended amount to give

C
- Ask the students to read the email again and work individually to underline all the phrases that could be used in any fundraising letter.
- Put the students in pairs to discuss their answers. Then check answers with the class and write them on the board.

Answer

Dear Community Supporter,
The Oakdene Wildlife Centre <u>was created in</u> 1987 <u>to serve the needs of</u> our area's wild birds of prey – red kites, eagles, osprey and falcons. <u>Each year</u>, we help rescue dozens of sick and injured birds. <u>Our trained volunteer staff works to</u> rehabilitate these birds so that they can be released back into the wild. <u>We also conduct</u> educational outreach programmes to inform the public about the place these beautiful birds have in our environment and how we can all work together to protect their habitat.
<u>I'm writing to ask for a donation to our annual fund</u>.
<u>Your gift helps pay for</u> food and shelter for the birds, their medical expenses, our educational outreach programmes in schools and community centres and our nature centre. <u>A donation of just £20 includes</u> an annual membership to the Oakdene Wildlife Centre, discounts on our gift shop items and free admission to any of our programmes. <u>For £50, you can</u> sponsor an individual bird, for which you'll receive a photo of the bird, an adoption certificate and regular updates about your sponsored bird's progress.
<u>Click here to donate £20 or any amount of your choosing</u>.
<u>Thank you for your generosity</u>.
<u>Sincerely</u>,

D
- Ask the students to read the instructions, and explain the task as needed. Then have the students look at the notes provided. Ask them to use the notes to write a formal email with a request for money for the shelter. Encourage them to supplement those notes with their own ideas to make their emails interesting and informative.
- Encourage the students to use the phrases they identified in Ex. C to help them draft their emails. Refer them to the structure of the sample email in Ex. A and encourage them to follow it. Circulate and help as needed.
- When the students finish writing, put them in small groups to review each other's work and offer tips on revision. Have them check their group members' emails to make sure that they all include a direct request for what their organisation wants, that they are right length (about 250 words) and that they are in the correct format.
- Remind each group to offer guidance on the quality of the points and the structure of the email by writing corrections, comments and suggestions on each page. Then ask the students to rewrite their emails based on the peer feedback they received and display their final emails on the classroom walls or on a noticeboard.

How are you doing?

- Ask the students to read the statements and tick the ones they believe are true.
- Ask them to discuss their email with a member of their group and identify things they could improve on next time.

▶ Workbook p. 32, SkillsStudio

UNIT 6 MORE THAN MACHINES?

The expression *more than machines* refers to the expanding role of machines in our lives, and how machines are taking over many tasks from humans. Some machines even simulate human speech and emotions. Scholars predict that in the future we will be able to upload our consciousness into computers, so that we can exist forever in the cloud.

Unit plan

Unit opener	(p. 68)	10 min.
1 **Grammar:** future perfect	(p. 70)	40 min.
2 **Speaking:** talking about automation	(p. 71)	30 min.
• Vocabulary: phrases with adjective + preposition		15 min.
3 **Reading:** an online news article	(p. 72)	20 min.
• Vocabulary: phrasal verbs		15 min.
4 **Listening:** inferring opinions	(p. 73)	40 min.
5 **Grammar:** future perfect continuous	(p. 74)	20 min.
6 **Pronunciation:** linking words with a /w/ or a /j/ sound	(p. 75)	40 min.
7 **Writing:** summarising	(p. 75)	20 min.
LifeSkills: organising an argument (Study and Learning)	(p. 76)	45 min.
• Optional downloadable *LifeSkills* lesson (Self and Society)		45 min.
• Optional downloadable *LifeSkills* lesson (Work and Career)		45 min.
Language wrap-up	(p. 78)	15 min.
Speaking workshop: comparing and contrasting photographs	(p. 79)	45 min.
Video and downloadable video worksheet		45 min.

Unit opener (p. 68)

Lead-in

Ask the students to look at the unit title and the photos and to predict what the unit will be about. Elicit the meaning of the title using the ideas in the panel above. Ask the students to describe new machines that are being developed (*driverless cars*, '*smart glasses' with GPS*, etc) and say which they would like to use most. Direct the students' attention to the points in the unit objectives box. To get your students to think about the skills being developed in this unit, ask them to look at the questions in the cogs.

Listening: inferring opinions
- Ask the class the meaning of the verb *infer*. Elicit that *to infer* means to make an educated guess, based on the information you have available. Have the students brainstorm answers to the question.

Writing: summarising
- Ask the students to define the word *summary* without looking it up (*a short statement of the main points of something, such as a text or a talk*). Direct the students' attention to the questions and discuss them as a class.

LifeSkills: organising an argument
- Refer the students to the **LifeSkills** panel. Explain that part of this unit will focus on how to organise an argument. Ask the students to read the question quickly and tick the first response they think of. Check to make sure they understand the meaning of *passion* (*strong feelings*). Ask for a show of hands for each answer choice.

Common European Framework: unit map

Unit 6	Competence developed	CEF Reference (C1 competences)
Grammar	can use and understand the future perfect	Table 1; Table 2; Sections 5.2.1.2; 6.4.7.7; 6.4.7.8
Speaking	can talk about automation	Table 1; Table 2; Sections 4.4.1.1; 4.4.3.1; 4.4.3.5; 4.5.2.1; 5.2.1.1; 5.2.1.2; 5.2.3.2
Reading	can understand an online news article	Table 1; Table 2; Sections 4.4.2.2; 4.4.2.4; 4.4.3.4; 4.5.2.2
Listening	can infer opinions	Table 1; Table 2; Sections 4.4.2.1; 4.4.2.4; 4.5.2.2
Grammar	can use and understand the future perfect continuous	Table 1; Table 2; Sections 5.2.1.2; 6.4.7.7; 6.4.7.8
Pronunciation	can link words with a /w/ or /j/ sound	Section 5.2.1.4
Writing	can summarise a text	Table 1; Table 2; Sections 4.4.1.2; 4.4.1.3; 4.4.4.2; 4.5.2.1; 5.2.1.1; 5.2.1.2; 5.2.3.2; 5.2.1.6

More than machines? UNIT 6 51

A

- Put the students in pairs and have them look at the photos. Direct their attention to the discussion questions.
- Allow enough time for the students to discuss the questions. Circulate and help as needed.
- Discuss the students' opinions as a class. Draw a Venn diagram (overlapping circles, with common attributes in the overlapping section) like the one below to show the differences and similarities between robots and machines. Have the students give their ideas and write them in the diagram.

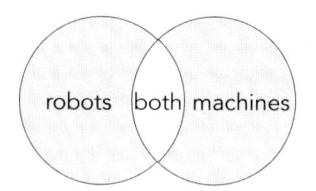

robots | both | machines

- Have the class vote on the most useful robot pictured, and ask the students to summarise the reason for their choice in one sentence.

Culture note

What can robots do? There are different types of robots that do many different tasks. In the field of medicine, robots not only perform surgery, but they also perform routine medical tests. In the area of public works, robots are used to do dirty jobs, such as cleaning water and sewer pipes. In the home, microwaves and cookers have robot-like microprocessors designed to prevent fires and damage, and in fact, the household might have a robotic 'pet dog'. Finally, some robots just are designed to be like humans – the Quiro robot can walk, run, dance, recognise faces, surf the Web and even talk a little.

B

- Put two pairs from Ex. A together to form groups of four. Direct the students' attention to the instructions. Circulate and help as needed.
- To conclude, elicit ideas from each group in a whole-class discussion. Make sure the students give reasons to justify their answers.

Extra: speaking

Ask the students to think of a machine or robot that they would like to own – real or imaginary. Put the students in pairs and have them take turns describing the robot or machine, and say why they would like to have it and what they would use it for. Encourage them to be as specific as possible.

Grammar: future perfect (p. 70)

Lead-in

Draw the following timeline on the board:
NOW _____ ONE YEAR FROM NOW
Ask the students for examples of things they will do in the next year and write them under the timeline (*finish school, find a job, go on a trip, get married, move to a different home*, etc). Write the following sentence on the board: *By this time next year, I _____*. Ask a volunteer to complete the sentence using one of the examples on the board (*will have finished school, will have found a job*, etc). Elicit or explain that this form indicates that the action has been completed by a future date.

A

- Direct the students' attention to the blog entry and the photo. Read the instructions to the class and ask them try to find the answer to the question as they read.
- Have the students read the article silently. When they finish, ask a volunteer to answer the question.

Answer

The writer thinks robots threaten our future by taking away some of the roles at work that were previously done by humans. There won't be enough jobs for people.

NOTICE!

- Direct the students' attention to the **Notice!** box.
- Have the students find one example of *will* and one of *won't* in the text. Write one example of each on the board, including the full clause.
- Ask a volunteer to answer the question, and then underline the answer in each clause (the word *have* and the past participle).

Answer

Each example of *will* or *won't* in the text is followed by *have* + past participle or by *have* + *been* + past participle.

B

Form

- Have the students read the blog entry again, paying attention to the future tenses.
- Direct the students' attention to the grammar table. Review when the passive is preferred (*when the agent is unknown or is unimportant*).
- Have the students work individually to complete the table with examples from the text in Ex. A. Check answers with the class.

Answers

1 will have changed
2 won't have disappeared
3 won't have been replaced

Culture note

When native English speakers say *will have*, they often pronounce *have* in its weak form, so it sounds like *will of*. Thus, *you will have known* sounds like *you will of known*. Sometimes they make the mistake of writing it this way, as well.

Function

- Have the students choose the correct option (*a*) to complete the rule. Direct the students' attention to the **What's right?** box and ask them to tick the correct sentence (*2*). Ask them what the difference is between the two sentences. Elicit that in the correct sentence, the action will be completed by 2025. Explain that when an action will be completed by a certain time, it requires the future perfect.

Extra: grammar

Write the following sentences on the board: *In 2020, we will build our new house. By 2020, we will have built our new house.* Ask the students how the two sentences differ in meaning (*in the first sentence, they will start building in 2020; in the second sentence, the house will already be finished in 2020*). Have the students work individually to write two similar sentences and then put them in pairs to compare their work.

C

- Write the words *by* and *in* on the board. Direct the students' attention to the sentence prompts.
- Ask the students which sentences would require *by* and which would use *in*. Encourage them to skim the blog entry for clues. Elicit that items 2 and 6 would use *by* and the rest would use *in* (or *within*).
- Ask the students if they can deduce a rule or pattern for using *by* and *in/within*. Elicit that *by* is used with definite dates or points in time (*2050, the middle of the century*), while *in* or *within* is used for time periods (*five years, another decade*).
- Have the students write the six sentences individually. Circulate and help as needed. Check answers with the class.

Answers

1 In 15 years / In 15 years' time / Fifteen years from now, robots will have become common around the home.
2 By the middle of this century, robots will have taken over many manufacturing jobs in my country.
3 In four or five years / In four or five years' time / Four or five years from now, smartphones will have been replaced by smartwatches in some cases.
4 In another decade / In another decade's time / Another decade from now, the PC will have become obsolete.
5 In a few years / In a few years' time / A few years from now, the last DVD rental shops in my city will have gone out of business.
6 By the year 2050, artificial intelligence still won't have been created.

Extra: grammar practice

Ask the students to choose three of the time phrases in Ex. C and write their own predictions for that date using the future perfect. Put the students in small groups to share their sentences. Have the groups discuss areas of agreement or disagreement.

D

- Put the students in pairs to discuss the questions raised in the blog entry in Ex. A. Circulate and help as needed.
- To conclude, have each pair share their ideas with the whole class. Monitor future perfect tense in their speech.

▶ Workbook p. 34, Section 1

Speaking: talking about automation (p. 71)

Lead-in

Ask the students if they enjoy flying, and why or why not. What makes them the most nervous? Elicit personal examples of good flights and bad flights the students have had.

A 1.27

- See p. 126 for the **audioscript.**
- Explain that the students are going to hear two people disagreeing with each other. Direct their attention to the two questions. Ask them to listen for the answer to the first question, and tell them not to worry right now about details or words they do not understand. Ask them to raise their hands as soon as they think they know the answer.
- Play the audio. Stop it when a student raises their hand, and check their answer. Then play the entire audio.

Answer

The man blames automation; the woman blames the pilots.

- Ask the students which speaker they agree with. Give several students a chance to speak.

B

- Explain that certain English adjectives are usually followed by certain prepositions. For example, we are afraid *of* something and good *at* something. Some adjectives can be followed by more than one preposition, such as *careful*, which can be followed by *with*, *about* and *of*.
- Have the students skim the two parts of the sentences. Ask them to listen to the audio to hear which preposition follows each adjective. Play the audio again and have the students listen for the phrases on the left. Then have them match the two halves of each sentence.
- Check answers with the class.

Answers

1 b 2 f 3 g 4 d 5 c 6 a 7 e

More than machines? UNIT 6 53

Extra: vocabulary

Write the following list of adjectives on the board, and tell the students to copy them: *proficient, careless, good, suited, capable*. Tell them to use dictionaries or other references works (or even online references) to find the prepositions that can follow them (there may be more than one). Ask them to write one sentence with each adjective + preposition combination. Have the students share with their sentences with a partner at the next lesson.

C

- Put the students in pairs and ask them to read the instructions. Have them read the text individually and circle the correct options. Then have them compare answers with their partner and refer to Ex. B.
- Check answers with the class.
- Have each pair brainstorm their own definition of *automation*. Emphasise that they should not look it up in a dictionary. Elicit answers from each pair and then write the dictionary definition (*the use of machines and technology to make processes run on their own without manpower*) on the board.
- Explain that *auto* is a Greek word meaning *self*. Elicit other examples of *auto* words (*automobile, autopilot, autograph, autocratic*, etc). Ask how each word connotes a sense of self.

Answers

1 aware of
2 dependent on
3 distracted by
4 overwhelmed by
5 suspicious of
6 alarmed by
7 focused on

Extra: game

Divide the class in half to create two teams. Write the adjectives and prepositions from Ex. B on the board in a mixed-up order. Explain that the students are going to use them in a game. To begin the game, say one of the adjectives (e.g. *dependent*). Choose a team to have first chance to pair it with the correct preposition (*on*). Give them ten seconds. If they name the correct proposition they get three points. If they are incorrect, the other team gets ten seconds to guess the correct answer for two points. After the first three or four words, the teacher should switch the order: state one of the three prepositions (*of, on, by*) and ask for an adjective it pairs with. For example, if the teacher says *by*, correct answers would be *alarmed, distracted* or *overwhelmed*. Keep score until all the adjectives and prepositions have been used once.

D

- Ask the students to read the instructions. Discuss with the class the kinds of automation found in cars and planes (*cars – GPS, automatic windscreen wipers, etc; planes – automatic pilot, individual TV screens for passengers*, etc).
- Give the students time to choose the option they agree with. Have them organise the ideas for their presentation and make notes if they wish. Remind them to include a list of types of automation to include or exclude. Circulate and help as needed.

E

- Put the students in pairs and direct their attention to the instructions. Have the students time their partners. Ask them to allow no more than two minutes for each presentation. Encourage partners to ask questions and give feedback. Circulate and help as needed.
- To conclude, ask for a show of hands to find out whether the students would prefer to increase or decrease the use of automation. Then have students share ideas on the types of automation they would like to add to or remove from cars and planes. List their ideas in two columns on the board.

Extra: discussion

Divide the students into sides (increase/decrease) and conduct a whole-class debate on the topic of automation in cars and planes. Make sure several different students get to speak for each side.

▶ Workbook pp. 34–35, Section 2

Reading: an online news article (p. 72)

Lead-in

With the class, brainstorm jobs or tasks that are done mostly by machines (*tasks in factories, such as making cars on assembly lines; self-checkout in supermarkets*). If the students have trouble thinking of examples, prompt them to think about their home (*washer/dryer, dishwasher, cooker*, etc). Ask why people use machines for these jobs or tasks. Then brainstorm a list of jobs or tasks that are mostly done by people, but that they think machines could do faster or better (*train driver, security guard*, etc).

A

- Direct the students' attention to the photo. Ask them to speculate on the idea that it shows. Invite several students to give ideas (*robots and humans can work together; robots do not need to replace humans*, etc).
- Direct the students' attention to the article. Have the students read the question.
- Give the students time to read the article silently with the question in mind. Elicit answers to the question as a class.

Answer

We don't see 'armies of robots' in the workplace because globalisation has led to the availability of cheap human labour.

B

- Direct the students' attention to the instructions. Point out that answers should be in their own words and not copied directly from Ex. A.
- Have the students complete the exercise individually, referring to Ex. A as needed.
- Put the students in pairs to compare their answers. Check answers with the class.

Possible answers

1 It is used to find tumours by a surgeon.
2 Because workers will have to use more technology in the future, the demands of low-skilled work will increase and even low-skilled work will become high-skilled work.
3 They will need to be resilient because they will need to continue developing new skills over the course of their whole career.

Culture note

Research conducted by the University of Oxford in 2014 predicted that approximately 35% of jobs in the UK would become redundant due to technological advances within the next 20 years. At the same time, the demand for people to work in the area of artificial intelligence (*development of software that can reason, gather knowledge, plan intelligently, learn to communicate, perceive and manipulate objects*) is growing rapidly.

Extra: speaking

Organise a class debate on the topic: *Will robots steal our jobs?* Divide the class into two opposing teams (agree/disagree). Allow each group to prepare their arguments. Then ask each side to choose two people to debate the statement. After the debate, ask the class to vote on the winning team.

Extra: homework

Ask the students to find an example of another online article on the topic of robots in the workplace. Tell the students to read the article and write the main idea of the article in one sentence. Tell them to bring a copy of the article to the next lesson. Put the students in pairs and have them each explain the main idea of their article. Also have each partner say if the article they read has the same position on robots in the workplace as the article in Ex. A.

C

- Direct the students' attention to the instructions. Make sure they understand the meaning of *phrasal verb* (*a verb followed by a particle acting together to form a verb*). Tell the students to work individually to come up with their own definition for each phrasal verb first before they check a dictionary.
- Check the answers with the class.

Answers

1 happen, occur
2 tell someone something they need to know
3 (of a situation, etc) happen, especially by chance
4 try to get something other people are also competing for
5 need something in order to continue living, existing or operating
6 learn a new skill

D

- Refer the students to the instructions. Make sure they understand that they are to fill in the gaps with the correct form of phrasal verbs from Ex. C.
- Allow the students enough time to complete the exercise. If they need help, suggest that the students review the definition they wrote for the phrasal verb in Ex. C and see if it makes sense in the sentence. Have the students compare their answers in pairs. Then check answers as a class.

Answers

1 point out
2 pick up
3 going on
4 rely on
5 going after
6 come about

Extra: practice

Put the students in pairs or groups, and provide each pair/group with a variety of English-language publications: books, magazines, newspapers, etc. Tell the students not to use the internet. Explain that they are going to work together to find as many phrasal verbs as they can in ten minutes. Have the students use the English publications to search for phrasal verbs. Tell them to write the phrasal verbs as they find them. After ten minutes, have each pair/group share their answers. Pairs/groups get one point for each phrasal verb they find that is *not* found by any other pair/group. The team that finds the most original phrasal verbs is the winner. To extend the activity, have each group find the meaning of their new phrasal verbs and share them with the class.

Extra: homework

Ask the students to write a sentence for each of the phrasal verbs in Ex. C. Tell them to use the sentences in a context that relates to their school. Put the students into small groups and have them read their sentences aloud in the next lesson.

▶ Workbook p. 36, Section 4

More than machines? UNIT 6 55

Listening: inferring opinions (p. 73)

Lead-in
Ask the students to read the information in the skills panel. Make sure they understand the meaning of *emphasis* (*stressing one word in a sentence more than others*). Ask if they know of examples of this in their native language. Have the students share examples with the rest of the class.

A 1.28
- See p. 126 for the **audioscript**.
- Make sure the students understand the meaning of *artificial intelligence* (AI) (*software that can reason, gather knowledge, plan intelligently, learn to communicate, perceive and manipulate objects*). Explain that they will hear a six-part conversation about AI. Direct their attention to the six parts of the exercise and ask them to decide which answer choice is the best paraphrase of the sentence on the audio.
- Play the audio. Stop after each part, and if necessary, play the audio for each part again.
- Check answers as a class.

Answers
1 b 2 b 3 b 4 b 5 a 6 b

B
- Explain that you will play the audio again. This time, the students should listen and decide which of the three techniques listed – a, b or c – was used by the speaker to help them understand the meaning.
- Have the students review the sentences and answers in Ex. A. Explain that if they think they already know the correct answer choice for one of the sentences in Ex. A, they should write a, b, or c next to that part of the conversation.
- Play the audio. Check progress, and if necessary, play the audio again.
- Put the students in pairs to compare answers, discussing any differences.
- Check answers with the class. How many of the students' predicted answers turned out to be correct?

Answers
1 c 2 a/c 3 c 4 b 5 b 6 a/b

C
- Put the students in small groups. Give them time to discuss each of the three questions. Circulate and help as needed.
- Ask each group to appoint a spokesperson to summarise the group's opinion on each question. The spokesperson should answer *yes* or *no* to each question on behalf of the group and explain in one sentence why the group chose this answer.
- Have each spokesperson share their group's answers with the class. Finally, take a vote by a show of hands to find out how most students answer the three questions.

▶ Workbook p. 35, Section 3

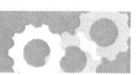

Grammar: future perfect continuous (p. 74)

Lead-in
Draw the following timeline on the board:
PAST _____ NOW _____ FUTURE
Under NOW, write the year and the sentence *I am studying English*. Ask a volunteer to tell you what year they began studying English. Write the year under PAST. Ask the student how long they have been studying English now and elicit the answer. Under NOW, write *I have been studying English for (six) years*. Write a future year under FUTURE. Ask the same student if they will still be studying English at that time. If so, ask how long they will have been studying English by that date. Write the sentence under FUTURE (*By 2020, I will have been studying English for (eleven) years*).

A
- Direct the students' attention to the instructions. Have them read the questions carefully.
- Give the students time to read the text and determine the writer's viewpoint. Ask the first question and elicit the answer (*positive*). Then ask the students to read phrases from the text that helped them reach their conclusion (*technology keeps on improving, people will have been living comfortably with robots*).

Answer

The author's view is positive because he uses robots in his business and because he is generally optimistic.

NOTICE!
- Direct the students' attention to the **Notice!** box.
- Read the instructions, and give the students time to find the verb form (*will have been living*).

B
Form
- Ask the students to read the blog post again, paying attention to the verb forms like *will have been living*.
- Draw the students' attention to the grammar table, and give them time to read it. Refer the students back to the Lead-in sentence on the board (*I have been studying English for (six) years*). Remind them that the verb tense in this sentence is called the *present perfect continuous*. Ask what the difference is between this verb phrase and the verb phrase in the **Notice!** box sentence. Elicit that the **Notice!** sentence adds *will* at the start of the phrase, making it the future perfect continuous.

- Have the students complete the table with examples from the blog post. Check answers with the class.

Answers
1 will have been using
2 will have been making

Extra: grammar practice
Elicit examples of other continuous forms using *the robots* as subject and the verb *work*. Make a list on the board. Direct the students' attention to the difference in the forms (*present continuous: The robots are working …; past continuous: The robots were working …; present perfect continuous: The robots have been working …; future continuous: The robots will be working …*). Point out that the future perfect continuous includes both *will* and *have*.

Function
- Have the students choose the correct option to complete the rule (*b*). Check the answer with the class. Remind the students that the present perfect continuous can be used to describe an action or a situation happening for a period of time up to a specific time in the *present* (e.g. *I have been working in this school for nine years.*). Contrast this with the future perfect continuous, which is about an action happening up to a specific time in the *future* (e.g. *By this time next year, I will have been working in this school for ten years* (future time – the future perfect continuous).
- Direct the students' attention to the **What's right?** box and ask them to tick the correct sentence (*2*). Ask them what the difference is between the two sentences. Elicit that in the correct sentence the action (*waiting*) began earlier and continues up to a specific time in the future (the arrival of the other person), and so the future perfect form is needed.
- Ask the students what else a future perfect continuous verb phrase must have in addition to *will*. Elicit the answer *have been*.

C
- Direct the students' attention to the instructions. Have the students complete the exercise individually and then check their answers in pairs, discussing any differences.
- Ask a different student to write an answer to each question on the board. After they write their answer, have the class correct it and make changes if necessary.

Answers
1 will have been working
2 will have been making
3 get, will have been taking
4 will have been using
5 retires, will have been collecting
6 will have been playing, finishes

D
- Put the students in groups. Direct the students' attention to the instructions. As a model, elicit several answers for the first sentence stem (*I will have been living overseas for several years. I will have been working in my father's business since graduation*, etc).

- Give the students time to think of how they will complete each of the sentences and to make notes if necessary. Then have the students in each group take turns sharing their future plans using the future perfect continuous.

Extra: grammar practice
Ask the students to complete the three sentences from Ex. D using the negative form of the future perfect continuous (*won't + have + been + -ing*). Have them share their answers in the same group they worked with in Ex. D.

▶ Workbook p. 36, Section 5

Pronunciation: linking words with a /w/ or a /j/ sound (p. 75)

Lead-in
Explain that native speakers of English commonly link certain sounds, or say them together. Write the following pairs of words on the board, say them, and have students repeat them linking the sounds as indicated: *turn‿off, most‿intelligent*. Point out that these pairs present an example of one type of linking – linking a consonant sound to a vowel sound. Explain that the students are going to study another type of linking – linking a vowel sound to another vowel sound. Indicate that, in this case, another sound is added when the words are linked, to allow both vowel sounds to be pronounced fully and separately without a pause between words.

A 🔊 1.29
- See the Student's Book page for the **audioscript**.
- Direct the students' attention to the title of the section and help the students review the sounds for the symbols. Write the following on the board, say the words and have the students repeat them:
/w/ **w**ild **w**ill, /j/ **y**ou **y**oung
- Direct the students' attention to Ex. A. Explain that when one word ends with a vowel sound and the next word begins with a vowel sound, another sound – /**w**/ or /**j**/ – can be added between the words to join the two vowel sounds together.
- Play the audio for the phrases in the first row. Have the students repeat each phrase as soon as it is played.
- Direct the students' attention to the pair of words in each phrase, and have them identify the two vowel sounds that are linked.

Answers
go on: /w/	he isn't: /j/
high altitude: /j/	I often: /j/
no idea: /w/	true answer: /w/
two apples: /w/	we allow: /j/

B 🎧 1.30

- See the Student's Book page for the **audioscript**.
- Put students in pairs and play the audio again.
- Have the students practise reading the sentences aloud to their partner. Circulate and help as needed.

Extra: pronunciation practice

Ask the students to write sentences for two of the pairs in the first row and for two of the pairs in the second row. Put the students in pairs. Ask the students to read their sentences to their partner, monitoring each other's pronunciation.

Writing: summarising (p. 75)

Lead-in
Ask the students to read the information in the skills panel. Ask them to close their textbooks and ask what the first step is in writing a summary. Then ask them what the second and third steps are.

A
- Direct the students' attention to the text. Make sure the students understand the instructions.
- Have the students work independently to complete the exercise. Put them in pairs to compare answers and discuss differences.
- Check answers with the class.

Answers
Main ideas: the past few years have seen some impressive developments in robotics, and the future looks even brighter for robot technology. My research is focused on using robots for search and rescue missions and environmental clean-ups.

If government agencies continue to fund our research at current levels, robots will have started working on every continent …

Information for summary: Dr Jake Helder, NowTech Institute, 8th Jan., Robots: a necessary expenditure

B
- Give the students time to read both summaries silently. Ask them to decide which summary they think is better and why. Elicit opinions and come to an agreement.

Answer
Summary (a) contains all of the necessary information presented in a logical order. Summary (b) lacks the name of the author and is not well organised.

C
- Direct the students' attention to the text and ask them to read it and write their own summary. You could suggest that they use the same technique as when they read Ex. A (*underline the main ideas, and circle the information about the text: title, author, source, date*).

- Allow the students time to write their summaries in class. Circulate and monitor, assisting where needed.

D
- Ask the students to read the instructions. Put them in groups and have them compare their summaries, discussing any differences.
- To conclude, ask the class to name the main idea(s) in the article and the important information in the text. Make a list of each on the board and ask the students to check whether they included all the points in their summaries.

Extra: homework

Ask the students to find a short online article on the topic of robots, or provide one for them. Ask the students to write a summary of it, using the process in the skills panel. In the next lesson, put the students in pairs and have them exchange their summaries. Ask the partners to read the summary and provide feedback, asking questions about any points that are not clear.

▶ Workbook p. 37, Section 6

LifeSkills: organising an argument (p. 76)

Step 1: Choose an appropriate organisational pattern for your argument. (Ex. A, Ex. C, Ex. D)
Step 2: Select points to include in your argument. (Ex. B, Ex. C, Ex. D)
Step 3: Organise the points you want to make according to the pattern you have chosen. (Ex. D, Ex. E)

Lead-in
- Read the target skill aloud and invite the students to tell you what they think *organising an argument* means. Ask them what *argument* means. Elicit that it has two meanings: 1) a quarrel or disagreement, and 2) a talk or a piece of writing that is intended to convince or persuade someone to accept one's opinion on an issue. Elicit that the second sense is used in this section. Then **highlight** the three-step strategy to develop the skill of *organising an argument*.
- Write the words *fact* and *opinion* on the board. Ask the students for a definition of each word, as well as for a few examples. Discuss with the class when opinions are appropriate in their writing and when facts are more important. Ask the students if they know what an *informed opinion* is (*an opinion based on fact*).

A
- Direct the students' attention to the webpage and the words and phrases in the box. Make sure they understand the meaning of all the words and phrases. Explain that a *counter-argument* is an argument that opposes one's opinion and that students are going to learn about counter-arguments in this exercise.
- Explain that they are going to match the phrases to the five gaps in the text.

- Have the students read the text and complete the exercise individually. Put them in pairs to compare answers and discuss any differences.
- Check answers with the class.
- Ask the students to discuss the kinds of assignments that they have done that are similar to the ones described in Ex. A, in which they have had to argue a point of view. Elicit some of the topics that they have had to talk/write about. Discuss whether it was easy or hard to do the assignment and whether they enjoy expressing their opinions for one side of an issue and arguing against the other side.

Answers

1 Context
2 Statement of your view
3 Supporting reasons
4 Counter-arguments
5 Responses

B

- Have the students read the instructions and the three statements individually. Explain that each student will choose one statement and then organise an argument to defend it. Give the students time to read and decide.

Alternative

Have the students close their books while you write the five words and phrases from the box on the board. Say each one aloud and invite individual students to tell the class what they know about it. Then have each student read the text and use what they learnt to complete the exercise individually. Check answers with the class.

Extra: class survey

Read each statement aloud and have the students raise their hands if they have chosen it to write about. Ask them to discuss why they think more students chose one answer than another.

C

- Explain that the students should now think of three reasons that support the statement they have just chosen. **Highlight** that they should put the reasons in order, with the first being the most important. Have them read the instructions and then give them time to prepare their outlines. Circulate and help as needed.

D

- Direct the students' attention to the instructions. Explain that the prefix *counter-* means *against* or *contrary to*. Read the examples in the box of a counter-argument and a good response. Then give the students time to think of two possible counter-arguments and write suitable responses.

E

- Tell the students they now have the main part of their argument organised, but they must add an introduction and conclusion. **Highlight** the roles of the introduction (*to grab attention*) and the conclusion (*to restate your opinion*).

- Direct the students' attention to the examples in the *How to say it* box and encourage them to use these expressions as they organise their arguments.
- Give the students time to prepare their arguments following the instructions.
- Have the students take turns presenting their arguments to the rest of the class. Discuss which were the most convincing, and why.

F

- Direct the students' attention to the questions. Lead a class discussion about the skill of organising an argument learnt in this lesson and how it can be useful to them in the domain of **Study and Learning**.
- Focus the students' attention on what they still need to work to improve their skill of organising arguments.
- Elicit some suggestions from the class for how the students might continue to practise and develop the skill of *organising and presenting an argument*, for example, by joining a school debate team, actively participating in class discussions on issues, writing letters to the editor of the school newspaper and answering essay questions that ask for an opinion on a topic.

REFLECT

- Ask the students to read the **Reflect** question.
- Give them time to think about different situations in the domains of **Work and Career** and **Self and Society** where the skill of *organising an argument* would be useful.
- Elicit the following ideas: *contributing to online forums that relate to issues they care about, writing letters to the local newspaper about issues, joining a community activist group*, etc.

RESEARCH

- Explain the task and make sure the students understand what they have to do.
- Suggest some possible websites for the students to look at for information. Encourage them to review at least three articles. Ask them to take notes on the information that they find the most interesting.
- Have them share their findings in class. At the next lesson, put the students in pairs and have them take turns giving and critiquing presentations.

Language wrap-up (p. 78)

For notes on how to approach the exercises in the Language wrap-up section, please refer to page 9.

1 Vocabulary

A

- Ask students to read the text before they fill in the gaps. Suggest that they do the ones they are sure about first.

B

- **Highlight** that students must fill in each gap, not only with the correct word, but also the correct preposition.

More than machines? UNIT 6 59

- Encourage them to read through the exercise before beginning to fill in the gaps.

2 Grammar
- Remind the students to read each sentence silently to themselves, substituting different verb constructions. They should trust the one that sounds the best.

Extra: setting goals
Ask the students to review all the activities in this unit and then write a set of goals for any of the skills and topics the unit covered that they would like to improve. Have them select their three top goals, write them on a piece of paper and hand them in. Keep the papers until the end of the school year and then hand them back to the students. Have them analyse which goals they have achieved.

Speaking workshop: comparing and contrasting photographs (p. 79)

Lead-in
Ask the students to look at the two photographs and say what they think is happening in each one. Explain to the students that in this workshop they are going to practise comparing and contrasting these photographs.

A 1.31
- See p. 127 for the **audioscript**.
- Direct the students' attention to the instructions and the question in the box.
- Explain that the students are going to listen to someone answer the question. They should take notes, listening for the speaker's main points for each photo.
- Play the audio, repeating it if necessary.
- Put the students in pairs to compare their notes and discuss any differences.
- Ask several students to present one of their summaries in front of the class and have the class comment on any of the speaker's points they disagree with.

Possible answer
Photograph 1
The photo shows someone supervising the work of robots in a factory. Because robots are doing the work, the person can just supervise and not do the tiring physical labour. But the supervisor may worry that someday robots will be able to do the job of supervising themselves.
Photograph 2
The photo shows a robot that is probably examining something suspicious in the road. Because the robot is doing the work, there is less danger, but the supervisor may worry that robot might break down. The supervisor probably feels that there will always be the need for his/her job because humans will always have to monitor such unsafe situations.

B
- Draw the students' attention to the list of phrases. Read them to the students and ask them to listen this time for phrases in the audio that have the same meaning as the phrases in the exercise.
- Play the audio, stopping and repeating as necessary.
- Check answers with the class.

Answers
1 looks as if
2 would think
3 other hand
4 guess
5 I'm sure
6 Unlike

C
- Refer the students to the question in Ex. A. Explain that they are going to present their own answer to the class, and they need to begin preparing an argument to support their opinion.
- Remind them they will have one-and-a-half minutes to present their answer, so they should keep their reasons brief and concise.
- Give the students time to prepare their notes and then put them in pairs to compare ideas.

D
- Have the students take turns presenting their answers to the class. Time each speaker. At one-and-a-half minutes, establish a signal that indicates that the speech must end.
- Elicit class feedback. Ask if it was difficult to fit the presentations into one-and-a-half minutes. Why or why not?

Extra: agreeing and disagreeing
Pause after each presentation and ask one or two students if they agree or disagree with the speaker. Encourage them to explain their reasons. Then ask another student to present their answer to the class.

How are you doing?
- Ask the students to read the statements and tick the ones they believe are true.
- Ask them to discuss their talk with another student in the class and identify things they could improve on next time.

Extra: homework
Ask each student to find and print two photos from the internet that show people working with robots in different situations. Ask them to write a short paragraph to explain what they think it would be like to work with robots in those situations. In the next lesson, put the students in groups and invite them to take turns showing their photos and sharing their ideas with their group.

▶ Workbook pp. 38–39, SkillsStudio

UNIT 7 THE CRITICAL CONSUMER

The expression *the critical consumer* means that consumers are becoming more aware of the ecological and health impact of what they buy. Cost is fast becoming less important than quality, value for money and ethics. Consumers want to make responsible choices.

Unit plan

Unit opener	(p. 80)	20 min.
1 **Reading:** understanding explanations and examples	(p. 82)	30 min.
2 **Grammar:** reduced adverb time clauses	(p. 83)	40 min.
3 **Grammar:** reduced adverb cause-effect clauses	(p. 84)	40 min.
4 **Listening:** to a discussion	(p. 85)	30 min.
• Vocabulary: adjectives ending in *-able* / *-ible*		15 min.
5 **Pronunciation:** /ʌ/, /ʊ/ and /u/	(p. 86)	15 min.
6 **Speaking:** modifying a statement	(p. 86)	30 min.
• Vocabulary: money and finances		15 min.
7 **Writing:** offering advice	(p. 87)	30 min.
LifeSkills: evaluating claims (Work and Career)	(p. 88)	50 min.
• Optional downloadable *LifeSkills* lesson (Self and Society)		50 min.
• Optional downloadable *LifeSkills* lesson (Study and Learning)		50 min.
Language wrap-up	(p. 90)	20 min.
Writing workshop: interpreting charts	(p. 91)	30 min.
Video and downloadable video worksheet		45 min.

Unit opener (p. 80)

Lead-in

Ask the students to look at the unit title and photos, and predict what the unit will be about. Elicit the meaning of the title using the ideas in the panel above. Ask them how they make choices about what food items to purchase. Then ask if their family has made any changes in their buying and eating habits recently, (e.g. *eating less meat*). Elicit reasons for these changes. Direct the students' attention to the points in the unit objectives box and review with them. To get your students to think about the skills being developed in this unit, ask them to look at the questions in the cogs.

Reading: understanding explanations and examples
- Elicit the ways examples help readers to understand the main point (*providing context, demonstrating ideas*, etc). Ask the students to recall a text where examples helped them understand the writer's argument.

Speaking: modifying a statement
- Ask the students if they have made a plan and changed it, or given an opinion and then changed their minds. Explain that speakers often modify their speech to adjust their ideas, clarify statements, choose better words or backtrack.

LifeSkills: evaluating claims
- Refer the students to the **LifeSkills** panel. Ask them to think about the statements in advertisements. Ask them if they expect these claims to be true. Ask them to explain and give examples. Point out that the skill of *evaluating claims* helps people to recognise exploitative commercial marketing.

Common European Framework: unit map

Unit 7	Competence developed	CEF Reference (C1 competences)
Reading	can recognise and understand explanations and examples	Table 1; Table 2; Sections 4.4.2.2; 4.4.2.4; 4.5.2.2
Grammar	can use and understand reduced adverb time clauses	Table 1; Table 2; Sections 5.2.1.2; 6.4.7.7; 6.4.7.8
Grammar	can use and understand reduced adverb cause-effect clauses	Table 1; Table 2; Sections 5.2.1.2; 6.4.7.7; 6.4.7.8
Listening	can understand a discussion	Table 1; Table 2; Sections 4.4.2.1; 4.4.3.1; 4.4.3.5; 4.5.2.2; 5.2.3.1
Pronunciation	can correctly pronounce /ʌ/, /ʊ/, and /u/	Section 5.2.1.4
Speaking	can modify a statement	Table 1; Table 2; Sections 4.4.1.1; 4.4.3.1; 4.4.3.5; 4.5.2.1; 5.2.2.2; 5.2.3.1; 5.2.3.2
Writing	can offer advice	Table 1; Table 2; Sections 4.4.1.2; 4.4.3.2; 4.4.3.4; 4.5.2.1; 5.2.1.1; 5.2.1.2; 5.2.1.6; 5.2.2.4; 5.2.3.2

A

- Have the students look at the photos and the words in the box. Go over the five different problems in the box and explain the terms if necessary. Put the students in pairs and have them decide which problems might be associated with each type of food/drink item pictured, if any. Point out that there may be several possible answers for each item, and that some answers may overlap with others.
- When checking the answers with the class, encourage the students to share their knowledge and opinions, and to justify their responses with as much detail as necessary.

Possible answers

Bottled water: Health, because plastic bottles can release chemicals and toxins into the water, especially if exposed to heat; Packaging, because the plastic bottles can be recycled in some places, but can also end up in landfills or pose a threat to wildlife; Pollution, because manufacturing plastic pollutes the environment; Sustainability, because one person needs six to seven glasses of water a day, so consuming bottled water every day is both expensive and bad for the environment; Transport, because bottled water has to be transported to shops after being packaged.

Seafood/Fishing: Health, because shellfish absorb pollutants and diseases from their environment, and these can be very dangerous to humans; Pollution, because pollution kills many sea creatures; Sustainability, because over-fishing has caused the near-extinction of many species of fish and shellfish, which in turn causes serious ecological imbalances in the sea; Transport, because food from the sea has to be transported to land-locked areas or areas further away from the sea, also causing fuel consumption and pollution. In addition, seafood has to be kept cool, and refrigeration uses energy.

Organic produce: Packaging, because organic produce usually does not come in recyclable packaging; Pollution, because organic foods frequently have to be transported long distances, and because of the plastic packaging; Sustainability, because organic foods are not yet mass-produced and are therefore more expensive for the consumer; Transport, because organic foods are not always available locally.

Beef/Cattle: Health, because beef is high in fat and cholesterol, and beef cattle are often fed growth hormones which can affect human development; Packaging, because beef and beef products are usually packaged in paper and plastic; Pollution, because bovine excrement releases methane gas into the air; Sustainability, because forests are cut down to provide more and more grazing land for larger and larger cattle herds; Transport, because meat has to be refrigerated and transported over long distances.

Fruit – also applies to vegetables: Health, because fruits and vegetables may have been sprayed with toxic pesticides; Packaging, because fruit (e.g. berries) is often packaged in plastic; Sustainability, because the sale of non-local fruit and vegetables raises prices; Pollution and Transport, because a lot of fruit and vegetables are transported by plane or lorry from where they are grown to where they are sold, which consumes fuel and adds carbon dioxide to the atmosphere. Fruit and vegetables also need refrigeration, which uses energy.

Culture note

Your carbon footprint is the amount of CO_2 produced directly or indirectly by your activities. If you travel by plane and eat a lot of imported food, then your carbon footprint is higher than someone who rides a bike and grows their own or eats local food.

B

- Ask the students to work in different pairs from in Ex. A. Ask them to discuss the kinds of compromises people sometimes make when they buy food (*buying the cheapest item even if the quality is low, buying expensive items when there are similar ones at a cheaper price, paying higher prices for convenience*, etc).
- Then ask them to discuss some positive and negative aspects of the food items pictured. Direct their attention to the example sentences and encourage them to use those as models for their discussion. Elicit their ideas and encourage them to justify their answers.

Reading: understanding explanations and examples (p. 82, p. 63 ⊚)

Lead-in

Give the students time to read the information in the skills panel. Ask them to think about the ways in which explanations and examples help readers to understand the ideas in the text. Point out that explanations and examples are also used by writers as evidence to make claims in different types of texts. Write the following words on the board: *fat-free, sugarless* and *light*. Ask the students if they know what these terms mean (*containing no fat, containing no sugar, containing little fat or fewer calories*). Then ask where they might see them (*on food packaging, in advertisements*, etc). Elicit what kind of information is usually found on food packaging (*nutritional values including calories and ingredients, product weight, comparative amounts of each ingredient, origin, recommended expiry date*, etc) and why people might read it (*if they have a food allergy, if they are watching their weight, if they want to maintain a healthy diet*, etc).

A

- Ask the students to read the questions and think about their responses.
- Put the students in groups to discuss their answers.
- Elicit ideas from volunteers from each group, and discuss the questions with the class.

Alternative

Ask the students to conduct a survey, moving around the class and noting their classmates' answers to each question. Have them form groups to analyse their results, and produce a set of basic statistics in the form of a bar chart for the class.

B

- Ask the students to read the first two paragraphs of the text carefully on their own. Then model the exercise by discussing the first underlined term with the whole class. Elicit why it is an example of the subject discussed in the sentence before it (*It is an example of terms that seem similar but don't really mean the same thing*). Also point out that the words '*for example*' can be easily inserted into the sentence (e.g. *Take 'sugarless' or 'sugar-free' for example; they mean …*).
- Have the students read the instructions carefully. Explain that the task has three aspects. The first aspect is to identify the underlined text as an explanation or as an example. In other words, the students will learn to identify whether the information is general (through an explanation) or specific (through an example). **Highlight** the fact that recognising explanations and examples will help the students become more effective readers.
- Explain that the second aspect of the task is to locate the main ideas supported by each explanation, as well as identify what the examples describe.
- Point out that the final aspect of the task is to decide how the explanations and examples help the reader to evaluate the strength of the claims in the text.
- Make sure the students understand the task. Then ask them to finish reading the text and completing the exercise. Check answers with the class.

Answers

a) **take:** example; terms that seem similar but do not mean the same thing
b) **which means that:** explanation; supports the idea that not all the terms mentioned mean the same thing
c) **or:** explanation; supports the meaning of 'fat free/non-fat'
d) **The implication of this is that:** explanation; supports the idea that serving size is one of the three main things to consider when reading a food label
e) **like:** example; unhealthy things
f) **What this means is that:** explanation; supports the idea that percentages are an important thing to check for daily intake figures
g) **Examples are:** example; food additives/ingredients that should be avoided completely
h) **which are:** explanation; what BHA/BHT mean

C

- Put the students in small groups, and have them read and discuss the two questions.
- Discuss the answers with the class. Ask the students if they will make changes to their food shopping habits as a result of information they learnt in the text.

Extra: homework

Ask the students to review the food packaging they have at home and to record the ingredients/calories/fat content to share in the next lesson. Put the students in groups and ask individual members to read the details of a food product for the rest of the group to guess what the food item is. This would also be a good introductory exercise for the next section.

▶ **Workbook p. 40, Section 1**

Grammar: reduced adverb time clauses (p. 83)

Lead-in

Ask the students to think about the contents of their own cupboards and refrigerators, and make a list of the kinds of packaged food they have at home right now. Elicit examples and write them on the board. Ask the students if they usually read the food labels on these food packages and, if so, elicit what kind of information they look for.

A

- Have the students read the survey to identify the general implication of the information. Do not encourage them to answer the questions at this stage.

Answer

Most of those surveyed do not do the activities listed, which smart consumers should do.

NOTICE!

- Direct the students' attention to the **Notice!** box.
- Have them look at the underlined clauses in the text. Ask them to focus on the clauses that don't have stated subjects, and circle the verb.
- Elicit the answer to the question.

Answer

You is the unstated subject of the underlined clauses which don't have a stated subject.

B

Form

- Ask the students to read the survey again, paying attention to the time clauses.
- Have the students read the grammar rule and its two options and ask them to choose the correct option (*the same in both clauses*). Point out that they should already have a good sense of how to use these adverbs of time. If necessary, explain how the full time clause is reduced by writing an example sentence on the board and deleting the appropriate words. (e.g. *Do you know the best food items to choose when* you are *shopping in a supermarket?*)
- Give the students a few minutes to read the information in the grammar table before circling the correct option. Check the answer, and explain that clauses containing adverbs of time can be reduced when the subject is the same in both clauses.
- Then ask them to complete the table with examples from the survey.
- Direct the students' attention to the **What's right?** box and ask them to tick the correct sentence (*2*). Elicit the difference between the two sentences (*the subject of the main clause is different*). **Highlight** the common error, pointing out that where the subject is not the same, the reduced clause cannot be used

The critical consumer UNIT 7 **63**

without producing a change in meaning or an incorrect sentence. Explain that the incorrect sentence would mean that the dog was studying!
- Point out that the reduced clause can come in first or second position. Stress the need for a comma when the reduced clause is first (e.g. *Since starting my new job, I've been tired all the time. / I've been tired all the time since starting my new job*).

Answers

1 shopping 2 going 3 reading

C

- Have the students work individually to rewrite the sentences, and then compare their answers in pairs. When checking the answers with the class, pay attention to comma placement.

Answers

1 Leo says he always reads labels when shopping for food.
2 I didn't realise how unhealthy diet soft drinks are before reading that article.
3 People who eat while working don't think about serving sizes.
4 After checking the label, Samira decided not to purchase the soup.
5 Before approving a new food, the government agency tests it on animals.
6 When processing foods, manufacturers add fat, sugar and salt to them.

D

- First, ask the students to look back at the survey in Ex. A and complete it by themselves.
- Then direct the students' attention to the model conversation. Put them in small groups, and have them discuss their results in a similar way. Circulate and help as needed.
- When they finish, ask the students whether or not they consider themselves to be smart food consumers. Then ask them for ideas on how to improve their own food shopping habits and practices. Make a list on the board.

Extra: homework

Have the students extend the survey by adding two questions of their own that are relevant to the topic of the critical consumer. (*Do you compare prices for the same food item in different shops? Do you avoid buying processed foods? Do you avoid food items that are high in sugar or fat? Do you buy some food items in bulk at wholesale outlets instead of in small amounts at food shops?* etc.)

▶ Workbook p. 41, Section 2

Grammar: reduced adverb cause-effect clauses (p. 84)

Lead-in

Ask the students if they have heard of Greenpeace, and if they can describe what it is (*a worldwide organisation that acts to help with environmental concerns, such as animal protection, oil spills and climate change*). Write *The Story of Stuff* on the board, and elicit anything the students may have heard about this.

A

- Refer the students to the question, and have them read the article to find the answer. Check the answer with the class.
- Then ask the students if they have seen the 20-minute video. If most of the students have not, have them watch *The Story of Stuff* as homework.

Answer

She became interested in what happens between the extraction of raw materials needed to produce a product and the final disposal of the used product.

NOTICE!

- Direct the students' attention to the **Notice!** box.
- Ask them to look at the underlined reduced clauses in the article and identify the understood subject of each one.

Answers

Having done research: Ms Leonard
Being convinced: Ms Leonard
wanting to create something: Ms Leonard
having been viewed: 20-minute video

Extra: summary writing

Ask the students to watch the video of *The Story of Stuff* on the internet and write a summary of its main points. In the next lesson, have them compare their summaries in pairs and make any necessary corrections or improvements.

B

Form

- Ask the students to read the article in Ex. A again, paying attention to the reduced clauses.
- Have the students read the examples of full clauses and reduced clauses in the grammar table. Elicit from the class how the two forms differ. Point out that they should already know the cause-effect adverbs *after*, *because* and *since*.
- Elicit that verbs that don't usually take the continuous form can be used in the *-ing* form in reduced clauses. Ask the students to find an example of such a verb in the text (e.g. *wanting to create something*). Elicit other verbs that don't usually take the continuous form but can be used in this way, *be*, *hope*, *wish*, *know*, etc.

- Explain that when the adverb clause has the meaning *after*, the students can use a reduced clause, either with or without the word *after*. To illustrate this point, write on the board: <u>After doing research</u> on the 'life cycle', ... = <u>Having done research</u> on the 'life cycle', ... **Highlight** that the negative is formed by putting *not* before the -ing form: *Not having done research* on the 'life cycle', ...
- Ask the students to complete the rule with the words given, based on the examples in the grammar table. Then have them complete the table. Check answers with the class.
- Direct the students' attention to the **What's right?** box and ask them to tick the correct sentences (*1 and 3*). Elicit what is wrong in the two incorrect sentences (*in the negative form,* not *always comes before the* -ing *verb*).

Answers
1 Having done
2 not being
3 wanting

Rules
1 subject
2 cause
3 main verb

C
- Ask the students to work individually to rewrite the sentences using reduced adverb cause-effect clauses. Then have them compare and discuss their answers in pairs.
- When checking the answers, invite different students to read their sentences aloud to the class, or write them on the board.

Answers
1 Not having seen the video before, we watched it together in class.
2 Having read about the video, I knew what it was about.
3 Not understanding the problems with consumption, most people don't worry about it.
4 Being recyclable, paper products are a good option for ecology-minded consumers.
5 Being concerned about global warming, some governments are taking strong action.
6 Wanting their students to know about climate change, many teachers use Ms Leonard's video.

D
- Put the students in groups. Direct their attention to the two examples below the questions. Encourage them to use these and other reduced adverb clauses in their discussion.
- Have the students read and discuss the three questions in their groups. Circulate and help as needed.
- When they finish, extend the discussion with the whole class.

▶ Workbook p. 42, Section 4

Listening: to a discussion (p. 85)

Lead-in
Write _____able and _____ible on the board. Point out that these are two forms of the same suffix. Put the students in pairs, and give them one minute to write as many words as they can which end with the suffix -*able* or -*ible*. Have them call out their words to you, and write all correct ones on the board. Ask the students what meaning this suffix adds to the stem word (*to be able*).

A
- Ask the students to read the information in the skills panel, and to look at the vocabulary words. Explain that they will hear the words later in a conversation. Put the students in pairs to work out the verbs these adjectives derive from, and the meaning of the words. Allow them to check their guesses with a dictionary.
- Check answers with the class.

Answers
account (for)
dispose (of)
recycle, afford
eat
return
biodegrade
perish
reuse

Extra: vocabulary practice
Ask different students to provide example sentences using each of the vocabulary words in context. Provide the first one as an example if necessary.

Example sentences
Corporations should be held *accountable* for their waste disposal practices.
It's more *affordable* to shop for food at wholesale outlets.
Some kinds of plastic are not *biodegradable*.
She prefers to use cloth nappies for her baby instead of *disposable* ones.
Some kinds of flowers are *edible*, like cauliflower and broccoli.
Fresh fruits and vegetables are *perishable*. Dry goods like rice, pasta and beans are not.
Paper, aluminium and glass are all *recyclable* materials.
Most items are *returnable* within 30 days of purchase, especially if you find that they are damaged.
You can buy *reusable* shopping bags at some supermarkets.

B
- Have the students complete the vocabulary exercise individually with the words in Ex. A. (Point out that one word is not used.) Remind the class to read all the sentences to get an idea of the context before completing them. Explain that they should use the context of each sentence and the information provided in it to make their choice.

The critical consumer UNIT 7

- Check answers with the class. Explain how the correct word choice is dependent on the explanation, cause-effect or contrast in the sentence (in 1, the second sentence is an explanation of *recyclable*; 2 provides an explanation for how to extend the life of *perishable* food; in 3, metal forks and spoons are contrasted with *disposable* plastic ones; 4 is a cause-effect using the conditional *if*: if companies don't recycle their waste, they will be held *accountable* for environmental damage; in 5, *biodegradable* is defined in the second part of the sentence; in 6, *expensive* contrasts with *affordable*; in 7, *poisonous* contrasts with *edible*; 8 defines *returnable* with 'bring … back to the shop to get your money back').

Answers

1 recyclable 2 Perishable 3 disposable 4 accountable
5 biodegradable 6 affordable 7 edible 8 returnable

C 2.01

- See p.127 for the **audioscript**.
- Have the students read the questions first. Ask the students to listen to the conversation to identify the first answer. Play the audio, and check progress. Play the audio again if necessary. Elicit the answers from several volunteers and ask the class to come to a consensus if they disagree.
- Play the audio again, and ask the students to make notes of the specific problems mentioned.
- Have the students compare answers in pairs, and discuss which of these problems they noticed previously in Ex. B.
- Check answers with the class.

Possible answers

Agreement:
In general, Hanna and Caitlin agree that shopping choices are important, and that their decisions impact the environment.

Problems:
Lettuce: it's perishable; organic produce is expensive; organic produce might leave a large carbon footprint due to transport; some organic produce is sold in plastic bags
Water: isn't sold in returnable bottles; isn't much different from tap water

D

- Ask the students to read both notecards and check the statements that they agree with or that are true for them. Point out that notecard A is about personal consumer decisions and notecard B is about wider issues.
- Put the students in groups to compare and discuss their ideas.
- Ask each group to share one or two interesting discussion points with the rest of the class.

▶ Workbook p. 41, Section 3

Pronunciation: /ʌ/, /ʊ/ and /u/ (p. 86)

A 2.02

- See the Student's Book page for the **audioscript**.
- Play the audio and have the students complete the table.

Answers

/ʌ/	/ʊ/	/u/
b<u>u</u>dget, c<u>u</u>t, imp<u>u</u>lse, inc<u>o</u>me, m<u>o</u>ney	l<u>oo</u>k, p<u>u</u>t, sh<u>ou</u>ld, s<u>u</u>gar, w<u>oo</u>d, w<u>oo</u>l	cons<u>u</u>me, f<u>oo</u>d, f<u>oo</u>lish, s<u>oo</u>n, s<u>u</u>per, tr<u>u</u>e

B 2.03

- See the Student's Book page for the **audioscript**.
- Play the audio, and ask the students to read the sentences, paying careful attention to the different vowel sounds.

Speaking: modifying a statement (p. 86)

Lead-in

Ask the students to read the information in the skills panel. Ask them if they usually plan what to say more carefully when speaking or writing (*writing*). Elicit what happens when we change our minds while speaking (*we rephrase, backtrack or hesitate as we speak*) and while writing (*we edit, revise or rewrite*).

A 2.04

- See p. 127 for the **audioscript**.
- Explain that the students will hear examples of speakers modifying what they say in the audio.
- Have the students read the questions. Remind them to make notes about Alex's problem and the solutions recommended by his friends as they listen.
- Play the audio once, and check progress. Play the audio again if necessary.
- Check answers with the class. The students may refer to their notes, but encourage them to use their own words to give the answers.

Answer

Alex doesn't have enough money. His friends advise him to make a monthly budget.

B

- Have the students read through the phrases before they listen to the audio again. Explain that they will hear all of the phrases, but they should only tick the ones that signal that the speaker is modifying something said earlier.
- Play the audio. Go over the answers by reading each of the phrases in turn and asking the students to raise their hands if they ticked that phrase.

> **Answers**
> That said, …
> But then again, …
> Although actually, …
> … having thought about it, I …
> On second thoughts, …
> … having said that, I …

Alternative
Have the students tick the phrases used for modifying statements before listening to the audio again to confirm their answers.

C
- Direct the students' attention to the two columns, and ask them to read through both columns carefully. Remind them that collocations are words that are commonly used together. Have them work individually to match the collocations.
- When checking answers with the class, elicit definitions of these four expressions: *to be broke* (to have no money); *to stretch your income* (to make your income cover more of your needs); *to stick to a budget* (to spend only what you planned to); *to cut down on expenses* (to reduce expenses).
- Point out that these expressions are idiomatic expressions. Idiomatic expressions are expressions with a specific meaning that is usually different from the definitions of the individual words in the expression. However, you can guess the general meaning of an idiomatic expression by thinking of them as images or descriptions. For instance, *to stretch something* means to make it longer, so *to stretch your income* means to extend it to fit your needs.

> **Answers**
> 1 e 2 b 3 d 4 f 5 a 6 c

D
- Ask the students to read the survey first, and then tick the answers that are true for them.

E
- Put the students in small groups, and have them read the questions. Direct their attention to the examples in the *How to say it* box, and encourage them to use similar expressions in their group discussion.
- Have each group nominate a member to represent them in a class feedback session. Ask each group representative to give a very brief report on the most interesting points discussed by their group.

▶ Workbook pp. 42–43, Section 5

▶ Workbook p. 43, Section 6

Writing: offering advice (p. 87)

Lead-in
Ask the students if they keep track of the things they buy every month. If they do, ask them what methods they use to keep track of their purchases. Ask them if they have ever bought items that are not strictly essential, and elicit their reasons for buying those items.

A
- Ask the students to work in pairs to make a list of everything they think they have to buy for themselves over the course of a year. Get each pair to come to a consensus on each item on their list.
- Then have each pair work with another pair to compare and discuss their answers.

B
- Ask the students to read the blog post with the questions in mind.
- When they finish reading, ask the students what experiment the blog writer tried (*going a year without buying anything new*). Elicit which piece of advice would be the easiest for them to follow and which would be the hardest. Ask the students to explain why. Elicit the tone of the blog post (*light-hearted, the language is informal*).
- To extend the discussion, ask the students to brainstorm more ideas for reducing product consumption and write the best suggestions on the board.

Extra: ranking
Ask the students to rank the ideas given in the blog post, and put them in order of effectiveness. Have them justify their answers and make exceptions for each idea if necessary.

Extra: vocabulary
Explain that *consumerism* is a social ideology that encourages the public to acquire more and more goods and services, with the idea that more is better than less, and new is better than old. However, *consumerism* also refers to the protection of consumer rights against low-quality or dangerous products, unfair prices and misleading advertising.

C
- Put the students in pairs to write more advice in the same style as the ideas in the blog post. Point out that they should write bullet points, that the tone should be informal and that they should include sufficient detail.
- Before the students start writing, review some modals of advice to use in their tips (*should, have to, could, ought to,* etc).

D
- Have the students display their ideas on the classroom walls, and ask them to walk around and read their classmates' advice. Encourage them to make a note of the tips that would be most useful for them.

The critical consumer UNIT 7 **67**

- Then put the students in pairs to discuss the ideas that they chose.

Alternative

If displaying the tips in the classroom is not possible, have the students exchange notebooks in groups to read each other's ideas.

LifeSkills: evaluating claims (p. 88)

Step 1: Identify the claims made. (Ex. B)
Step 2: Think of questions to test the validity of the claims. (Ex. B)
Step 3: Do research to check the validity of the factual claims. (Ex. C)

Lead-in

Read the target skill aloud, and invite the students to tell you what they think *evaluating claims* means (*deciding if a claim is a fact that can be proved, or an opinion*).
Highlight the three-step strategy to develop the skill of *evaluating claims*. Model this by showing the class a video of a popular or interesting TV advertisement of your choice. Then show them several pictures of well-known magazine adverts. Ask the students to identify the slogans used in these adverts.
Then ask the students to name their favourite TV or print advertising campaign and briefly describe it. Elicit why they like it, and have them recall the slogan if they can.

Alternative

Ask each student to bring a print advert to the lesson. Have the students take turns showing their adverts to the class and talking about why they like or dislike it. Then take a class vote to determine how many students like/dislike the advert.

Extra: slogans

If possible, show the class advertisements with catchy slogans. These may include:
Apple: Think different
Nike: Just Do It
McDonald's: I'm lovin' it
Kentucky Fried Chicken: Finger lickin' good
Sky: believe in better
Elicit other slogans that students know. Put the students in groups to discuss what they like about the slogans and why they think catchy slogans help sell a product.

A

- Ask the students to think about what makes a great advertisement, and ask them how much influence advertising currently has on their choice of products as individual consumers.
- Direct the students' attention to the two adverts. Clarify any vocabulary items they might have difficulty with. Then put the students in groups and have them discuss the questions.
- To discuss the answers with the class, invite a volunteer from each group to share their ideas and to provide reasons justifying their responses. Encourage the rest of the class to offer alternative points of view.

B

- Ask the students to work in the same groups. Ask them to study the adverts in order to complete the table. Make sure they understand the table headings. Explain that *Claims* refers to both factual claims and opinion claims. Opinion claims are based on opinions instead of facts, and factual claims are presented in the adverts as facts or research-based findings. Then explain that formulating questions about these claims is the first step in deciding whether the claims are valid or not.
- Give each group time to complete the *Claims* section of the table. Then ask them to discuss how the factual claims made in each advert can be proved or disproved. Limit their discussion to the factual claims only, since differences of opinion are not generally based on evidence. Encourage them to ask questions about the factual claims to start the discussion, and have them write the questions that they find most useful. (Possible questions: **Sugar-free gum**: *Is daily gum-chewing recommended for people of all ages? What are the ingredients in the sugar-free gum? Could some of these ingredients be potentially harmful?* **Milk**: *Are there any problems associated with drinking a lot of milk every day? Is milk good for everyone?*)
- Discuss the answers with the class, and elicit responses from different students. Have volunteers raise questions about each factual claim during the discussion. Write several of these on the board to provide a focus for the next task.

Answers

Claims:
Sugar-free gum:
Research shows that chewing sugar-free gum:
- Promotes dental health
- Aids in weight control
- Increases concentration
- Reduces stress
Approved by dentists

Milk:
The calcium in milk makes your bones stronger.
An everyday essential
Teenagers should drink four glasses a day.
Milk is a delicious and refreshing drink for any time of day.
For everyone

Extra: homework

Have each student create their own advertisement. They can use information they learnt from research or class discussions. If possible, the students should draw the advertisement and use catchy language to talk about the product. Encourage them to use some of the vocabulary words ending in *-able* and *-ible* that they learnt in this unit. Display the students' advertisements around the classroom. Give the students time to walk around the classroom, and read and comment on the advertisements.

C

- Elicit or explain the meaning of *lactose intolerance* (*a condition in which lactose, a primary component of dairy products, cannot be processed by the body, which means that consuming such products makes the person feel unwell*), and *osteoporosis* (*a medical condition leading to bones becoming more easily breakable, which means that a minor fall could result in major fractures; this condition is more common in older women and said to be linked to a lack of calcium in the diet*).
- Direct the students' attention to the questions. Give the students time to read the text individually, with the questions in mind.
- Once the students finish reading, make sure they understand the text well enough before beginning their discussion. Go over any vocabulary items or clarify any points made in the text if necessary.
- Have the students discuss the first question with their groups from Ex. B. Remind each group to refer to the questions they raised about the factual claims in each advert and decide which of these were answered in the text they just read. Discuss their answers briefly with the class. Then ask the students to discuss the three remaining questions in their groups.
- Direct the students' attention to the examples in the *How to say it* box, and encourage them to use the expressions in their group discussions. Circulate and help as needed.
- Check answers with the class.

Answers

1. Sugarless gum does help promote dental health. None of the claims about milk were supported.
2. The claims about gum were not directly contradicted, as the article said the claims are not well documented enough to say whether they are true or false. The claims about milk (teens should drink four glasses daily, milk makes bones stronger, milk is for everyone) were all contradicted.

Culture note

The FDA, or Food and Drug Administration, is a government agency within the US Department of Health and Human Services. It is responsible for protecting public health by monitoring the safety of food and drug products. One of its responsibilities is to regulate prescription drug advertising to ensure the validity of the claims made.

REFLECT

- Ask the students to read the **Reflect** question.
- Give them some time to think about different situations in the domains of **Self and Society** and **Study and Learning** where the skill of *evaluating claims* would be useful.
- Elicit the following ideas: *deciding if an argument is valid, prioritising one claim over another, detecting flaws in logic, allocating funding to a particular project instead of another, identifying fact vs opinion*, etc.

RESEARCH

- Explain the task and make sure the students understand what they have to do.
- Suggest possible sources for advertisements online, in magazines or newspapers or on TV or radio. Ask the students to read or listen carefully to their chosen advert and make a list of the claims made about the product. Then have them identify the claims as factual claims or opinion and do research on checking the factual claims.
- Ask the students to present the results of their research to the class. First, have them show the class the advertisement they have chosen, identify its source (i.e. magazine, website, television, etc) and draw attention to the claims that it makes.
- Then have them discuss whether those claims are factual or based on opinion. If they checked on the factual claims, encourage them to report on their findings, and discuss whether the claims could be true. If not, have them explain why not.

Extra: research

Have the students brainstorm the type of websites they could visit to determine whether or not some claims are true. These could include the FDA, and sites that provide medical information. Ask the students to visit these sites to see the type of information available in each.

Language wrap-up (p. 90)

For notes on how to approach the exercises in the Language wrap-up section, please refer to page 9.

1 Vocabulary

- Ask the students to read the whole paragraph first to get a sense of the context before completing it with the words and phrases from the box. Remind them that there are three options in the box that will not be used.
- Once the students finish filling in all the gaps in the paragraph, encourage them to read it through on their own to see if their paragraph makes sense. Remind them that they can change their answers if necessary.
- Go over the answers with the whole class. If more than half the class makes the same error with an item, explain the answer.

2 Grammar

- Ask the students to read the instructions and make sure that they understand the task. Explain that they should first identify whether each sentence is correct or incorrect by putting a tick next to each correct one and a cross next to each incorrect one.
- Then ask them to rewrite the incorrect sentences by using a correct reduced clause if possible. Encourage them to draft their rewrites, and read them over carefully to help them decide if they have used the reduced clause correctly.
- When the students finish writing the final versions of their sentences, check the answers as a whole class. Ask the students to refer to the grammar charts in this unit again for guidance, and/or explain the answers if necessary.

Writing workshop: interpreting charts (p. 91)

Lead-in

Explain that in this workshop the students are going to practise writing an article based on information taken and interpreted from a pie chart.

A

- Ask the students to read the assignment in the box. Make sure they understand that there are two parts to the task. The first part of the task asks the students to summarise the information given in the pie chart by selecting and reporting the main points. The second part asks them to *interpret* the information (*to decide what it means, or to give possible reasons for it*), draw conclusions and/or make recommendations.
- Have them read the student's response carefully and identify the recommended change. Point out that this recommendation is not explicitly made in the text, but is in the form of an observation.
- Check the answer with the class.

Possible answer

The writer might recommend changing the recycling programme to allow residents to mix their recyclables in one container.

B

- Ask the students to read the response again with the questions in mind. Explain the questions if necessary. Encourage the students to notice how the information in the pie chart is presented and interpreted in the response.
- Put the students in pairs to discuss and answer the questions. Circulate and help as needed.
- Check answers with the class.

Possible answers

Answers for initial part of items 1 and 2:

The chart shows what types of material were recycled in a particular year. The amount of each material is indicated as a percentage of the total materials recycled. Slightly more than half of all recycled material is paper. This could be because paper is very widely used and one of the easiest materials to recycle. Most offices and schools have collection containers for paper recycling, and residential recycling collects newspapers, post and other household paper goods.

The fact that residential recycling is popular can be seen from the next largest category, garden waste, which accounts for slightly less than a quarter of all recycled material. Garden waste includes grass, leaves and bits of plants and trees that are biodegradable. The local council collects these materials directly from residences for a small fee. Larger pieces of wood, however, must be taken by the resident to a special recycling area, which is probably the primary reason the recycling rate for wood, although it is also biodegradable, is so low – less than 3%. Metal, glass and plastic make up about 16% of recycled materials. This figure could increase if recycling these materials were easier. People must separate plastic, glass and metal into different containers. Additionally, only some types of plastic can be recycled. Cities where residents can mix plastic, metal and glass into one container show significantly higher recycling rates for these materials.

Possible answers for final part of items 1 and 2:

1 The information on individual items is presented in words (half, quarter) or gathered together and expressed as a percentage of the whole.
2 The information is based on the student's own knowledge.

C

- Explain that the students will use the information in a pie chart to write an article about what people in a particular community throw away.
- Have the students look at the pie chart and use the questions as a guide to make notes about the information in it. These notes will help them plan out their articles.

D

- Ask the students to read the instructions carefully. Remind them to summarise the information in the pie chart accurately, and select and report the main features. Encourage them to interpret this information, draw reasonable conclusions and include recommendations as part of their analysis.
- Have the students limit their summaries to about 250 words. Their summaries should not be significantly shorter (because key information will be left out) or longer (because including too many details/opinions will reduce the impact of the reported information).

How are you doing?

- Ask the students to read the statements and tick the ones they believe are true.
- Ask them to discuss their article with another student in the class and identify things they could improve on next time.

▶ Workbook pp. 44–45, SkillsStudio

UNIT 8 ARTISTIC LICENCE

The expression *artistic licence* describes a situation when an artist interprets their subject artistically, and isn't accountable to factual accuracy. The artists mentioned within the unit all use an element of artistic licence when representing the world as they see it, rather than as it actually is.

Unit plan

Unit opener	(p. 92)	20 min.
1 **Listening:** inferring factual information	(p. 94)	30 min.
• Vocabulary: describing art		15 min.
2 **Grammar:** inverted conditionals	(p. 95)	40 min.
3 **Pronunciation:** words ending in *-ical*	(p. 96)	15 min.
4 **Speaking:** talking about meaning in art	(p. 96)	30 min.
• Vocabulary: negative prefixes: *un-, non-, mis-, im-, in-*		15 min.
5 **Grammar:** adjective phrase + indirect question	(p. 97)	40 min.
6 **Reading:** an article about art	(p. 98)	30 min.
7 **Writing:** a review	(p. 99)	30 min.
LifeSkills: developing curiosity (Self and Society)	(p. 100)	50 min.
• Optional downloadable *LifeSkills* lesson (Work and Career)		50 min.
• Optional downloadable *LifeSkills* lesson (Study and Learning)		50 min.
Language wrap-up	(p. 102)	20 min.
Speaking workshop: proposing a solution	(p. 103)	30 min.
Video and downloadable video worksheet		45 min.

Unit opener (p. 92)

Lead-in

Ask the students to look at the unit title and photos, and to predict what the unit will be about. Elicit the meaning of the title using the ideas in the panel under the title on this page. Ask the students if they think they view the world with their own set of ideas, or follow the ideas of others. Direct the students' attention to the points in the unit objectives box and go through the information with them. To get your students to think about the skills being developed in this unit, ask them to look at the questions in the cogs.

Listening: inferring factual information
- Answer the question as a class. **Highlight** that in this unit the students will practise inferring facts, as opposed to Unit 6 where they were inferring opinions.

Writing: a review
- Make sure the students understand the meaning of *review*. Then answer the questions as a class.
- Ask the students if they have ever written an online review. What did they review? Make a list on the board. Ask why they wrote their review and if they were positive, negative or in between.

LifeSkills: developing curiosity
- Refer the students to the **LifeSkills** panel and discuss the questions. Ask the students what they usually do when they encounter new situations, circumstances or people. Ask why it might be useful to ask questions in those situations.

Common European Framework: unit map

Unit 8	Competence developed	CEF Reference (C1 competences)
Listening	can infer factual information	Table 1; Table 2; Sections 4.4.2.1; 4.4.2.4; 4.5.2.2
Grammar	can use and understand inverted conditionals	Table 1; Table 2; Sections 5.2.1.2; 6.4.7.7; 6.4.7.8
Pronunciation	can correctly pronounce words ending in *-ical*	Section 5.2.1.4
Speaking	can talk about meaning in art	Table 1; Table 2; Sections 4.4.1.1; 4.4.3.1; 4.4.3.5; 4.5.2.1; 5.2.1.1; 5.2.1.2; 5.2.3.2
Grammar	can use and understand adjective phrases followed by indirect questions	Table 1; Table 2; Sections 5.2.1.2; 6.4.7.7; 6.4.7.8
Reading	can understand an article about art	Table 1; Table 2; Section 4.4.2.2; 4.4.2.4; 4.4.3.4; 4.5.2.2
Writing	can write a review	Table 1; Table 2; Sections 4.4.1.2; 4.4.1.3; 4.5.2.1; 5.2.1.1; 5.2.1.2; 5.2.1.6; 5.2.3.2

Artistic licence UNIT 8

A
- Ask the students to take a quick look at the six pictures. Explain that they are going to rank the art by writing a number ranging from 1 (favourite) to 6 (least favourite) in the box at the corner of each picture.
- Point out that the way to describe this ranking system is *on a scale of one to six*. Tell the students that *on a scale of* implies ranking, and that the ranking can go from lowest to highest or highest to lowest. Make sure the students understand that *lowest* means worst and *highest* means best. **Highlight** that the ranking system in this exercise goes from highest to lowest.
- Have the students complete the exercise quickly, based on their first impressions of the art.

Culture note

Art can be presented in many different forms.
Paintings: The first known paintings were cave paintings, painted with pigments on the walls of caves between 40,000 and 10,000 BC. Today, paintings are often made with oil paints, acrylics, watercolours or gouache.
Drawings: Drawings are images drawn directly on a flat surface such as paper. The first drawings were done on parchment, before the invention of paper.
Prints: Prints are an impression made by transferring art from one surface to another. For example, an **etching** is made by transferring an image from a metal plate to a piece of paper. The image is scratched into a waxy ground on a metal plate and then dipped in acid. The acid leaves the lines marked in the metal. Then the metal plate is inked and the image is transferred to a sheet of paper. A **lithograph** is another form of print. The artist draws the work on a flat stone or metal plate with a greasy crayon. The stone is inked and the drawing can be transferred to a sheet of paper.
Photographs: Photographs are made by the exposure of light on a light-sensitive material, e.g. photographic film. Digital photography is made by the exposure of light through a lens and recorded as a digital file.

Extra: discussion

Put the students in pairs and have each pair study the pictures and discuss the art forms of each of the pieces of art. Encourage the students to use what they know to identify the art forms. Then have the students discuss their ideas with the whole class.

B
- Put the students in pairs to compare their rankings in Ex. A, discussing any differences. Then have them take turns describing each work of art to their partner.
- Briefly review phrases the students can use when describing the art. Elicit the following verbs and write them on the board: *looks like, shows, illustrates, has a feeling of, suggests, includes*. Then explain the following terms used to describe art and write them in a separate list on the board: *modern, traditional, ethnic, portrait, landscape*, etc. Circulate and help as needed.

Alternative

After comparing rankings, have each student describe one of the works of art without telling the other student which one it is. See if the other student can identify the work of art from the description.

Extra: class ranking

Find out through a show of hands which picture received the highest ranking (the most 1s) and which pictures received the lowest ranking (the most 6s). Then discuss with the class the reasons they did and did not like these particular works of art.

Extra: ranking practice

Put the students into groups. Write the following words on the board: *apple, chocolate bar, pizza, salad, crisps, chicken*. Tell the students they are going to rank these items according to specific criteria. For example, *healthiness, taste, size, price, number of calories*, etc. Tell each group to select their criterion, then rank the food items on a scale of 1 to 6, with 1 being best and 6 worst. When they are finished, have each group read its rankings to the rest of the class, which then tries to guess what criterion the group used. For example, if a group ranks the items 1 salad, 2 chicken, 3 apple, 4 pizza, 5 chocolate bar, and 6 crisps, the criterion might be *healthiness*. You could repeat this process by selecting other possible groups to rank, and eliciting criteria from the class.

Listening: inferring factual information (p. 94, p. 73)

Lead-in
Ask the students to read the information in the skills panel. Write on the board: *'Be sure to take an umbrella if you're going outside', her mother said*. Ask the students what they can infer from the sentence. (*It's raining*.) How do they know? (from the words *umbrella* and *outside*) Remind them that *inferring* is looking for the meaning behind what we hear, read or see.

A
- Direct the students' attention to the two paintings. Ask the students if they have heard of the artists before. Make sure the students understand the meaning of *surreal* (*bizarre, dream-like*). Elicit what the students know about surrealism and surrealist artists, and discuss as a class.

Culture note

Surrealism, which emerged in the 1920s, was most notably an art movement, but also extended to music, theatre and politics. Surrealist works feature the element of surprise or juxtaposition. Leonora Carrington, Frida Kahlo and Salvador Dali are three of the most famous surrealist artists.

B 🎧 2.05

- See p. 128 for the **audioscript.**
- Refer the students to the quiz and have them read the five questions individually.
- Suggest that they take notes as they listen to the audio, and remind them to circle the correct answer for each question.
- Play the audio, repeating if necessary.

Answers

1 a 2 c 3 a 4 c 5 b

C

- Put the students in pairs and play the audio again. Have the students check and then compare their answers to the questions in Ex. B. Then ask them to discuss how they inferred each answer.
- Circulate and help as needed. Make sure the students point out to their partners the words in the audio that led to each inference.
- Check answers with the class.

D

- Refer the students to the words in the vocabulary box. Encourage them to read all the sentences before completing the definitions. Point out that they heard all of the words in the lecture in Ex. B.
- Give the students time to complete the exercise individually. Then check answers with the class.

Answers

1 Controversial 2 A concept 3 represent 4 A symbol
5 proportion 6 An illustration 7 Unconventional
8 a school

Extra: vocabulary practice

Have the students write one or two new sentences for each vocabulary word. Put the students in pairs to compare sentences, and then elicit class examples to write on the board.

E

- Put the students in pairs and ask them to read the instructions.
- Ask the students to describe the pictures together, and to discuss what they think the pictures mean. Based on what they have learnt about surrealism, ask them to decide how typical of the movement they think the pictures are. Encourage use of the vocabulary words in Ex. D. Circulate and help as needed.
- To conclude, ask the students which picture they prefer and why.

▶ Workbook p. 46, Section 1

▶ Workbook pp. 46–47, Section 2

Grammar: inverted conditionals (p. 95)

Lead-in

Write these phrases on the board: *Size matters not. Always moving forward is the future. Here am I.* Ask the students what they notice about the sentences. Elicit that the words are out of their typical order, or stated in an unusual way. Elicit more common ways to say each sentence (*Size doesn't matter, The future is always moving forward,* and *Here I am*). Ask why they think the authors chose to write this way (*to sound more formal in style, or to attract the reader's attention*).

A

- Direct the students' attention to the photo and the text. **Highlight** the question in the instructions.
- Have the students read silently, with the question in mind. Check the answer as a class.

Answer

The modern style he developed used paints which contained toxic materials. He died of lead poisoning at 59.

NOTICE!

- Direct the students' attention to the **Notice!** box.
- Have them examine the underlined phrases and explain what is unusual about the word order. Ask if these are questions.

Answer

The word order is inverted. In regular statements, the subject comes before the verb(s). In the underlined phrases, however, the subject comes after the auxiliary verb or the modal verb. This is the case even though the sentences are not questions.

B

Form

- Ask the students to read the text in Ex. A again, paying attention to the underlined phrases.
- Refer them to the table and have them complete it with examples from the text in Ex. A.
- Check answers with the class. Point out that *should* is added to inverted conditionals in the present tense in the absence of an auxiliary verb.
- Put the students in pairs, and have them practise reading aloud the standard conditional sentences in the chart, and then the inverted conditional sentences.

Answers

1 Should, choose 2 Had, not won 3 Had, listened

Function

- Have the students chose the correct option to complete the rules.
- Check answers with the class.

Artistic licence UNIT 8 73

- Draw the students' attention to the **What's right?** box and ask them to tick the correct sentence (*2*). Ask them to read through both sentences before eliciting/explaining that contractions are not possible in inverted conditionals because the subject must always come before *not*.

Answers

1 formal **2** writing

C

- Have the students read all the sentences and determine which are in past tense (1 and 3) and which are in the present tense (2 and 4).
- Ask the students to rewrite the sentences as inverted conditionals. Then put them in pairs to check their answers, discussing any differences.
- Check the answers as a class.

Answers

1 Had Claude Monet not been short-sighted, he might not have painted objects as soft and blurry.
2 Should you paint with colours such as cadmium red or cobalt blue, wear gloves to protect your skin.
3 Had she known how dangerous the paint fumes were, she would have used a fan.
4 Should you melt metal or glass with a blowtorch, always wear protective goggles.

D

- Put the students in pairs and direct their attention to the exercise.
- Circulate and monitor as the students write and help as needed.
- When they finish, put each pair with another pair to compare sentences.
- Have each group share at least one example with the class. Write the examples on the board.

Extra: grammar practice

- Ask each student to write four short standard conditional phrases for the past, and four for the present. For example, past: *If he had run ..., If she had thought ..., If Tom had read ..., If the dog had barked ...*; present: *If you decide ..., If you want ..., If she likes ..., If the President says ...*, etc.
- Put the students in groups. Have them take turns reading one of their phrases. As soon as a student finishes, another group member should try to say the phrase as an inverted conditional as quickly as possible. For example, *If he had run/Had he run ...; If you decide/Should you decide ...*, etc. The first person to respond correctly earns a point, and then has the opportunity to complete the sentence correctly for an additional point (e.g. *Had he run, he would have won.*). The champion of each group could earn a small prize or reward.

▶ Workbook p. 47, Section 3

Pronunciation: words ending in *-ical* (p. 96)

Lead-in

Practise the correct pronunciation of *-ical* as a class. Ask the students to identify the vowel sound in the second syllable (/ə/). **Highlight** that the /ə/ sound here is spelt with the letter *a*. Point out that in multisyllable English words, it is common for an unstressed syllable to become a schwa, i.e. to sound like /ə/. The schwa is typically not spelt with the letter *u*. It can be spelt with any other vowel letter – *a, e, i, o* – except *y*.

A 2.06

- See the Student's Book page for the **audioscript**.
- Direct the students' attention to the words and the instructions.
- Play the audio. Ask the students what changed in each pair of words (*the -ical word was one syllable longer; in the 3- and 4-syllable words, the stress moved to the syllable before the -ical ending.*)
- Play the audio again, and have the students repeat each pair of words.

Answers

biographical (5 syllables), historical (4 syllables), political (4 syllables)

B 2.07

- See the Student's Book page for the **audioscript**.
- Put the students in pairs. Ask them to listen to the sentences, paying special attention to the words they practised in Ex. A.
- Play the audio once. Play it again, and have the students repeat each sentence.
- Give the students time to practise saying the sentences in pairs. Circulate and help as needed.

Speaking: talking about meaning in art (p. 96)

Lead-in

Ask the students what *meaning* is in the phrase *meaning in art*. Explain that *meaning* communicates something that is not directly expressed. Ask how they think art can convey meaning.

A

- Have the students look at the painting and read the description of it. Ask them to think about the questions individually and decide on their answers.
- Discuss the answers with the class. Encourage the students to cite specific words and phrases from the text to support their opinions.

B 🎧 2.08
- See p. 128 for the **audioscript**.
- Explain that the students will hear two speakers discussing the description of the painting in Ex. A. Refer students to the question.
- Make sure students understand that *objections* are disagreements or complaints. Encourage them to take notes as they listen.
- Play the audio, repeating if necessary.
- Check the answer as a class, listing the woman's objections on the board.

Answer
The second woman thinks the person who wrote the description doesn't know much about non-traditional art, and the information given is unoriginal and uninteresting. She thinks the description is also misleading.

C
- Refer the students to the words in the box and the table. Ask them to complete the table individually.
- Direct the students' attention to the *im-* words. Ask why these words use *im-* instead of *in-*. Elicit that the *n* changes to an *m* when the following letter is an *m* or a *p*.
- Point out that all of the words in the table were used in the text in Ex. A or in the audio for Ex. B.
- Check answers with the class.

Answers
un: unable, uninteresting, unloving, unoriginal, unwilling
non: non-standard
mis: misinterpreted, misunderstood
im: immovable
in: incomprehensible, invisible

D
- Explain that the students they will now give their own opinion of the painting in Ex. A. Ask them to look at it and decide quickly if they like it.
- Have them read the questions in Ex. D, and explain that these questions will help them form their own opinion of the painting. Give them time to think about their answers to the questions and to make notes. Assure them there are no correct or incorrect answers, as each person responds to art differently.
- Ask the students to use as many words from Ex. C as they can in their opinions.
- Give the students time to prepare for their discussion. Circulate and help as needed.

E
- Explain that the students will each present their opinion of the painting to a partner.
- Assign partners to keep time and listen without interrupting. Remind the students that each partner must speak for at least two minutes. Monitor while the students take turns presenting their opinion of the painting.

Extra: homework
Ask the students to find a work of art that evokes strong emotion for them. It could be a photo, painting, hand-made object, etc. Ask them to bring a picture of the work of art to school and give a three-minute review in front of the class or in small groups. Have the students vote for the best presentation.

▶ Workbook p. 48, Section 4

Grammar: adjective phrase + indirect question (p. 97)

Lead-in
Ask the students if they know what *non-permanent art* is. Elicit materials it could be made of, (*ice, sand, clay, balloons*, etc). Ask students to share any examples of non-permanent art they might know of, and why this art genre might be interesting.

A 🎧 2.09
- See the Student's Book page for the **audioscript**.
- Explain that the students are going to listen to a conversation between three people. Ask them to determine the speakers' ideas about the meaning of non-permanent art.
- Play the audio, repeating if necessary. Discuss the answer with the class.

Answer
The speakers aren't sure they understand the meaning of non-permanent art, but they do think it's interesting.

NOTICE!
- Direct the students' attention to the **Notice!** box.
- Ask the students to find and underline the question words in Ex. A. Discuss the answer to the question as a class. Encourage the students to give examples of direct questions. (*What is your name? Where do you live?* etc)

Answer
No, they are not being used in direct questions.

B
Form
- Ask the students to read the conversation in Ex. A again, paying attention to the question words.
- Focus the students' attention on the table, and ask them to scan the text for the missing information. Ask them what each example listed in the table has in common (*It + be, adjective, infinitive, indirect question*).

Artistic licence UNIT 8

- Review with the students the rules for word order in indirect questions in the affirmative form (question word, not inversion of subject and verb, no auxiliary *do/does/did* and no question mark at the end).
- Have them complete the table independently, and then check answers with the class.

Answers

1. It would be
2. good
3. why people go to all that trouble to create non-permanent art!
4. what the non-permanent aspect really means.
5. It's
6. natural
7. for people
8. what the deeper meaning of everything is
9. to see
10. where the deep meaning is in something that will be a pool of water in a few hours!

Function

- Complete the rules as a class. After each answer, have a student find an example from the table and explain why/how the example proves the answer to be correct.
- Refer the students to the **What's right?** box and ask them to tick the correct sentence (*2*). Ask them to read both sentences and identify which words were not used in any of the examples in Ex. A. Elicit the answer *if/whether*. **Highlight** that with *if* and *whether*, the constructions is *if/whether* + noun/pronoun + *could*. **Highlight** the words *could I take a course in ice skating* in the incorrect sentence. Point out that *could + pronoun* is used only in questions, such as *Could I have a hamburger?* or *Could you give me a lift to work?*

Answers

1. not known   2. don't expect

C

- Encourage the students to refer to the grammar table in Ex. B as they do this exercise.
- Ask them to rewrite the direct questions as indirect questions individually and then compare their answers in pairs, discussing any differences.
- Check answers with the class.

Answers

1. It would be interesting to find out where they have sand sculpture exhibits.
2. It would be nice to know whether/if there is any non-permanent art in our community.
3. It's easy to see why non-permanent art is so popular.
4. It's difficult to know if/whether there have always been forms of non-permanent art.
5. It's hard for me to understand what abstract art symbolises.
6. It's important for us to consider what the world was like when abstract art began.

D

- Put the students in groups. Ask them to discuss other types of non-permanent art they know about or would like to know more about.
- Write a list on the board to help them get started: *sand castles, graffiti, origami, ice/snow sculptures*, etc. Remind the students that, as you listen to their discussions, you want to hear sentences beginning with *It's* and *It would be*. Circulate and help as needed.

▶ Workbook p. 48, Section 5

Reading: an article about art (p. 98)

Lead-in

Ask the students why art might be controversial. Ask if they have read any articles or seen any videos about controversy in art. Make a brief list of some examples. Ask the students if there are limits to art, or if there should be. For example, how much nudity (if any) should be allowed in public art displays? How much violence?

A

- Put the students in pairs. Direct their attention to the art accompanying the text in Ex. B, and ask what kind of art this is (*graffiti*). Ask them whether they think graffiti is art or vandalism, and if so, a crime. Elicit several opinions. Have the students discuss the question with their partners. Circulate and help as needed.
- Discuss answers with the class. Encourage the students to expand on their answers.

Extra: comprehension questions

Ask the students the following questions.
1. What subject matter is commonly present in graffiti art?
2. Why did Haring prefer graffiti to commercial art?
3. Why did Haring feel that his subway drawings were performances as much as art?
4. How did MadC become a graffiti artist?

Answers

1. comments on social or political topics, the artist's name, or simple drawings
2. He found graffiti creative, spontaneous, and provocative.
3. People watched him draw and asked about the meaning of his work.
4. She created the largest graffiti mural painted by a single person.

B

- Keep the students in the same pairs. Explain that they are going to read an article about two famous graffiti artists. Have them read the instructions, and remind them to look for similarities and differences as they read the article. Suggest that they write the words *same* and *different* on a piece of paper and make a list of examples under each word as they read the article.

- Have the students read silently. When they finish, have the students compare their lists with their partner's, discussing any differences.
- Discuss answers with the class. Ask the pairs to share some of their examples. Make a list on the board.

Possible answers
Some similarities: Both did their graffiti on public property; both were influenced by popular culture; both produced large-scale works
Some differences: MadC is European; Haring quickly became well-known, MadC still believes graffiti artists are quite anonymous to the wider creative world.

C
- Put each pair together with another pair for a group discussion. Ask the students to read the questions silently before they begin discussing them. Circulate and help as needed.
- To conclude, have each group share their opinions with the class. Ask the students to consider again if they think graffiti is art or vandalism, and whether their opinions have changed since the beginning of the lesson.

Extra: grammar
Challenge the students to find one inverted conditional and one adjective phrase + indirect question in the article in Ex. B. Make it a contest by setting a time limit, e.g. one minute.

Answers
Inverted conditional: ... *had he not relocated, he might not have met the musicians and artists* ...
Adjective phrase + indirect question: ... *it was impossible to remain invisible while drawing in such public spaces.*

Writing: a review (p. 99)

Lead-in
Ask the students to read the information in the skills panel. Give them time to read, and then tell them to close their books. Ask for volunteers to state the three parts of a review in their own words.

Answers
1 introduction **2** opinion **3** recommendation

Write this outline format on the board, and go over it with the students. Remind them of the importance of outlining, which they learnt in Unit 2. Do not erase the outline format, as the students will need it for Ex. B.

i. *Introduction*
   a) *What event*
   b) *Where*
   c) *When*

ii. *What I liked*
   a) *Point 1*
   b) *Point 2*
iii. *What I didn't like*
   a) *Point 1*
   b) *Point 2*
iv. *Conclusion*
   a) *Summary of my opinion of the event*
   b) *Whether I recommend the event*

Highlight the fact that the opinion part of the review includes two paragraphs. Typically, one paragraph deals with what the reviewer liked and one with what they didn't like.

A
- Have the students read the questions first. Then ask them to read the review in Ex. B with the questions in mind. Give the students time to read the review individually, and to think about their answers.
- Discuss the answers as a class.

Possible answers
1 The first paragraph explains where the event is taking place, how much it costs and when you can attend.
2 The second paragraph defines the event and discusses what the reviewer liked about it.
3 The third paragraph discusses what the reviewer didn't like about the event.
4 The final paragraph summarises her opinion and gives her recommendation, which is negative.

B
- Ask the students to read the review again, and compare it with the outline format on the board.
- Discuss with the students how closely the essay matches the outline format. Direct their attention to paragraphs 2 (likes) and 3 (dislikes). **Highlight** how much longer paragraph 3 is (eleven sentences to four). Ask the students if they could have predicted the author's opinion by looking at the review, without reading it, and comparing it with the outline.
- Ask the students to find the transition words between the points in paragraphs 2 and 3 (*For one thing, Second, Finally, In conclusion*).

C
- Ask the students to think of an event they have attended, a concert, play, film, fair, exhibition, show, comedy act, etc. Explain that they are going to write a review of this event.
- Ask them first to make an outline similar to the one on the board. Remind them to include their specific points in the outline, instead of 'Point one' and 'Point two', and to include as many points as they wish.
- Give them time to create their outlines. Circulate and help as needed.

D
- When the students finish their outlines, give them time to write their reviews. Ask them to assume that the event they are reviewing is still going on, or playing, and remind them to give a recommendation in the final paragraph.

Artistic licence UNIT 8

E

- Put the students in pairs. Ask them to read each other's outline and review, and then 'review the review'. Explain that they should compare their partner's review with the outline, noting places where the review and outline do and do not match. Encourage the students to be honest. Instruct them to find specific examples from the review to support their opinion.

Extra: practice

Have the students say or write one sentence that summarises their partner's opinion in Ex. E. Suggest that the sentence begins *XX recommends/does not recommend the (name of show, fair, etc being reviewed), because ...*

▶ **Workbook p. 49, Section 6**

LifeSkills: developing curiosity (p. 100)

Step 1: Understand the value of curiosity. (Ex. A, Ex. B, Ex. E)
Step 2: Develop curiosity-building techniques such as careful observation and asking questions. (Ex. C)
Step 3: Apply these techniques to new situations. (Ex. D)

Lead-in

Read the target skill aloud, and invite the students to tell you what they think *developing curiosity* means (*developing a strong desire to learn or know something*). Ask them what the root word of *curiosity* is (*curious*). Do they know any curious people? Have them share examples. Ask them if they associate this characteristic with any particular age group, and why or why not.
Highlight the three-step strategy to develop the skill of developing curiosity. Ask the students if they think curiosity is mostly genetic, or if it can be learnt.

Alternative

Find video and/or books and pictures of *Curious George*, a famous children's book about a young monkey who lives in a big city. Start off by showing a short video clip, or by sharing a few of the cartoon drawings, before asking the students to define *curiosity*.

A

- Put the students in groups. Have them read the questions, and think about their answers before beginning their group discussion.
- Give the students time to discuss the questions. Circulate and help as needed, especially with questions 2 and 3.
- Check answers with the class.

Possible answers

1 Curious people are always looking for new ways to see or do things. Other professions: architecture, medicine, scientific research, engineering, etc.
2 Curious can mean *interested in learning new things* or *strange and unusual*. The sentence could be interpreted either way.
3 *Curiosity killed the cat* is a proverb meaning that if you are overly inquisitive about other people's affairs, you can get into trouble.
4 Many adults find this annoying and become impatient. Others encourage their children's natural enthusiasm for learning new things.

B

- Keep the students in the same groups as in Ex. A. Explain that they are going to read the article in two parts, stopping for a discussion after each part.
- Direct their attention to the title of the article. Ask the students if they can infer the author's opinion from the title. (*Yes, because the question mark indicates that the author doubts this popular saying.*)
- Have the students read the first section. Circulate and help as needed. When the students finish, discuss the two statements, encouraging groups to share their ideas.
- Have the students read the second section of the article, and discuss why curiosity can be referred to as a life skill.
- Discuss the answers with the class.

Answers

1 The two statements are contradictory, so the challenge they present is how to reconcile steadily declining curiosity with employers' need for creative, innovative workers.
2 Curiosity can be considered a life skill because it makes us want to learn, and learning new things develops our ability to think, adapt and solve problems. It strengthens our mind by making our brains active, rather than passive.

Extra: alternative schools

Put the students in pairs or groups. Explain that they are going to work together, and they have complete freedom to design a school (or a single classroom) that fosters curiosity and creativity. They should decide whether to design a primary, middle school or secondary school classroom or school. Encourage them first to brainstorm a list of ideas. **Highlight** that this is an *ideal* school, so they shouldn't factor cost into their design. When they finish, have each group choose a spokesperson to present the group's ideas to the class. Have the class vote on the best presentation.

Extra: practice

Make a list of 20–40 common subjects, such as *horses, Australia, coconuts, coffee, rainforests, dogs, explorers, flowers, films, summer, books, ghosts, holidays,* etc. Make the subjects broad, and make sure there is at least one subject for each student. Write each subject on a slip of paper, then fold the strips in half and put them in a container. Have each student draw a slip of paper without looking. Tell the students to write three facts they would like to know about the subject they have drawn. Have them find the answers to these facts, then share with the rest of the class.

C

- Direct the students' attention to the question at the top of the quiz, and give them time to think about it and answer it. Ask if they have ever heard of CQ before. Elicit or explain what *IQ* means (*intelligence quotient*). Have them complete the quiz individually and total their scores. Take the quiz with them at the same time.
- Share your own score, and invite the students to share theirs. Ask them what they thought of the quiz. Was it accurate for them? Do they consider themselves similar to classmates who got about the same score? Is it a reliable way to measure curiosity, in general? Was their score similar to their original self-assessment?

D

- Put the students in different groups from those they were in for Ex. A and Ex. B. Tell each group to try the two activities. Circulate and help as needed.
- Have each group choose a spokesperson to give a brief summary to the class. They should say what they did, how it went, and what they learnt.

E

- Ask the students to name as many reasons as they can why curiosity is a useful and important trait. Encourage brief answers. Make a list on the board.

Possible answer

Curiosity leads people to investigate and question things, which can help them to: meet new people, visit new places, try new activities and experiences, widen their knowledge of the world, make new discoveries, invent new things and generally do things that people who are not curious may never get to do.

Extra: discussion

Ask the students if they can think of circumstances where curiosity could be a bad, or unwise trait. Have them share examples (*you could find out information you weren't supposed to know, you could try to drink or eat something that is bad or harmful for you, you could discover a criminal activity and endanger yourself, you could get a reputation for being nosy,* etc).

REFLECT

- Ask the students to read the **Reflect** question.
- Give them some time to think about different situations in the domains of **Work and Career** and **Study and Learning** where the skill of *developing curiosity* would be useful.
- Elicit the following ideas: **Work and Career:** being curious shows your supervisors you are eager to learn, which could lead to a promotion. If your job is in sales, being curious about your clients might help you make a sale. Curiosity could help you invent something, etc. **Study and Learning:** Being curious makes you want to learn more, which could give you a higher mark. It activates your mind, so you are able to learn more. Teachers might like a curious student better, etc.

RESEARCH

- Explain the task and make sure that the students understand what they have to do. Brainstorm places where they could find quotations. Which key words should they type into an internet search engine? (*curiosity, quotations, sayings*) Where else, besides the internet, might they find sayings and quotations? (*in books, magazines, newspapers*)
- Set a deadline for students to complete their research and be ready to give their presentations in class.

Extra: posters

Have the students make posters displaying some of the quotations that they found. Put the students into groups to write and design the posters. Encourage them to decorate the posters with drawings or photos. Display the posters on the classroom walls.

Language wrap-up (p. 102)

For notes on how to approach the exercises in the Language wrap-up section, please refer to page 9.

1 Vocabulary

- Ask the students to read through the text before they fill in the gaps. You could suggest that they do the ones they are sure about first.

Extra: double negative

Ask the students to look at answer choice 10, and to read the sentence containing that answer choice. **Highlight** the word *not* just before the answer choice. Explain that whichever answer is correct (*unwilling* or *unoriginal*) this type of sentence construction is called a double negative. *Not* + *un-*, *in-*, or *im-* literally means *not not*. Write this on the board: *not not = is*. Then write this sentence: *It is not impossible.* Ask the students what the sentence literally says (*it is not not possible*) and what that means (*It is possible*). Do the same for this sentence: *She is not unintelligent.* (*She is not not intelligent. She is intelligent*).

Artistic licence UNIT 8 79

2 Grammar

A
- Ask the students to rearrange the phrases to make sentences. Remind them to read each phrase first, and then decide which other phrases make sense with it. Have them read their finished sentences carefully and ask themselves if they sound correct.

B
- Ask the students to check the tense of other verbs in the sentence to determine the form of the verb phrase in brackets.

Extra: practice
- When the students have completed the exercise and checked their answers, have them write each sentence again starting with the word *If*.
- Ask the students when it might be appropriate to write sentences using inverted conditionals, and when it might be appropriate to write sentences using *if*-clauses. Why? Elicit the idea that writers need to consider the audience they are writing for. Inverted conditionals are generally considered more formal than *if*-clauses.

Speaking workshop: proposing a solution (p. 103)

Lead-in
Explain that in this workshop the students will propose a solution to a problem, and then present their proposal to the class. First, they will listen to a speaker propose three different solutions to a problem and explain the one they like best. Then they will practise thinking of three possible solutions to a different problem and decide which solution is the best.

A 2.10
- See p. 129 for the **audioscript.**
- Direct the students' attention to the question in the box. Ask them to listen to a student's response to this question, and then complete the exercise. Ask them to list the solutions in the order they are mentioned.
- Play the audio, repeating if necessary. Check answers with the class.

Answers
The speaker prefers the third solution.
1 poisoning the pigeons   **2** hiring people to chase them away   **3** covering the carvings with metal nets

B
- Direct the students' attention to the checklist of phrases. Ask them to listen for these phrases and tick the ones they hear clearly. Remind them that they may not hear all of the phrases.
- Play the audio again. Check to see how many phrases most of the class heard. Play the audio one more time, pausing it for a moment after each of the phrases.

Answers
… it's important to …
… in several ways …
Three solutions … have been proposed.
… is a better idea …
The best of these solutions is …

Extra: writing
Have each student choose two or three of the phrases for talking about problems and solutions. Have them write one sentence for each phrase. Then put the students into small groups to check their work.

C
- Put the students in pairs. Ask them to read the problem described in the box. Then ask them to brainstorm possible solutions to the problem together.
- When they finish brainstorming, have the students return to their seats. Ask them to decide individually on the three strongest solutions to present to the class.

Alternative
Have the whole class brainstorm possible solutions to the problem. Then put the students in pairs. Ask them to work together to decide on the three strongest solutions.

D
- Have the students work individually to prepare their presentations.
- Ask them to make an outline first, and review the outline format with them if necessary. Refer them also to the list of phrases in Ex. B.
- Remind the students to limit their presentations to one and a half minutes. Have them practise timing themselves, or work with a partner to time each other.
- Give each student one and a half minutes for their presentation.

How are you doing?
- Ask the students to read the statements and tick the ones they believe are true.
- Ask them to discuss their presentation with another student in the class and identify things they could improve on next time.

Extra: voice recording
Have the students record their presentation. They should limit their presentation to one and a half minutes. Then have the students play back their presentation and listen to themselves speak. Ask students to think about ways they could improve their presentation.

▶ Workbook pp. 50–51, SkillsStudio

UNIT 9 JUST PLAYING?

The expression *just playing* implies that play is often considered unimportant to a healthy lifestyle. Anti-social or destructive forms of social behaviour in children, like bullying or cruel pranks, are sometimes excused as 'just playing' by parents. This unit talks about the wider impact of play, both positive, as an important developmental stage in children and a beneficial social activity in adults, and negative, when gaming becomes addictive.

Unit plan

Unit opener	(p. 104)	20 min.
1 **Reading**: understanding intent	(p. 106)	30 min.
• Vocabulary: childhood development		15 min.
2 **Listening**: to a radio talk show	(p. 107)	30 min.
3 **Grammar**: the subjunctive	(p. 108)	40 min.
4 **Speaking**: making and responding to invitations	(p. 109)	30 min.
• Vocabulary: making and responding to invitations		15 min.
5 **Grammar**: alternatives to the subjunctive	(p. 110)	40 min.
6 **Pronunciation**: assimilation	(p. 111)	15 min.
7 **Writing**: a short article	(p. 111)	30 min.
LifeSkills: recognising contradiction (Work and Career)	(p. 112)	50 min.
• Optional downloadable *LifeSkills* lesson (Self and Society)		50 min.
• Optional downloadable *LifeSkills* lesson (Study and Learning)		50 min.
Language wrap-up	(p. 114)	20 min.
Writing workshop: writing a short article	(p. 115)	30 min.
Video and downloadable video worksheet		45 min.

Unit opener (p. 104)

Lead-in

Ask the students to look at the unit title and photos, and predict what the unit will be about. Elicit or explain the meaning of the title using the ideas in the panel under the title on this page. Elicit their opinions on whether play is important for children and teenagers. Then ask them whether play is important for adults. Direct the students' attention to the points in the unit objectives box and go through the information with them. To get your students to think about the skills being developed in this unit, ask them to look at the questions in the cogs.

Reading: understanding intent
- Explain that every text is written with *intent*, i.e. to achieve a purpose. A text can be written *to inform*, i.e. to provide information. Ask the students to think of other types of intent that a writer might have (*to entertain, to argue, to persuade, to describe, to complain*, etc).

Speaking: making and responding to invitations
- Ask the students to think about ways in which they refuse invitations. Elicit indirect as well as direct methods of refusal and examples of actual language. Write the answers on the board and discuss.

LifeSkills: recognising contradiction
Refer the students to the **LifeSkills** panel. Ask them why *recognising contradiction* is an important skill to learn.

Common European Framework: unit map

Unit 9	Competence developed	CEF Reference (C1 competences)
Reading	can recognise the writer's intent to aid understanding	Table 1; Table 2; Sections 4.4.2.2; 4.4.2.4; 4.5.2.2
Listening	can understand a radio talk show	Table 1; Table 2; Sections 4.4.2.1; 4.4.3.1; 4.4.3.5; 4.5.2.2
Grammar	can use and understand the subjunctive	Table 1; Table 2; Sections 5.2.1.2; 6.4.7.7; 6.4.7.8
Speaking	can make and respond to invitations	Table 1; Table 2; Sections 4.4.1.1; 4.4.3.1; 4.4.3.5; 4.5.2.1; 5.2.2.1; 5.2.2.2; 5.2.3.2
Grammar	can use and understand alternatives to the subjunctive	Table 1; Table 2; Sections 5.2.1.2; 6.4.7.7; 6.4.7.8
Pronunciation	can correctly use assimilation	Section 5.2.1.4
Writing	can write a short article	Table 1; Table 2; Sections 4.4.1.2; 4.5.2.1; 5.2.1.1; 5.2.1.2; 5.2.1.6; 5.2.2.4

A

- Direct the students' attention to the photos. Elicit the ages of the people shown and the activities they are doing (*teenagers, playing video games; 3–6, playing dressing-up; 8–9, playing tug-of-war; 16–17, playing team sports; 40–50, playing a board game*).
- Ask the students to read the statements and choose the ones that best reflect their own attitude towards play. Point out that they can choose more than one statement each. Encourage them to articulate their ideas about play, and remind them to give reasons explaining how and why their chosen photo(s) reflects these ideas.
- Discuss answers with the class, inviting the students to explain their choices.

Extra: class poll

Read each of the statements aloud. Pause after each statement to ask how many students feel it reflects their own attitude towards play. Write the results on the board. When all votes are tallied, invite volunteers to talk about the results, e.g. *Ten students thought the first statement best reflected their own attitude.*

B

- Put the students in groups, and have them read the questions. Give them time to discuss their ideas.
- Then discuss their ideas as a class. Elicit ideas from different students, and encourage them to justify their answers.

Extra: speaking

Put the students in small groups and have them look at the photos again. Ask them to discuss which one of these games they would most enjoy playing, and why. Then ask them which game they would enjoy least, and why.

Culture note

The concept of play for people of all ages has become increasingly important in contemporary culture in many parts of the world. Technology and tools developed for communication, like computers and mobile phones, usually have games and other interactive software which are built-in or downloadable. In the same way, video games and interactive devices can often be used as simulations for practising real-world activities. The transformation of technology and tools into toys (and vice versa) is becoming very common today. This reflects a growing awareness of the ways in which the processes of work and play are inter-related instead of separate.

Reading: understanding intent (p. 106)

Lead-in

Ask the students to read the information in the skills panel. Have them think about the idea of intent behind a piece of writing. Point out that writers have reasons for writing what they do and organising their texts in the way that they do. For instance, the writer of an advertisement wants to attract and maintain readers'/listeners' attention with short, memorable statements. Elicit examples of different types of writing, and the writer's probable intent in each case.

A

- Elicit examples of playtime activities that the students remember clearly from childhood. Ask them to consider the ways in which their types of play and leisure activities have changed over the years.
- Have the students read the questions, and give them time to think about their responses.
- Discuss answers with the class, and remind the students to justify their points with evidence from their experiences.

B

- Explain that the students are going to read a magazine article on the importance of play for children. Elicit what they think the intent/purpose of such a text might be (*to inform and/or persuade*). Ask them to predict points they think the writer might mention.
- Have the students read the questions. Then give them time to read the article with the questions in mind. Ask them to decide if the writer sounds generally optimistic or pessimistic, and mark the sections of text that support their opinion. Tell them to ignore the words in bold, as they will look at these carefully later.
- Check answers with the class, and ask if all the students agree. Elicit references to the text to support the answers.

Answer

She seems pessimistic about current developments in children's play because she feels that there is less and less play and more and more structure in children's lives and that this will limit their development.

Extra: comprehension questions

Ask the students the following questions.
1 What is electronic entertainment?
2 How does electronic entertainment affect how children play?
3 What outcomes does the author anticipate if children have less time for free play?
4 What is the author's conclusion?

Answers

1 television, DVDs, tablets, smartphones and video games
2 Their games are full of media characters and stories, so it is harder for them to make up their own creative stories.
3 The author anticipates difficulties in the way children socialise and communicate with each other, more aggression in social relationships, and less creative thinking.
4 For the sake of children and society, play needs to be restored as an essential part of childhood.

C

- Direct the students' attention to the paragraphs in the article and ask them to number them 1–6. Ask them to read the list of purposes (a–f) and to match each one to a corresponding paragraph. Emphasise that they do not need to understand every word to make a good answer choice, and remind them to read for the general intent in each paragraph. Circulate and help as needed.
- Encourage the students to compare their answers in pairs before discussing as a class. When checking the answers, ask the class to come to a consensus if they disagree on any point.

Answers

Paragraph 1: d
Paragraph 2: b
Paragraph 3: e
Paragraph 4: c
Paragraph 5: f
Paragraph 6: a

Extra: speaking

Ask the students to discuss the following questions in small groups (write them on the board or dictate them):
1 Compare the nursery school programme described in the text with early childhood education programmes in your country.
2 Do children in your country usually attend pre-school or kindergarten?
3 Do children aged 3–6 often watch TV or play electronic games?
4 If you have children, or younger siblings, has this article influenced how you feel about their play?

D

- Put the students in pairs to think about the overall intent of the article in Ex. B. Check that all the students have the right answer (c – *persuade the reader that we need to encourage creative play for children*). If necessary, explain why a and b are incorrect. (The text does not explicitly compare how children play now with how they played in the past; the writer limits her argument to young children aged of 3–6.)
- Ask the students to consider how each paragraph contributes to the intent of the text. Focus their attention on the example answer given for Paragraph 1. Ask them to read the text again closely, making notes about Paragraphs 2–6.
- Check answers with the class.

Answers

Paragraph 1 helps the writer achieve her purpose by telling the reader that she knows what she's talking about because she's been working with children for over 30 years.
Paragraph 2 explains how types of play affect children's development and that play is very important in children's development.
Paragraph 3 shows that young children now spend more time on academic subjects than playing.
Paragraph 4 states a concern about the effects of a lack of play.
Paragraph 5 explains what the negative consequences will be if children no longer play.
Paragraph 6 explains that the problem is worldwide and says that there is a need for change.

Alternative

If time is short, assign different paragraphs to different pairs to evaluate before checking the answers as a class.

E

- Ask the students to match the definitions to the words and phrases in bold in the article. Remind them to use the context for help.
- When checking the answers with the class, point out that *literacy* and *numeracy* are technical terms, used by professionals, whereas the remaining vocabulary could be used in everyday speech.

Answers

1 outcomes 2 emerge 3 outlet 4 numeracy 5 engage in 6 imitate 7 open-ended 8 literacy

F

- Put the students in groups to read and discuss the statements and their reasons for agreeing or disagreeing. Circulate and help as needed.
- Invite volunteers to share their ideas with the class.

▶ Workbook p. 52, Section 1

▶ Workbook p. 53, Section 2

Just playing?

Listening: to a radio talk show (p. 107)

Lead-in
Explain that the students are going to listen to a radio programme about how we play. Ask the students with children or young relatives or friends if they have noticed any differences between how children play now compared with how they themselves used to play.

A
- Ask the students to describe the differences between the two photos. Then have them choose one that most closely reflects their own childhood. Encourage volunteers to explain their choices to the class.

B 2.11
- See p. 129 for the **audioscript.**
- Have the students read the instructions and the four statements. Explain that they need to identify the two main points that the speaker makes.
- Play the audio once, and check progress. Play the audio again, if necessary, before checking answers with the class.

Answer
I understand why the way children play has changed. Children used to engage in more imaginative play.

C 2.12
- See p. 129 for the **audioscript.**
- Ask the students to listen to the rest of the radio programme and make notes on the two main points made by each of the other speakers.
- Play the audio once, and check progress. Give the students time to read their notes, and decide on their answers. Play the audio again, if necessary, before checking answers with the class.

Answers

Becky
Children play different types of games now because of new technology, and some of the games are very good for numeracy and literacy.

Maarten
Parents used to leave their children to play on their own. Now parents organise their kids' play and take them to play centres.

D
- Put the students in pairs. Have them discuss their notes and say which points they think are true, and why.
- Discuss the answers with the class.

Grammar: the subjunctive (p. 108)

Lead-in
Ask the students to describe a typical office environment that they are familiar with. Ask them what changes they would make to such an environment to improve it.

A
- Have the students read the text with the question in mind. Elicit suggestions and discuss the answer (they think the employees will be more productive).
- Ask the students if they would like to work in the environment described in the text and have them explain why or why not.

Extra: classroom design
Ask the students to work in small groups to design an ideal classroom that incorporates opportunities for play. Show them some images of offices of well-known companies to stimulate their imaginations. Brainstorm some ideas and write them on the board. Ask each group to present their classroom design to the class.

NOTICE!
- Direct the students' attention to the **Notice!** box.
- Have them circle the verbs that come after *that* and decide what form those verbs are in. Then ask them to identify the verbs and adjectives that come immediately before *that*.
- Elicit the answers to the questions.

Answers
They're in the base form.
Verbs: insist, ask, recommend, demand, suggest
Adjectives: essential, important, recommended

B

Form
- Have the students read the paragraph again, paying attention to the underlined sentences.
- Ask the students to read the grammar table carefully. Remind them that the subjunctive uses the root form of the verb (*go, take, do,* etc). Ask them to look back at the text and place the underlined sentences in the correct places in the table.
- Check answers with the class.

Answers

1 His boss asks that he take a break every couple of hours to do something fun.
2 Of course, most companies don't *demand* that their employees take time off to play.
3 Some simply suggest that workers not spend the whole day at their desk.
4 They say it is essential that people relax and have fun in order to be more productive.
5 It definitely isn't recommended that you play *all* the time!
6 They also say it is important that a person not work too many hours without taking a break.

Function

- Ask the students to refer to the table again before they decide whether each sentence is true or false.
- Check answers with the class. **Highlight** the fact that the subjunctive is formal in tone, and is used to emphasise the importance of what is being said (the importance of the requests, orders or recommendations being made).
- Direct students' attention to the **What's right?** box and ask them to tick the correct sentence (*2*). Discuss why the other sentence is incorrect.

Answers

1 T 2 F

C

- Ask the students to work individually to choose the appropriate verb form for the eight sentences. Encourage them to refer to the patterns in the grammar table for guidance as they complete the exercise. Give them time to compare their answers in pairs.
- When checking the answers with the class, ask different pairs to give their answers. If the sentence is incorrect, explain why (*the subjunctive uses the root form of the verb, subject-verb agreement, the infinitive to*, etc).

Answers

1 check 2 is 3 not take 4 allow 5 be 6 to work
7 not work 8 be

D

- Put the students in pairs, and direct their attention to the two example statements. Ask them for ideas about how an employer can increase employee motivation and productivity, and how employees can improve their work environment. Remind them to use words and phrases from the grammar table in their discussion.
- Invite volunteers to share their ideas with the class, and encourage other students to agree or disagree. Ask them to give reasons for their opinions.

Extra: grammar

Dictate the following sentence stems or write them on the board:
It is recommended that ...; I think it is important that ...; I suggest that ...
Ask the students to complete these sentences individually. Then have them compare their sentences in pairs.

▶ Workbook p. 53, Section 3

Speaking: making and responding to invitations (p. 109)

Lead-in

Ask the students to read the information in the skills panel. Ask them if they ever feel uncomfortable when they can't or don't wish to accept an invitation. Elicit some of the excuses they usually give (*someone else won't allow them to go, they have another appointment*, etc). Ask them how they feel, on the other hand, when someone declines their invitation (*hurt, disappointed, annoyed*, etc).

A 2.13

- See p. 129 for the **audioscript.**
- Direct the students' attention to the instructions and the table, and make sure they understand the task. Explain that they will listen to three conversations, decide if each conversation is formal or informal and then decide if the invitation was accepted or not.
- Play the audio once, stopping after each conversation if necessary.
- Invite different students to share their answers with the class. When discussing the invitations that were declined, ask the students if they felt that the person really wanted to accept, or if they were just making an excuse. Elicit the reasons for their opinions.

Answers

Invitation 1: Informal, Accepted
Invitation 2: Formal, Paul – accepted, Olivia – declined
Invitation 3: Informal, Declined

B

- Have the students read the table carefully before they listen to the audio for a second time. Ask them to complete the table with the phrases that they hear. Point out that they are probably already familiar with most of these phrases.
- Play the audio. If necessary, pause briefly after each conversation to give the students time to write their answers.
- Check answers with the class.

Just playing? **UNIT 9** 85

Answers

1 You up for it?
2 Want to go?
3 I'd like to invite you to …
4 Would you like to …?
5 Sounds great!
6 Yes, I'd love to …
7 Sorry, can't do it … I have to …
8 Can I take a rain check?
9 Maybe later …?
10 I'd really like to go, but unfortunately, I won't be able to.

Extra: expanding vocabulary

Write the following expressions on the board: *You up for it? Don't start without me! Want to go? Can I take a rain check? Can't you get out of it?* Make sure the students understand the meaning of each. Elicit that these expressions are used in informal speech. Put the students in small groups and have each group prepare a conversation using as many of these expressions as possible. Invite a group or two to perform their conversation for the class.

C

- Put the students in pairs and assign them the roles of Student A and Student B. Explain that they are going to roleplay two different situations and that they will have the opportunity to play both roles.
- Give the students time to read through both of their own roles and to plan what they are going to say. In both situations, Student A must think about the details of the invitation: the kind of activity or talk, where this takes place, what time, how to get there, etc. Student B must think about the appropriate language to accept or decline politely. Ask them to use language from the table in Ex. B.
- Ask the pairs to begin their first roleplay. Circulate while they are working and encourage them to improvise. When they finish, have them move on to the second roleplay. Them ask them to swap roles and roleplay both situations again, changing the details of the activity and the talk.

Extra: speaking

In a whole-class roleplay activity, have each student invite a classmate to join them for a trip or activity. Encourage the classmate to accept or decline as they wish, but point out that if they decide to decline the invitation, they should try to do so as nicely as possible.

▶ Workbook p. 54, Sections 4 and 5

Grammar: alternatives to the subjunctive (p. 110)

Lead-in
Ask the students if they play video games. If so, ask them what games they play and how often. Ask the students who don't play video games to explain why not.

A
- Have the students read the text with the questions in mind. Then ask them if they were surprised by the results of the studies or not. Prompt them to explain their answers.

NOTICE!
- Direct the students' attention to the **Notice!** box.
- Have them look at the text to find and underline the verbs and adjectives that are normally followed by a verb in a subjunctive form.
- Elicit the answer to the question.

Answer
Only the first verb is followed by a subjunctive.

Alternative
Give the students the following focus question before they read: *What are the positive effects of playing video games?* Have the students read the text. Then check the answers with the class.

B
Form
- Ask the students to read the paragraph again, paying attention to the words they underlined.
- Give the students time to read through the grammar table. **Highlight** the three alternatives to the subjunctive (which was introduced earlier in this unit), and ask them to pay attention to the key differences in structure. Explain that their main focus should be on developing accuracy with these forms.
- Have the students complete the table with examples from the text in Ex. A.

Answers

1 The fast pace of life <u>demands that your brain function</u> is at its top capacity.
2 … video games of the type that <u>require you to think and react</u> very quickly.
3 Some researchers <u>recommend increasing</u> brain function by …
4 … if your job <u>requires sitting</u> in front of a computer screen …
5 … it's <u>important for you to include</u> games …

Function

- Have the students complete the rule by selecting the correct option (*the same meaning as*). Then go over the alternatives to the subjunctive, and point out that the different forms have the same meaning.
- Direct the students' attention to the **What's right?** box and ask them to tick the correct sentences (*1 and 2*). Then elicit what is wrong in the incorrect sentence (the verb *suggest* must be followed by a gerund, not an infinitive).

C

- Ask the students to read through the five sentences before starting to rewrite them using alternatives to the subjunctive. Remind them to refer to the table in Ex. B for guidance as they construct their sentences. Circulate and help as needed.
- Check answers with the class.

Answers

1 It is vital for us to exercise our brains as well as our bodies.
2 The company recommends learning to play at least one video game.
3 It is essential for you to keep your brain active.
4 I propose giving the employees free video games.
5 Our boss is asking us to attend a brain-training workshop.

D

- Give the students time to read the discussion question and to prepare some notes individually. Then put the students in pairs to discuss. Encourage them to use the three sample sentence stems in their discussion.
- Circulate while the students are working, and make a note of any errors to correct at the end.

Alternative

Make a note of errors you hear while you are monitoring. Afterwards, write the sentences with errors on the board and have the students correct them. Remind them that it is important to develop accuracy when they use the subjunctive and its alternatives.

▶ Workbook p. 55, Section 6

Pronunciation: assimilation (p. 111)

A 2.14

- See the Student's Book page for the **audioscript**.
- Explain that *assimilation* in speech happens when the pronunciation of one sound is affected by the sound immediately after it. Assimilation contributes to fluency, where spoken language sounds smooth and connected instead of like a series of single or disjointed sounds. These sounds can be words that are next to each other, or they can be sounds in words with two syllables or more. Direct the students' attention to the final consonant sounds in the table, and the addition of /j/ to make a new consonant sound.
- Play the audio, and have the students complete the table with the phrases in the box.
- Play the audio again, and give the students time to repeat the words.

Answers

/s/ + /j/ = /ʃ/	/z/ + /j/ = /ʒ/	/t/ + /j/ = /tʃ/	/d/ + /j/ = /dʒ/
this year	does your	that your	would you

B 2.15

- See the Student's Book page for the **audioscript.**
- Ask the students to read the three sentences, and think about how to pronounce the pairs of words which are underlined. Then have them practise saying the sentences in pairs, paying attention to assimilation.
- Play the audio, and have the students compare and practise their pronunciation. If necessary, play the audio again, and ask the students to practise after each sentence.

Writing: a short article (p. 111)

Lead-in

Elicit from the class their thoughts on the future of video games. Ask them if they think the popularity of video games will continue growing, or if it will reach a peak and then decline. Elicit ideas about how they think the technology of video gaming will develop. Encourage the students to share their ideas about the effects these improved video games will have on young people in the future, and ask them to speculate on the kind of game that might eventually replace video games altogether.

A

- Direct the students' attention to the announcement. Have them read it with the question in mind. Elicit the answer. Ask the students what type of publication this announcement comes from and who its target audience is (*a teenage/young adult magazine*). Ask them if it sounds like the type of magazine they would like to read.

Answer

an opinion article on a controversial subject

B

- Explain to the students that *opinion articles* reflect the writer's opinion on a particular subject. They are usually published in newspapers and magazines.
- Have the students read the winning opinion article and decide if the statements are true or false. Give them time to do this. To check the answers, ask one student to read each statement and the rest of the class to call out *true* or *false*.

Just playing? UNIT 9 **87**

Answers
1 F 2 T 3 T

C
- Ask the students to read the topic and decide on a viewpoint. Then ask them to brainstorm some ideas for their opinion article before choosing a title and drafting their 200 to 300 word article. Remind them that their readership/target audience means the text should be informal in style. Circulate while they are working and help as needed. The article may need to be completed in the next lesson if time runs out.

Alternative
Ask the students to write their opinion article individually as homework. In the next lesson, put the students in pairs to read each other's work and offer comments on how effective the argument is, how well it is structured and how interesting it is overall.

LifeSkills: recognising contradiction (p. 112)

Step 1: Learn to recognise points that contradict each other. If two points cannot both be true, then they are contradictory. (Ex. A, Ex. B)

Step 2: When you hear or read an argument, try to identify the main idea and the main points. Then decide whether any of the points contradict each other. (Ex. B, Ex. C, Ex. D)

Step 3: Decide whether an argument is strong or weak based on how many contradictory points there are. (Ex. E, Ex. F)

Lead-in
Read the target skill aloud, and invite the students to tell you what they think *recognising contradiction* means. Ask the students to define the word *contradiction (a combination of statements or ideas that are fundamentally opposed to each other)* and to give a few examples (saying there is no right or wrong answer and then telling someone their answer is incorrect). Explain that part of thinking critically about an argument is to analyse how the different parts of an argument relate to each other. Sometimes, one part of an argument contradicts another part. In other words, they cannot both be true. Recognising this allows us to evaluate how strong the argument is and how to improve it. Then **highlight** the three-step strategy to develop the skill of recognising contradictions.

A
- Ask the students to read and match the contradictory statements individually. To check the answers, ask one student to read a statement and a different student to read its contradiction. Ask the rest of the class if they agree. Then ask volunteers to specify the key words that helped them make their decisions.

- Invite different volunteers to say which of these statements they agree with. Encourage further discussion from the rest of the class.

Answers
1 c 2 a 3 d 4 b

B
- Put the students in pairs and have them read the instructions. Ask them to read both texts first. Suggest that they work with one text each to identify and underline the contradiction, and then share their ideas in a discussion. Circulate while the students are working and help as needed.
- Elicit and discuss the answers with the class.

Suggested answers
Text 1
The writer says that he/she supervises his/her daughter's play so that she plays 'properly', but then he/she says that children learn to make their own decisions and how to socialise when they play. If everything is supervised, it is a contradiction to think they will learn how to make their own decisions.

Text 2
The speaker says he/she doesn't think playing video games did him/her any harm, but then continues by saying that children can become isolated when they play electronic games. The speaker goes on to say that he/she is nervous in large groups, so it seems that playing video games as a child may have been harmful.

Alternative
Put students in pairs to read and analyse the texts. Ask them to work together to identify and underline the contradiction in each. Then have the pairs combine to form groups of four to discuss their answers.

C
- Review some of the negative effects of playing video games that have been discussed in this unit. Write a list of the students' ideas on the board.
- Ask the students to read the essay individually and to locate the three main points the writer makes. Give them just enough time to do this. Then check the answers with the class by inviting different students to give the answers. Encourage the students to compare the main points in the essay with the students' own ideas on the board.

Answer
Three main points:
1 Video games can be addictive.
2 Video games can cause antisocial behaviour because kids spend less time with other people.
3 Spending too much time playing video games limits the time kids spend doing other activities.

D

- Give the students time to read the essay again and locate the contradictions. Remind the students to underline the statements that contradict each other.

Answer

Contradictions:
1 In some countries, young people are sent to special clinics to cure them of their addiction even though there is no real evidence that it is actually a physical or psychological condition.
2 Gamers these days often play games that take place online and that involve interacting with a wide range of people.

E

- Put the students in pairs to compare their ideas before discussing the answers as a class. Point out that the use of contrastive linking words such as *even though* can indicate a contradiction is coming, as with the first example.
- Elicit other words that could indicate a contradiction: *however*, *nevertheless*, *although*, etc. Challenge the pairs to edit the essay to correct the contradictions.

F

- Put the students in groups to discuss whether or not they agree with the argument in the essay. Encourage them to refer directly to the points made in the essay in their discussion as they state their own points of view.
- Extend the discussion with the whole class. Ask the students if reading this text, and others in the unit, has made them think about how much time they spend gaming, or involved in other activities that are considered play. Ask them if they are likely to change their habits in any way, and to explain these adjustments to the class: increase, decrease or adjust the time they spend on these activities; modify their play in other ways as a consequence of their reflections. Remind them to be as specific as possible, and encourage them to justify their answers by giving reasons for maintaining their current habits or making adjustments.

G

- Have the students work in the same groups as in Ex. F. Ask them to read and discuss the questions.
- When they finish, discuss the responses with the class. Ask the students to say what they feel are the most useful points they learnt from this lesson and how the skill of *recognising contradiction* might be useful in the domain of **Work and Career**, either now or in the future.

REFLECT

- Ask the students to read the *Reflect* question.
- Give them time to think about different situations in the domains of **Self and Society** and **Study and Learning** where the skill of *recognising contradiction* would be useful.

- Elicit the following ideas: evaluating the logic of an argument, improving an argument (by eliminating contradictions and other logical flaws), comparing and contrasting information in different texts, identifying assumptions, identifying incorrect conclusions, deciding which viewpoints are more valid than others, etc.

RESEARCH

- Explain the task and make sure the students understand what they have to do.
- Suggest some possible sources where the students could find written opinion articles, such as newspaper columns or editorials, blogs, magazines or websites.
- Ask the students to take turns presenting the results of their research to the class. First, have them say what controversial topic they chose and which type of written opinion they looked at. Then have them summarise one or two of the arguments and **highlight** the contradictions, if any. If necessary, have them explain how the points contradict one another.

Language wrap-up (p. 114)

For notes on how to approach the exercises in the Language wrap-up section, please refer to page 9.

1 Vocabulary

A

- Encourage the students to read the whole paragraph before attempting to complete it with the words from the box. Explain that reading the text first provides them with the context and helps them to identify the correct answers and their placement in the paragraph.
- Once they have completed the exercise, have them read through the paragraph to check if their answers make sense. Allow them to adjust their answers if necessary.

B

- Read the instructions aloud. Point out that the students have to complete the conversations by writing one or two words in each gap. Remind them that they have come across suitable words and phrases in this unit.
- Have the students read through each conversation before completing it. If necessary, explain that they should look at the response in each conversation to first decide whether the person is accepting or declining the invitation.

2 Grammar

- Ask the students to recall what they have learnt about the subjunctive and alternatives to the subjunctive in this unit. Then have them read the text (a letter to a head teacher) carefully, and elicit the reason for doing so (*to get a sense of the context*).
- Ask the students to complete the text by choosing one of the two options for each item. Encourage them to experiment with both options in the sentence if they are unsure of any answer.

Just playing? UNIT 9

Writing workshop: writing a short article (p. 115)

Lead-in
Explain to the students that in this workshop they are going to practise writing a short opinion article.

A
- Ask the students to read the assignment and take note of what the requirements are (*to choose a game/sport and explain how it helps people develop various skills*). Then ask them to read the response to the assignment and decide whether the four statements are true or false.
- Put the students in pairs to discuss their answers. Then check answers with the class and discuss any difficulties.

Answers
1 T 2 F 3 T 4 T

Extra: false to true
Ask the students to rewrite the false statement in Ex. A to make it true.

Answer
The writer says dominoes helps people develop numeracy skills.

Extra: categorising games
Put the students in small groups and ask them to write a list of games that help people develop mental, physical or social skills. Tell them that some games could be included in more than one category. Give them a few minutes to write their lists. Then discuss their ideas as a class.

B
- Ask the students to read the article again, paying particular attention to how the writer has structured it. Have them look at the title, and elicit ways in which it sets the tone for the content of the article. (It clearly states the game that is going to be discussed (dominoes). It suggests that there are several positive benefits of the game (in the words *more than*). It tells the reader to expect to learn something about this game, etc).
- Have the students look at the introduction, the second paragraph and the conclusion, and identify the main points in each of them.
- Then ask the students to complete the outline. Point out that what they are doing is producing a *reverse outline*. *Reverse outlining* is a useful method of extracting the main ideas of the text and examining the way in which it is organised. It also helps a writer decide if a text is structured logically. For example, if it is difficult to summarise the main point of a paragraph, it might need to be revised.
- Check answers with the class.

Answers
Paragraph 1:
Topic sentence: In my opinion, dominoes is a game that has many advantages and no disadvantages.
Paragraph 2:
Topic sentence: Here is why dominoes is much more than just a game, and why it is definitely not a waste of time.
Also develops analytical skills
Paragraph 3:
Topic sentence: In conclusion, playing dominoes requires thinking and planning, so it is a good way to train your brain.
doesn't cost money to play

C
- Explain that the students are going to write a short article that responds to the same assignment. Have them reread the assignment in Ex. A and think of a game or sport that they would like to write about.
- Have the students work individually to prepare an outline for their article, similar to the one in Ex. B. Encourage them to brainstorm ideas before selecting and condensing the best ones into main ideas. Once they are ready, encourage them to use these main ideas to write topic sentences. Remind them that each topic sentence must contain the main idea for each paragraph.
- If they wish, ask the students to compare their outlines in pairs and incorporate peer feedback into a revised outline. Encourage each pair to contribute ideas to make each other's articles stronger and more interesting.

D
- Ask the students to use their outlines to write their articles. Remind them to limit their article to 250 words.

How are you doing?
- Ask the students to read the statements and tick the ones they believe are true.
- Ask them to discuss their article with another student in the class and identify things they could improve on next time.

▶ Workbook pp. 56–57, SkillsStudio

UNIT 10 FACT OR FICTION

The expression *fact or fiction* is an idiomatic way of distinguishing between true and false or between what's real and what's imaginary. As more and more images are circulated online (often through social media) there is a growing awareness of the importance of being able to distinguish genuine or fake photos and videos.

Unit plan

Unit opener	(p. 116)	20 min.
1 **Speaking:** talking about popular beliefs	(p. 118)	30 min.
• Vocabulary: falsehood		15 min.
2 **Grammar:** inversion with negative expressions	(p. 119)	40 min.
3 **Reading:** a wiki entry	(p. 120)	30 min.
• Vocabulary: word forms (proving and disproving)		15 min.
4 **Writing:** a wiki entry	(p. 121)	30 min.
5 **Grammar:** ellipsis and substitution	(p. 122)	40 min.
6 **Pronunciation:** thought groups	(p. 123)	15 min.
7 **Listening:** difficult situations	(p. 123)	30 min.
LifeSkills: evaluating internet source reliability (Study and Learning)	(p. 124)	50 min.
• Optional downloadable *LifeSkills* lesson (Work and Career).		50 min.
• Optional downloadable *LifeSkills* lesson (Self and Society)		50 min.
Language wrap-up	(p. 126)	20 min.
Speaking workshop: responding with an opinion	(p. 127)	30 min.
Video and downloadable video worksheet		45 min.

Unit opener (p. 116)

Lead-in
Ask the students to look at the unit title and photos, and to predict what the unit will be about. Elicit the meaning of the title using the ideas in the panel under the title on this page. Direct the students' attention to the photos, and ask if they know what the strange shape cut into the field is called (*a crop circle*). Ask the students what they know about crop circles. Tell them they will learn more about them in this unit. Direct the students' attention to the points in the unit objectives box and go through the information with them. To get your students to think about the skills being developed in this unit, ask them to look at the questions in the cogs.

Listening: difficult situations
- Elicit answers to the question. Ask the students to share personal experiences of someone talking too fast. What did they do?

Writing: a wiki entry
- Make sure the students understand the meaning of *wiki* (*a collaborative website that allows anyone to write and edit its material*). Then answer the questions as a class.

LifeSkills: evaluating internet source reliability
- Refer the students to the *LifeSkills* panel. Ask the students how they use the internet to get information. Which websites do they use the most? Why? Encourage the students to share personal experiences with unreliable internet information.

Common European Framework: unit map

Unit 10	Competence developed	CEF Reference (C1 competences)
Speaking	can talk about popular beliefs	Table 1; Table 2; Sections 4.4.1.1; 4.4.3.1; 4.4.3.5; 4.5.2.1; 5.2.1.1; 5.2.1.2; 5.2.3.2
Grammar	can use and understand inversion with negative expressions	Table 1; Table 2; Sections 5.2.1.2; 6.4.7.7; 6.4.7.8
Reading	can understand a wiki entry	Table 1; Table 2; Sections 4.4.2.2; 4.4.2.4; 4.4.3.4; 4.5.2.2
Writing	can write a wiki entry	Table 1; Table 2; Sections 4.4.1.2; 4.4.3.2; 4.4.3.4; 4.5.2.1; 5.2.1.1; 5.2.1.2; 5.2.1.6; 5.2.2.4
Grammar	can use and understand ellipsis and substitution	Table 1; Table 2; Section 5.2.1.2; 6.4.7.7; 6.4.7.8
Pronunciation	can correctly pause between thought groups	Section 5.2.1.4
Listening	can deal with difficult situations	Table 1; Table 2; Sections 4.4.2.1; 4.4.3.1; 4.4.3.5; 4.5.2.2

A

- Put the students in pairs and direct their attention to the photos. Ask the students to decide individually whether each photo is real or fake and then tell their partner why they think so. Circulate and help as needed.
- When the students finish, take a class vote on each photo: real or fake?

Answers

Real: giant coconut crab, scorpions on sticks, rabbit-shaped fruit
Fake: world's smallest cat, UFO, hole in the pavement
(The hole in the pavement is an example of 3D pavement art, where the artist creates the illusion of a 3D scene on the pavement.)

Extra: idioms

Write the following idiom on the board: *Seeing is believing*. Put the students in pairs to discuss what they think this means. Ask them to give concrete examples of some things they would have to see in order to believe that they exist. Have the students think about any similar idioms they have in their first language. Give partners a few minutes to talk about their ideas. Then discuss as a class.

Extra: discussion

Either put the students in groups or lead a class discussion on this question: *Why do people fake things, such as the photos above?*

Possible answer

for fun, to earn money, to become famous

B

- Put the students in groups and refer them to the instructions. Ask what is meant by *to what extent …* Elicit that *extent* refers to range or scale, like a scale of one to five or a three-star review.
- Review expressions the students could use if they completely agree or disagree with a statement (*I completely/absolutely/totally agree/disagree. I couldn't agree/disagree more*, etc).
- Give the groups time for their discussion. Then discuss together as a class. Draw two lines on the board to represent a scale of 1 to 10 for each statement, with 1 being 'completely disagree' and 10 being 'completely agree'. Ask the students, by show of hands, to what extent they agree with each of the two statements. For each statement, **highlight** the number on the scale that receives the most student responses. Ask the students to translate those numbers into percentages (the class agreed 60% with the first statement and 40% with the second).

Extra: class discussion

As a class, have the students discuss technological advances that make it easier to fool people than ever before. Begin by naming the computer program Photoshop, which is used to digitally enhance photographs. Point out that an adept user can enhance or change colours, delete items in the photograph, and even place items from another photo in the photograph they are editing. Elicit other technological advances that make falsification easy. Ask the students to talk about how these advances affect us.

Extra: practice

Play this popular game, or your own variation of it. Put the students in small groups. Tell them to write three facts about themselves, but that one of the 'facts' must be untrue, or fiction. The students then take turns reading their list of facts to each other. The listeners try to guess which fact is not true.

Variation: Have the students make two of their facts untrue, and listeners guess which fact is true.

Culture note: falsehood

- *Fiction* means *not factual, untrue*. It is most commonly used as an adjective to classify books. When writing or speech is labelled as fiction, it implies that whatever was written or said was created from the author or speaker's imagination.
- *False* is similar to fiction, as both adjectives apply chiefly to language. False, however, does not necessarily imply that the false words were invented or made up. It simply means they are not true.
- *Fake* means not genuine and implies an intention to deceive. It applies mostly to objects and persons. Popular synonyms for *fake* include *phony, imitation,* and *counterfeit*. (*That's a phony moustache. The car has imitation leather seats. Those trainers are counterfeit Nike.*)
- *Fake* can also be used as a verb: *He faked his own death. Magicians fake cutting people in half.* In this case, *fake* means to falsify – to make, write, or produce something that is not genuine.
- Another word, *forgery*, applies to falsely signing someone else's name on a legal document, such as a contract or cheque. It stems from the verb *forge*: *He forged his mother's signature on the letter.*

Speaking: talking about popular beliefs (p. 118)

Lead-in
Write this on the board: *After eating, you should wait for an hour before you swim.* Ask the students how many believe it. Point out that this is an example of a popular belief. It is not true, because there is no medical evidence showing you need to wait an hour. Ask the students for other popular beliefs and write them on the board. Ask the class which they believe are true and untrue, and why. Why do some beliefs become popular?

Culture note
Popular beliefs with no medical evidence to back them up are also known as *old wives' tales*. This refers to the oral tradition of older women passing on helpful hints to the next generation. Science has proven some old wives' tales to be at least partially true (chicken soup will cure your cold), and others completely false (Don't go outside with wet hair. You will catch a cold.).

A 2.16
- See p. 130 for the **audioscript**.
- Direct the students' attention to the photos. Explain that they will listen to three different conversations about popular beliefs. Ask them to take notes and fill in the gaps. Explain that, after listening, they will tell their partners in their own words why these beliefs are false.
- Play the audio. Pause after each conversation to give the students time to write.
- Put the students in pairs. Ask them to take turns explaining the three beliefs and why they are false.
- Discuss the answers as a class.

Answers
1 *Great Wall of China*
belief: The wall can be seen from space.
reality: It can't.
2 *human brain*
belief: We only use 10% of our brains.
reality: We use all of our brains.
3 *shaving*
belief: Shaving makes hair grow back thicker and stronger.
reality: Shaving has no effect on hair growth.

B
- Direct the students' attention to the vocabulary words and explain that they were all used in the conversations. Point out that they all have to do with falsehood.
- Have the students circle the word or phrase on the right that is closest in meaning to the word on the left.
- Check answers with the class.

Answers
1 incorrect belief 2 general false belief 3 trick
4 not genuine 5 not real 6 easy to trick

C
- Ask the students to read the blog entry first, before choosing the correct words to complete it.
- Check answers with the class.

Answers
1 gullible 2 misconception 3 hoax 4 fake 5 myth

Culture note
Get real and *be real* are popular English idioms. They are both ways of expressing total disagreement with someone and bewilderment that the person would make such a statement or hold such a belief. The phrases carry the connotation of '*You can't be serious*'.

D
- Have the students read both statements. Then ask them to choose one of the statements.
- Give the students time to make notes on whether they agree with this statement or not, and why.

E
- Put the students in pairs. Have the students talk to their partner about whether or not they agree with the statement they chose. Encourage them to use their notes to help them stay focused and remember everything they want to say.
- Ask each student to speak for about two minutes while their partner listens without interrupting.
- Have the students take turns talking about whether they believe the statement they chose, and why or why not.

▶ Workbook p. 58, Section 1

Grammar: inversion with negative expressions (p. 119)

Lead-in
Write the date *September 11, 2001* on the board, and ask the students what happened on that date. (*The World Trade Centre in New York City was attacked.*) Ask them what they remember about that day. How did they hear the news? What did they think was happening? Elicit that when a crisis occurs, it is important not to jump to conclusions or to believe everything you hear.

A
- Direct the students' attention to the photo and the text. Ask the students who is in the picture (*former US President John F. Kennedy*) and what they know about him. Write the words *conspiracy theory* on the board. Ask the students if they think they know what it means, but do not ask for an explanation.
- Have the students read the text with the question in mind. Then ask different students to explain what a conspiracy theory is. Create a definition with the class.

Fact or fiction UNIT 10 93

Answer

A conspiracy theory is the idea that a group of people secretly worked together to cause a particular event.

NOTICE!

- Direct the students' attention to the **Notice!** box.
- Ask them to look at the words and phrases in bold and tell you what they notice about word order in those sentences.

Answer

These words and phrases are followed by an inverted word order: a verb phrase and then the subject of the sentence.

B

Form

- Have the students read the article in Ex. A again, paying attention to the inverted sentences.
- Ask the students to read the table. Point out that the types of sentences being studied in this unit can be divided into three general groups: phrases with time, phrases with *only*, and other negative expressions, such as *never* and *seldom*.
- Ask the students to complete the table with the bold words in the text in Ex. A.
- Check answers with the class.

Answers

1 No sooner 2 Not only 3 Only when 4 Rarely 5 Little

Function

- Ask the students to choose the correct option to complete each rule (*both a*). Then check the answers as a class.
- Direct students' attention to the **What's right?** box and ask them to tick the correct sentence (*1*). Discuss why the other sentence is incorrect.

C

- Encourage the students to refer to the table in Ex. B as they rewrite the sentences. Circulate and help as needed. Check answers with the class.

Answers

1 have I heard such a ridiculous theory
2 will they (ever) admit what really happened
3 sooner had I begun to talk, than he interrupted me with his own theory
4 only is your theory illogical, (but) it also ignores the evidence
5 if you examine the evidence, will you come to the right conclusion

D

- Explain that the students are going to write a short paragraph stating their opinion of conspiracy theories. Encourage them to outline the paragraph first. **Highlight** that they must include three sentences with inversions, and cover the three points listed.
- Give the students time to pre-plan and write. When they finish, put the students in pairs to exchange their paragraphs. Have their partners check to make sure there are three sentences with inversions and that all three points have been covered.

▶ Workbook pp. 58–59, Section 2

Reading: a wiki entry (p. 120)

Lead-in

Ask the students whether they generally check facts on the internet, and if so, which sites they use (e.g. Wikipedia). Elicit issues to consider if they use this site for homework assignments (e.g. reliability, because anyone can write and edit it). Point out that colleges do not accept Wikipedia as a source for students' work. Explain that they are going to read a wiki-type entry. (For a definition of *wiki*, see the skills panel on p. 121 of the Student's Book.) Write this sentence on the board: *Kangaroos are reptiles that live only in Austria.* Ask if there is anything wrong with it. Elicit that kangaroos are *mammals* (or *marsupials*) that live only in *Australia*. Point out that mistaking Austria for Australia is easy because the two words look alike. Erase the incorrect words and replace them with the correct ones. Invite different students to state one fact about kangaroos (*they hop, they carry babies in a pouch, they have powerful back legs*, etc). Add a sentence to the end of the one on the board for each fact. Stop after three or four. Tell the students this is the same process of correcting errors and adding information that is used to create paragraphs for wiki articles and Wikipedia.

A

- Ask the students to read the instructions and the question. Then have them read the opening paragraph with the question in mind.
- Check the answer with the class. Ask them if they have ever heard of www.snopes.com or used it. Elicit the students' thoughts on whether or not this type of website is useful.

Possible answer

You might use snopes.com to verify information when someone sends you an email warning you about a virus or other threat, or when you see something online that sounds suspicious or false, etc.

B

- Ask the students to read the rest of the article individually and then check if the four statements below the article are true, false or not mentioned. Remind them that the article may contain errors, both factual and grammatical.
- Allow the students enough time to read the article and complete the exercise.
- Check answers as a class.

Answers

1 F 2 NM 3 T 4 F

Extra: change *false* and *not mentioned* to *true*

Have the students rewrite the statements they marked *false* or *not mentioned* to make them true.

Answers

1 Snopes was David's old internet name and the Mikkelsons decided to use it when they launched their website.
2 The Mikkelsons research the stories, but the text does not mention what sources they use.
4 The Mikkelsons are apolitical people. FactCheck.org conducted an investigation and could not find any confirmation of the charge that the Mikkelsons hold strong political views.

C

- Ask the students if they noticed any errors when they read the article. Tell them to read the whole article again very carefully to find not only spelling and grammar mistakes, but facts that need to be checked and corrected. Remind them that the article begins in Ex. A.
- When the students finish, put them in pairs to compare their answers. Then check answers with the class.

Answers

Fact to be checked: The date when Snopes was founded needs to be checked. At one point the wiki entry says: 'Snopes was founded in 1995 by Barbara and David Mikkelson, who still run the site today.' and at another it says: 'The Mikkelsons decided to use the name when they launched the site in 1997.'
Students should also find the following mistakes:
The site, located at www.snopes.com, owned and operated entirely by the Mikkelsons, should be *The site, located at www.snopes.com, **is** owned and operated entirely by the Mikkelsons,;* Not only the Mikkelsons debunk or confirm stories, should be *Not only **do** the Mikkelsons debunk or confirm stories,;* email hoxes should be *email **hoaxers**; Snopes has been accused having* should be *Snopes has been accused **of** having*

Alternative

Put the students in pairs and have them identify the four grammar mistakes and one spelling mistake in the wiki entry. Write each sentence on the board. Ask students to work individually to correct the mistakes. Then have them check their answers with their partner. Have volunteers share their corrections with the class. Encourage discussion if anyone in the class disagrees with the correction or if someone corrected it differently.

D

- Ask the students to look at the table and study the listed word forms.
- Ask them to complete the table by filling in the gaps, without any form of assistance. If they are not sure of a word, ask them to make their best guess.

- When they finish, have them look at the text in Ex. A and Ex. B to check their answers.
- Then check answers with the class.

Answers

1 validity 2 verify 3 confirmation 4 confirm 5 support
6 prove 7 dismiss 8 debunk 9 disprove

Extra: vocabulary practice

Put the students in two groups: one to prove a claim and the other to disprove a claim. Ask each group to choose one noun, one verb, one adjective and one participial adjective and write a sentence using each. Invite volunteers from each group to share their sentences with the class.

E

- Direct the students' attention to the sentences and have them work individually to choose the correct word forms.
- Check answers with the class.

Answers

1 validation 2 confirm 3 support 4 verifiable 5 dismissed
6 proof

F

- First, ask the students to read the sentences in Ex. E again and check the ones they agree with.
- Put the students in pairs. Ask them to discuss their answers and explain why they do or do not agree with each statement. Circulate and help as needed.
- When they finish, ask different pairs to share what they agreed or disagreed on with the class.

▶ Workbook p. 59, Section 3

Writing: a wiki entry (p. 121)

Lead-in

Ask the students to read the information in the skills panel. Make sure they understand the meaning of *a neutral point of view* (not favouring one side or the other), and what it means to *cite sources* (to reveal where you found a fact or quotation that you are using in an article). Ask the students if they have ever contributed to a wiki site or if they would like to.

A

- Read the instructions to the class. Tell the students they will now pretend to be reporters for a new website, called DebunkerWiki. Their first assignment is to write a short article – one or two paragraphs – on a popular belief and explain whether that belief is true or false. They may choose their own topic or one of the three listed in the Student's Book.
- Have the students make an outline before writing their article. Allow time for them to work individually, giving help where needed.

Fact or fiction UNIT 10

B

- Put the students in groups, and tell them they are going to 'wiki' each other's articles. Have each student pass their article to the student on their left. Then tell the students to read the articles they now have in front of them and edit them any way they like. They can correct spelling, grammar and punctuation, add information, remove information or change information. Tell the students that each group member must make at least one edit to each article they read. Tell the students to stop when their own article returns to them.

C

- Have the students read their own articles again, with all the changes that their group has made. Give the groups time to talk about the changes and whether or not they improve the article.

Alternative

Tell the students that, after they have finished reading, they should state their opinion of the changes. Did the changes improve the article? How? Which version is better, the new one or the original? Which changes would they keep? Which would they omit or correct?

▶ Workbook p. 60, Section 5

Grammar: ellipsis and substitution (p. 122)

Lead-in

Ask the students if they have ever been approached in an internet or telephone scam, or if they know someone who has. What happened? Did they get involved in the scam, or not? If not, what made them suspicious?

A 2.17

- See the Student's Book page for the **audioscript**.
- Write the word *phishing* on the board. Ask the students to raise their hands if they know or remember what it means, but not to say the meaning out loud or tell the other students.
- Explain that the students are going to listen to a conversation between two friends. Ask them to listen for an explanation of what phishing is. Play the audio as students read along silently. Ask for volunteers to explain what *phishing* means in their own words.

Answer

Phishing is the sending of fake emails with the aim of finding out someone's password, account details or other personal information.

NOTICE!

- Direct the students' attention to the **Notice!** box.
- Have them search the text in Ex. A for examples of incomplete sentences and underline them. Ask the students if the meaning of those sentences is different because of the missing words.

Answer

The meaning is the same, even without the missing words.

B

Form

- Ask the students to read the conversation in Ex. A again, paying attention to the shortened sentences.
- Have the students read the table. Ask them to complete the table with examples from the conversation.
- Check answers with the class.
- Have the students look at the completed table. Ask if they can explain the meaning of *ellipsis* and *reduced relative structures* in their own words. Ask them what *so* substitutes for in numbers 5 and 6 (*this* or *that*). Point out that in 5, *so* can also be left out.
- Put the students in pairs. Have them practise saying the full version of each of the examples in the table as if ellipses or substitution were not used. Model the first one: *I haven't seen you around.*
- Direct the students' attention to the **What's right?** box and ask them to tick the correct sentence (*2*). Discuss why the other sentence is incorrect.

Answers

1. Cost me a lot of money. / Heard of those? / You going to get any of it back?
2. Cost me a lot of money. / Heard of those? / You going to get any of it back?
3. The person receiving the email
4. And then the password entered
5. do so
6. in doing so

Function

- Have the students circle the correct options (1 leave out; 2 so), and then check the answers with the class.

C

- Direct the students' attention to the instructions, and give them time to proofread the text. Ask them to find and correct six mistakes with ellipsis and substitution.
- When they finish, put the students in pairs to compare their answers.
- Check answers with the class.

Answers

Mistake: *Had you any* – Correction: *Had any*
Mistake: *If is so* – Correction: *If so*
Mistake: *The person who sending* – Correction: *The person sending*
Mistake: *can't do* – Correction: *can't do so* (or *can't*)
Mistake: *doing so* – Correction: *in/by doing so*
Mistake: *done it so* – Correction: *done so*

D

- Explain that the students will now pretend to be social media managers. **Highlight** that *social media manager* is a real position and that this exercise simulates a future job assignment.
- Have the students read the instructions. Ask how many students have written tweets. Explain, if necessary, that a *tweet* is a short message with a maximum of 140 characters.
- Have the students read the example tweet. **Highlight** the use of ellipsis and substitution. Ask the students to work individually to write similar short messages on the three topics listed. Circulate and help as needed.
- When they finish, have the students share their tweets with the class. Write some of their examples of ellipsis and substitution on the board.

Possible answers

identity theft
Had your identity stolen? If not, make sure it doesn't happen to you. Keep all personal information secret.
online scams
Got an email from someone needing help to transfer money? Think it looks too good to be true? If so, then it probably is! Delete it now!
phishing
Ever received a phishing email? If so, be careful! Never give anyone your details in an email.
Could cost you a lot if you do!

Culture note

The term *tweeting* derives from the US based website Twitter. Twitter sends instant text messages, called tweets, to mobile phones and computers, but each message can contain no more than 140 characters. Because of this limitation, the use of ellipsis and substitution is widespread in tweets. Senders need to keep their messages short!

▶ Workbook p. 61, Section 6

Pronunciation: thought groups (p. 123)

Lead-in

Write the term *thought groups* on the board and ask what it means. Elicit that it is a group of words, such as a phrase or a clause, that implies a question or requires thought. For example, write *according to Marcus Miller* on the board. Ask students what question the phrase invokes. (*Who is Marcus Miller?*) Then write on the board: *on the other hand*. Ask the students what this phrase means (e.g. that an opposing or contrasting statement/viewpoint is about to follow). **Highlight** that speakers and writers often pause after a thought group, either to answer a question or to allow time to think.

A 🎧 **2.18**

- See the Student's Book page for the **audioscript.**
- Have the students read the instructions. Ask them to circle all the punctuation marks.

- Play the audio. Ask the students to mark the thought groups in the sentences using slashes (/). Ask them to tell you what they notice about the commas (they are used to separate thought groups.)

Answers

1 According to a survey by Gartner, / a leading information technology research and advisory company, / 4.3% of targets of email hoaxes / lost money.
2 Ordinary mass email marketing campaigns, / on the other hand, / have a success rate / of only 1.5%.

Extra: practice

Ask the students to turn to page 120 in the Student's Book and choose one or two sentences from the reading selection 'WikiWorld'. Have them write the sentences and use slashes to separate the thought groups. Put the students in pairs and have them read their sentences to their partner. Ask the partners to correct each other's mistakes. Move around the room and provide help as needed.

B 🎧 **2.19**

- See the Student's Book page for the **audioscript.**
- Put the students in pairs. Ask them to listen to each sentence and then take turns repeating it, pausing between thought groups.
- Play the audio. Stop after each sentence and allow the students time to practise. Encourage the students to read the sentences, first with pauses and then without them.

Extra: practice

When they finish, have the students close their books. Ask if anyone can correctly repeat all three sentences from Ex. B from memory. If the students are struggling, allow them to look at the sentences briefly before trying again.

Listening: difficult situations (p. 123)

Lead-in

Ask the students to read the information in the skills panel. Point out that it's all right to stop a conversation and ask for help. Explain that they will learn ways to do so in this lesson.

A

- Put the students in groups and have them read the questions.
- Give the students time to think about their answers in preparation for their discussion. Circulate while the students are talking and help as needed.
- Have the groups share their answers with the class.

Fact or fiction UNIT 10 **97**

B 🎧 2.20

- See p. 130 for the **audioscript.**
- Explain that the students are going to listen to a discussion in five short parts. Ask them not to worry if any part is difficult for them to understand and to tick the appropriate column in the table that describes the problem. Point out that they should tick only one column for each part. If there is more than one cause, they should tick only the primary cause.
- Play the audio, pausing after each part to give the students time to tick.

C

- Ask the students to listen again. This time they should tick the correct phrase or sentence they hear in each part of the conversation.
- Play the audio, and then elicit answers from the class.
- Play the audio one more time so that the students can hear the correct answers.

Answers
Part 1 a Part 2 a Part 3 b Part 4 b Part 5 a

D

- Put the students in pairs to discuss the questions. Circulate and help as needed.
- Discuss the answers with the class.

▶ Workbook p. 59, Section 4

LifeSkills: evaluating internet source reliability (p. 124)

Step 1: Know what questions to ask in order to determine a website's reliability. (Ex. A, Ex. B)
Step 2: Find the answers to the questions. (Ex. C, Ex. D)
Step 3: Use the answers to determine whether the website is reliable. (Ex. E, Ex. F)

Lead-in
Read the target skill aloud, and invite the students to tell you what they think *evaluating internet source reliability* means. Ask the students what *reliable* means. Elicit answers, such as *dependable, consistent, trustworthy,* etc. Ask for examples of people and things the students rely on (*parents, bus drivers, teachers, classmates, mobile phones, the internet, waiters/waitresses, sales assistants,* etc). Ask them how they decide who or what is reliable. Then **highlight** the three-step strategy to develop the skill of *evaluating internet source reliability*.

A

- Direct the students' attention to the questions. Ask the students to read through the entire list before beginning to tick the questions they usually ask when doing research online. Give them time to complete the exercise individually.

B

- Put the students in groups. Ask them to discuss why each question in Ex. A is important to ask. Encourage them to think of as many reasons as they can. Circulate and help as needed.

Alternative
Put the students in groups. Explain that members of each group must work together to produce a group ranking of the seven questions, from most important (1) to least important (7). The entire group must agree on the order of the rankings. If some group members do not agree, they must keep negotiating until they have a list that they all agree on. Have each group share their rankings with the class.

C

- Direct the students' attention to the list of ways to find the answers. Ask the students to match each of these to one of the questions in Ex. A.
- Put the students in pairs to compare their answers, and then check answers as a class.

Answers
a 3 b 5 c 2 d 6 e 7 f 1 g 4

Alternative
Ask the students how they would find the answer to each question in Ex. A. Have them write this information for each of the seven questions. When they have finished writing, have them look at Ex. C. Which of their answers are similar? Which are different? Have them then use their answer list, as well as the questions in Ex. A, to complete Ex. C. Check the answers as a class.

D

- Put the students in pairs. Explain that they are going to look for information in the online article to answer the questions in Ex. A.
- Give the students time to read the article and find the answers.
- Check answers with the class.

Answers
1 It is an article on a website.
2 There is no information on who the author of the blog is. Sharon Fowler is the author of the study.
3 There is no bias, and the writer has a fairly informed point of view, based on available research. While he/she recommends limiting intake of diet soft drinks, he/she does accept that the research doesn't prove that diet soft drinks cause obesity.
4 The claim is that individuals who consume diet soft drinks are more at risk of being overweight. There is a study with statistics to back up this claim.
5 Yes, there are a number of references and links to other sources.
6 It could be verified by following the links and checking the references, as well as by searching online using key words such as *obesity* and *diet soft drinks*.
7 Although the article does not have a precise year on it, it should be possible to follow the links and see how recent the information in the references is. This article was written after 2008.

E
- Put each pair with another pair to make groups of four. Explain that they are going to discuss the reliability of the article they just read.
- Direct the students' attention to the examples in the *How to say it* box, and encourage them to use the expressions in their discussion. **Highlight** that these phrases are typical ways to state opinions. Ask the students to suggest alternative phrases. Write three or four of these on the board.
- Give the groups time to discuss. Circulate and help as needed.
- When the groups finish, ask each group to state their assessment of the reliability of the article.
- Extend the discussion with the whole class by asking the students if they agree with the content of the article. Do they believe there is a connection between diet soft drinks and obesity? What other behaviours does the article mention that might also lead to weight gain? Do the students agree? Why or why not?

Extra: vocabulary expansion

Highlight some of the challenging vocabulary from the reading: *dramatically* (suddenly and surprisingly), *socioeconomic* (dealing with a combination of social and economic matters), *intake* (the amount of something that enters your body) and *impair* (to make less effective, often by causing damage that affects the way something works). Before reading, write the words on the board. Ask the students to use the context to help them understand the meaning of each word.

F
- Discuss the two questions with the whole class. (**1** *learnt what to look for, learnt to verify information, learnt to look for point of view, etc.* **2** *Yes, because now I know what to look for.*)
- Ask the students how they will apply what they have learnt in this lesson in the domain of **Study and Learning**. How could reliance upon an unreliable source affect their school work? Or a work report?

REFLECT
- Ask the students to read the *Reflect* question.
- Give them some time to think about different situations in the domains of **Work and Career** and **Self and Society** where the skill of *evaluating internet source reliability* would be useful.
- Elicit the following ideas: the same steps can be used to evaluate information from any type of source, it helps us know if the government is telling the truth, it gives us a deeper understanding of society, etc.

RESEARCH
- Explain the task and make sure the students understand what they have to do. Ask them to choose a topic to research and then compare three different websites, ranking their reliability by using the questions in Ex. A. Set a deadline for the assignment. Schedule time in the next lesson for students to present their findings.

Language wrap-up (p. 126)

For notes on how to approach the exercises in the Language wrap-up section, please refer to page 9.

1 Vocabulary
A
- Ask the students to read through the text before they fill in the gaps. Point out that there could be more than one correct answer. Students should choose the answer they think is best.

B
- Ask the students to complete the words by adding the appropriate ending. Remind them to pay attention to the form of any other verbs in each sentence. Suggest that they read each sentence silently in their head to check the answer, listening to see if it sounds correct.

2 Grammar
A
- Have the students rewrite each sentence, starting with the word or phrase in brackets.
- Remind the students that if they are not sure of an answer, they should make their best guess. Remind them to note verb tense.

B
- Ask the students to rewrite each sentence, using ellipsis and substitution where possible.
- Point out that there could be more than one correct answer.

Extra: practice

Give each student the following sentences with inversions, ellipses and substitutions or make similar ones. Tell the students to rewrite each sentence without inversions, ellipses or substitutions.
1 Never have I heard such an eloquent speech.
2 Not only did I see the film, but I also read the book.
3 Only if you listen will you hear the call of nature.
4 Don't reply to spam, because in doing so you might get a virus.
5 Go to the cinema last night? Was it good?

Speaking workshop: responding with an opinion (p. 127)

Lead-in
Explain that in this workshop, the students will answer a question that asks for a choice. They will listen to a speaker answering the question and explaining her choice, and then answer a similar question themselves. **Highlight** that people everywhere make choices every day – usually many a day. Explain that English speakers often want to know why you made a decision – especially an important one, such as to take a job or move to a new city. Being able to explain and, when necessary, defend your choices is an important social and business skill.

A 2.21
- See p. 131 for the **audioscript**.
- Direct the students' attention to the question in the box. Explain that the students will listen to someone answering that question. Ask them to listen for the speaker's main points, and take notes as they listen.
- Play the audio, repeating if necessary.
- Put the students in pairs to compare their notes. Then discuss the answer as a class.

Answer

The main points are: Schools should teach students about online scams and do what they can to protect students online. Students spend a lot of time online, making them vulnerable. They need to learn to avoid the risks. The speaker also has personal experience of phishing emails. Most time should be spent on academic subjects, but some time should be spent on potential dangers online.

Culture note

Phishing (pronounced /ˈfɪʃ.ɪŋ/) refers to online identity theft. It refers to fraudulent email messages, websites and phone calls that are designed to steal your personal information, such as credit card numbers, bank account data, usernames, passwords and other information. The people behind these scams are known as *cybercriminals* or *con artists*. Through their schemes, they can convince you to install malicious software on your computer or provide information under false pretences. They can then use this information for many kinds of fraud, from stealing money from your accounts, to opening new accounts in your name or obtaining false documents using your identity.

B
- Ask the students to read the six phrases first. Then ask them to listen to the audio again and fill in the gap in each sentence with a word or phrase that they hear.
- Play the audio again. Check answers with the class.

Answers

1 firmly of 2 do I believe 3 primary 4 based on 5 doubt 6 seems

Alternative
Have the students fill in the gaps first, and then listen to the audio to see if they were right.

C
- Direct the students' attention to the question in the box in Ex. D. Explain that the students are going to answer that question and that this exercise will help them prepare their answers.
- Ask the students to read and answer the questions. Remind them that they are making notes, so they should just write short answers and not complete sentences.
- Allow the students time to work individually on preparing their answers. Circulate and help as needed.

D
- Put the students in groups or have them speak to the whole class. Remind them to include details and examples in their answers to support their view. Point out that they must explain their choice in just one minute. Time each student, giving them a countdown and then cutting them off after one minute.
- Have the group or class vote on the best presentation.

Extra: research
Have the students do online research on how to recognise phishing scams and how to protect themselves against this cybercrime. Ask them to take notes and share what they have learnt with the class.

How are you doing?
- Ask the students to read the statements and tick the ones they believe are true.
- Ask them to discuss their talk with another student in their group or class and identify things they could improve on next time.

▶ Workbook pp. 62–63, SkillsStudio

UNIT 11 MUSIC TO MY EARS

The expression *music to my ears* means that you think something is very good news – as pleasant as beautiful music. Here it refers to the fact that there are many kinds of musical styles, and everyone enjoys different kinds of music according to individual tastes.

Unit plan

Unit opener	(p. 128)	20 min.
1 Reading: understanding intent	(p. 130)	30 min.
• Vocabulary: idiomatic expressions with *take*		15 min.
2 Grammar: past tense for unreal situations	(p. 131)	40 min.
3 Listening: to an informal discussion	(p. 132)	30 min.
4 Grammar: cleft sentences	(p. 132)	40 min.
5 Speaking: softening language for refusals	(p. 134)	30 min.
• Vocabulary: sharing music		15 min.
6 Pronunciation: intonation in cleft sentences	(p. 135)	15 min.
7 Writing: posting an opinion	(p. 135)	30 min.
LifeSkills: identifying bias (Self and Society)	(p. 136)	50 min.
• Optional downloadable *LifeSkills* lesson (Work and Career)		50 min.
• Optional downloadable *LifeSkills* lesson (Study and Learning)		50 min.
Language wrap-up	(p. 138)	20 min.
Writing workshop: writing a review	(p. 139)	30 min.
Video and downloadable video worksheet		45 min.

Unit opener (p. 128)

Lead-in

Ask the students to look at the unit title and photos, and predict what the unit will be about. Elicit the meaning of the title using the information in the panel above. Ask the students to name as many different musical styles as possible (*rock, classical, reggae, hip-hop*, etc). Elicit different reasons for listening to music (*entertainment, relaxation, dancing, expressing feelings, political protest*, etc). Direct the students' attention to the unit objectives box and go through the information with them. Have students read and think about the questions in the cogs.

Reading: understanding intent

- Explain the terms italics, quotation marks and bold type. Show the students samples. Ask if these conventions are used in their language(s), and if so, how.

Speaking: softening language for refusals

- Elicit what *softening language* means, and ask the students why language might need 'softening'. Remind the students about *hedging*. Explain that this is similar, and ask them to brainstorm examples of softening language.

LifeSkills: identifying bias

- Refer the students to the **LifeSkills** panel. Ask them to discuss who might have the strongest opinions about free music downloads. Explain that *identifying bias* is an important skill because everyone is biased according to their own interests. Learning to identify bias can help create a sense of fairness and objectivity.

Common European Framework: unit map

Unit 11	Competence developed	CEF Reference (C1 competences)
Reading	can recognise the writer's intent to aid understanding	Table 1; Table 2; Sections 4.4.2.2; 4.4.2.4; 4.5.2.2
Grammar	can use and understand the past tense for unreal situations	Table 1; Table 2; Sections 5.2.1.2; 6.4.7.7; 6.4.7.8
Listening	can understand an informal discussion	Table 1; Table 2; Sections 4.4.2.1; 4.4.3.1; 4.4.3.5; 4.5.2.2; 5.2.3.1
Grammar	can use and understand cleft sentences	Table 1; Table 2; Sections 5.2.1.2; 6.4.7.7; 6.4.7.8
Speaking	can use softening language for refusals	Table 1; Table 2; Sections 4.4.1.1; 4.4.3.1; 4.4.3.5; 4.5.2.1; 5.2.2.2; 5.2.3.2
Pronunciation	can use correct intonation in cleft sentences	Section 5.2.1.4
Writing	can write a response to a web post expressing an opinion	Table 1; Table 2; Sections 4.4.1.2; 4.4.3.2; 4.4.3.4; 4.5.2.1; 5.2.1.1; 5.2.1.2; 5.2.1.6; 5.2.2.2; 5.2.2.4; 5.2.3.2

A

- Ask the students to read the five quotes on music individually and think about what they might mean. If necessary, discuss one of them with the class as an example.
- Put the students in groups to discuss what each quote means and whether or not they agree with it. Encourage them to use details and examples where possible.
- When they finish, invite volunteers to tell the class about the most interesting ideas that came up in their group discussion on each quote. Remind the students to make sure their comments are relevant to the quotes.

Culture note

- **Heinrich Heine** (1797–1856) was one of the most significant German poets of the 19th century and also a journalist, essayist and literary critic. He is best known for his early poetry which was set to music as *lieder* (art songs) by the composers Robert Schumann and Franz Schubert.
- **Nick Hornby** (b. 1957) is an English novelist, essayist and screenwriter, who is best known for writing the novels *High Fidelity* and *About a Boy* and the football memoir *Fever Pitch*.
- **Jack Kerouac** (1922–1969) was an American novelist and poet, best known for the novel *On the Road* which pioneered the Beat Generation in the 1950s.
- **Friedrich Nietzsche** (1844–1900) was a German philosopher, essayist and cultural critic of the late 19th century, best known for his challenges to traditional religion, and his belief in the creative power of the individual and life lived fully in the present.
- **will.i.am** (b. 1975), whose real name is William Adams, is a Grammy Award-winning American rapper, singer/songwriter, entrepreneur and philanthropist, best known as founder of his hip-hop band, The Black-Eyed Peas.

B

- Have the students work in the same groups to create a quote about music. As a first step, encourage them to brainstorm as many ideas as possible. Then have them choose one or two ideas and connect these ideas together to form a message about music.
- If they need help, ask them to write down some nouns that represent what they think are the most important things in life (*joy, success, peace,* etc). Then ask them to create their quote about the connection between music and their chosen noun.
- If they still have difficulty coming up with ideas, encourage them to imitate and adapt one of the quotations from Ex. A (*the only truth is music* can be changed to *music never lies,* etc). Point out that they can be as creative as they like, as long as they can justify their choices.
- Ask each group to read their quote to the class and vote for the most memorable ones. Encourage the students to ask questions, offer comments, and share their ideas on each quote.

Alternative

Ask each group to write their quote on a large piece of paper, and display them on the classroom walls. Have the students go around the class to read their classmates' quotes before voting on the most memorable ones.

Reading: understanding intent (p. 130, p. 106)

Lead-in

Ask the students to read the information in the skills panel. Elicit from the students a few texts that they have read recently (*a novel, a cartoon, a recipe, a newspaper article, a film review, an advert,* etc). Ask them what the writer's general intent was when writing those pieces (*to argue, to describe, to entertain, to persuade, to inform, to make the reader reflect,* etc). Then explain that, within the general intent of the whole text, writers also have specific intentions when it comes to particular parts of the text. Elicit the specific techniques mentioned in the skills box (*italics, quotation marks, direct speech*) and check that the students understand what these are. Ask the students to recall what they learnt about understanding intent in Unit 9. Explain that in this lesson they will be looking at this topic again, but this time specifically at how the writer uses techniques such as punctuation to make intentions clear within different sections of the same text.

A

- Ask the students to look at the photo that accompanies the text. Ask the students what kind of music they think the man is playing and if they think he is getting a positive reaction. Encourage them to explain their ideas.
- Ask the students to read the article, reflect and answer the first question truthfully. Invite volunteers to share their answers with the class. Then ask them to read the second question and identify the intent of the text.

Answer

For question 2, the answer could be that the intent is either to entertain or to persuade people to pay more attention to street musicians, or the answer might be that it's a combination of those two things.

Extra: punctuation

- Ask the students to look back at paragraphs 2 and 3 in the text to answer these questions:
  1 *Why does the writer use direct speech in paragraph 2?*
  2 *Why does the writer use quotation marks in paragraph 3?*
  3 *Why does the writer have the word* really *in italics in paragraph 2?*
- Ask the students if the use of these three techniques helped the writer achieve his intent. (*Yes, these techniques helped to make the description interesting and entertaining, but also thought-provoking.*)

Answers

1 to create drama
2 because it is ironic that Joe calls the violin a fiddle
3 because the speaker emphasised the word

Extra: discussion

Put the students in small groups, and have them discuss street musicians in their country. Elicit typical descriptions of the people who perform on the streets in their area. Ask the students how they feel when they pass street musicians, and ask if they have ever given these musicians money.

B

- Ask the students to read the instructions and work individually to match each of the numbered phrases in the article to one of the purposes.
- Check answers with the class.

Answers

a 3 b 1 c 4 d 2 e 5

C

- Ask the students to work individually to locate the underlined expressions in the article in Ex. A. Encourage them to use the context to help them choose the correct idiomatic expression to complete each sentence. Remind them that they may need to change the form of the expression to fit grammatically into the sentence.
- Invite different students to give their answers, and write the complete sentences on the board.

Answers

1 taken out of context 2 take, seriously 3 have what it takes 4 take, for granted 5 take into account

Extra: vocabulary

Ask the students to locate the following words in Ex. A and guess their meaning from context: Paragraph 4, *mundane* (ordinary, not interesting); Paragraph 6, *struggling* (experiencing financial difficulty); Paragraph 6, *think out of the box* (to think of something in a different or unexpected way).

D

- Have the students read the questions. Explain any of the vocabulary items if necessary.
- Put them in groups and have them share their experiences and discuss their ideas. Point out that this is a good opportunity to practise using the idiomatic expressions with *take* that they encountered in Ex. C, and encourage them to do so. Circulate and help as needed.
- Invite volunteers from each group to share their conclusions with the class.

▶ Workbook p. 64, Section 1

▶ Workbook p. 65, Section 3

Grammar: past tense for unreal situations (p. 131).

Lead-in

Ask the students if they have ever thought about how famous people spend their free time. Ask the students to consider that, because of their fame, famous people may not often be able to do some of the things that we take for granted (visiting a shopping centre, visiting a local tourist attraction, going to the cinema, walking along a beach, etc). Elicit how they think famous people deal with the negative aspects of fame.

A

- Ask the students to read the question. Give them time to read the text with the question in mind, and then elicit ideas from the class.

Answer

The musicians probably thought that performing on the street was a way to get noticed and start a professional music career.

NOTICE!

- Direct the students' attention to the **Notice!** box.
- Ask them to identify which events in the text are hypothetical (unreal or imaginary scenarios).
- Elicit answers from whole class.

Answers

Suppose you were walking down the street and you heard a street performer playing. Would you take him or her seriously and stop to listen? Unless you really liked the song, you probably wouldn't stop. Well, maybe it's time you stopped taking street performers for granted. … next time you want to see a show and wish you had tickets, … Imagine how you would feel if you stopped to listen and saw that it was your favourite musician. What if that happened? Wouldn't that be amazing?

Culture note

Paul McCartney put on a disguise to be filmed playing his own tunes in the film *Give My Regards to Broad Street* (1984). Jon Bon Jovi has apparently given street performances in several places, including London's Covent Garden and Russia's Red Square. Sting has disguised himself and given street performances, earning around £40.

B

Form & Function

- Have the students read through the grammar table. Elicit the meaning of *hypothetical* (*not real/imaginary*).
- Ask the students to read the text in Ex. A again, paying attention to the forms used for hypothetical situations. Have them complete item 1 in the table as a class, and explain as necessary. Then ask the students to complete the rest of the grammar table individually with examples from the text.

Music to my ears UNIT 11

- Ask different students to give the answers and go over them as a class.
- Remind the students that they are already familiar with the structure used in item 4, as it is the second conditional (*if*).
- Ask the students whether we are talking about the past when we use these structures (*no*). Some students may recognise these structures as a form of subjunctive. Point out that the common feature is a removal from reality. Remind them that this tense shift also occurs when we are being very polite and/or very formal (e.g. *Did you want cheese with your burger?*).
- Direct students' attention to the **What's right?** box and ask them to tick the correct sentence (*1*). Discuss why the other sentence is incorrect.

Answers

1 you were walking 2 you stopped 3 happened
4 you stopped 5 you really liked; wouldn't stop

C

- Have the students work individually to rewrite the six sentences. If necessary, do the first one together as a class. Then give the students time to compare their answers in pairs before checking answers with the class.

Answers

1 I wouldn't give a street performer money unless I really liked the song. / Unless I really liked the song, I wouldn't give a street performer money.
2 Suppose you wanted to become a musician.
3 It's time we banned street performers because they put pressure on people to give money.
4 I would give a street performer money if they had talent. / If a street performer had talent, I would give them money.
5 I wish people wouldn't take music and street performers for granted.
6 What if you met your favourite performer at a party?

Extra: pronunciation

After checking the answers, model the sentences and ask the students to practise their intonation.

D

- First, ask the students to work individually to write hypothetical statements or questions about music or musicians using the structures given. Then put them in pairs to share and discuss their statements. Remind the students to give reasons for their opinions.
- Have several pairs of students report on their discussion to the class.

Alternative

If the students need more support, give them a few minutes to make brief notes about their statements. When they have done this, put them in pairs to have their discussion.

▶ **Workbook p. 65, Section 2**

Listening: to an informal discussion (p. 132)

Lead-in

Ask the students if any of them plays an instrument or sings well. Ask whether they know anyone who is musically gifted. Elicit the students' thoughts on whether musical talent is something people are born with, or if people can become musically accomplished through practice.

A 2.22

- See p. 131 for the **audioscript**.
- Explain to the students that they will hear the beginning of a discussion about musical intelligence. First, have them read the instructions and the statements, and decide whether each statement is true or false.
- Remind the students to check their answers as they listen. Play the audio once, and check progress.
- Play the audio again, if necessary. Discuss the answers with the class.

Answers

1 T 2 F 3 T 4 T

B 2.23

- See p. 131 for the **audioscript**.
- Ask the students to read the instructions and look at the grid. Remind them to take notes on the main points each speaker makes about themselves.
- Play the audio once, and check progress. Put the students in pairs to compare their notes.
- Check the answers with the class by inviting volunteers to share their ideas.

Answers

Amy: Thought she didn't have musical intelligence, but now thinks she may because she loves music and listens to a lot of music.
Emma: Doesn't listen to music much and says it isn't a big part of her life.
Andrew: Plays an instrument, but can't sing. He says he has one kind of musical talent, but not others.

Extra: discussion

Put the students into small groups. Ask them to discuss what they know about the three speakers and rank them in probable order of musical intelligence (Amy, Emma and Andrew).

C

- Direct the students' attention to the quiz. Make sure they understand *whistle* and *tap (out) a song with my fingers* by demonstrating these actions.
- Have them work individually to complete the quiz.

D

- Put the students in pairs to compare their answers to the quiz and decide what level of musical intelligence it reveals about them. Then ask them to discuss the role of musical intelligence in their lives and justify their responses with descriptions and examples.
- Extend the discussion by referring back to the question in the Lead-in. How many of the students believe they can raise their musical intelligence through practice and study? How many disagree? Ask the students who believe they have high musical intelligence how they plan to use it.

Grammar: cleft sentences (p. 132)

Lead-in
Ask the students what they know about The Jackson Five. (*They were a musical group of five brothers that became extremely popular in the 1970s. Michael Jackson was the youngest brother.*) Elicit what type of music Michael Jackson sang (*pop*) and ask them if they like his music.

A

- Ask the students to read through the text quickly to answer the question. Point out that the writer presents several reasons for the group's success, and remind the students to identify them all.
- Discuss the answers with the class. Then ask them if they are convinced by the writer's explanation for The Jackson Five's success.

Answers

They appealed to different generations and to people around the world. They spent long hours rehearsing. Their father pushed them to succeed.

NOTICE!

- Direct the students' attention to the **Notice!** box.
- Have them look at the underlined sentence in the text and determine if the word order can be changed to make a new sentence with the same meaning.
- Elicit the answer to the question.

Possible answers

It was their strict father, Joseph Jackson, who (was the person that) pushed them to succeed.
Their strict father, Joseph Jackson, was the person who pushed them to succeed.

Extra: reading
Remind the students about identifying intent. Ask them if they think the writer is *in favour of* or *critical of* Joe Jackson's approach, and why. (*The article is broadly favourable because it doesn't mention the problems that the children developed as a result of their father's behaviour. It only mentions the positive aspects of their success.*)

B

Function

- Ask the students to read the text in Ex. A again.
- Then focus the students' attention on the explanation of cleft sentences. Demonstrate the point by writing the following example on the board: *This group launched the career of Michael Jackson.* **It was this group that launched the career of Michael Jackson.** Point out how dividing the sentence into two clauses creates emphasis.

Form

- Have the students refer to the grammar table. Draw their attention to how it is divided into two patterns: the non-cleft form and the cleft form. Ask them to work individually to complete the table with examples of the cleft sentences from the text in Ex. A.
- To check the answers, ask four students to identify the corresponding sentences from the text.
- Direct the students' attention to the **What's right?** box and ask them to tick the correct sentence (*1*). Elicit and review when relative pronouns can be omitted and when they are required. (*They can be omitted when the relative pronoun refers to the object of the relative clause.*) Ask the students to explain what is incorrect in the second sentence. (*There is no relative pronoun. It is required because it is the subject of the relative clause.*)

Answers

1. It was this group that launched the career of Michael Jackson.
2. One reason why they were so successful was that they appealed to people …
3. The person who pushed them to succeed was their strict father, Joseph Jackson.
4. … what really made the group a success was his vision.

C

- Ask the students to work individually to complete the sentences.
- Check answers with the class. Go over any difficulties and provide explanations if necessary.

Answers

2. The reason (why) Jay Z is so successful is that/because he understands the music industry.
3. The place (where) Elvis Presley lived is/was called Graceland.
4. The day (when) the concert took place was my birthday.
5. What I like about music these days is the wide variety of styles. / It is the wide variety of styles that I like about music these days.
6. What I like about this album is the lyrics.

Music to my ears UNIT 11

Alternative

Put students in pairs and have them work together to complete the sentences. Then put the pairs in groups of four to discuss their answers.

Extra: grammar

If the students need further guidance, write this sample sentence on the board: *The thing that makes his music memorable is the emotion he puts into it.* Point out that the relative pronoun is required because it refers to the subject. However, in this sentence – *The thing (that) I like about his music is the emotion he puts into it.* – the relative pronoun is optional because it refers to the object.

Extra: grammar practice

After the students complete Ex. C, put them in pairs to talk about which relative pronouns are required and which are not. Have the students identify the subject or object in each sentence to support their answers.

Extra: writing

Put the students in small groups. Ask them to write a short text like the one in Ex. A about a music artist the students are interested in. If there is access to the internet in the classroom, encourage them to do some research. If not, assign this research task as homework, and ask the students either to complete their text or make notes for group-writing in class. Suggest that each member of the group be responsible for leading one of the writing stages (making an outline, writing the introduction, writing the body paragraph, writing the conclusion, revising, proofreading, etc).

D
- Direct the students' attention to the sentence stems, and give them time to think of some ideas individually. Then put them in pairs, and have them discuss their opinions. Circulate and help as needed.
- Have the pairs share their opinions with the class and encourage class discussion.

▶ Workbook p. 66, Section 4

Speaking: softening language for refusals (p. 134)

Lead-in

Ask the students to read the information in the skills panel. Invite volunteers to tell the class about the last time they refused an invitation, why and how they did it, and how both sides felt about the refusal. Ask the students to recall and discuss the strategies they practised in Unit 9 for politely refusing invitations.

A
- Refer the students to the list of requests, and ask them to read them. Then ask them to tick the boxes for the requests they would be happy to do for their friends.
- Ask volunteers to give their responses to the class. Then elicit their reasons for refusing some of these requests.

B 🎧 2.24
- See p. 131 for the **audioscript**.
- Explain that the students will listen to a conversation between two friends. Ask them to listen to the conversation, identify what Nicole wants Liam to do, and underline that item in the list in Ex. A. Then ask them to notice Liam's response.
- Play the audio. Elicit the answers from several volunteers, and discuss them with the class.

Answer
Nicole wants Liam to download pirated music. He refuses to do it and explains why it makes him feel uncomfortable. Nicole asks Liam to download the music so she can copy it to her computer. Students may include copying music from his computer to hers as a second answer. However, the main idea is that she wants him to download pirated music.

C
- Direct the students' attention to the two categories in the table: *phrases for saying 'no' or 'probably not,'* and *phrases for softening explanations or excuses*. Elicit the difference between the two categories. (The first category gives the refusal in a polite way. The second category softens the refusal by offering explanations or excuses for the refusal.)
- Contrast the ideas of saying something *harsh* (hard and unpleasant) with something *soft* (pleasant). Refusing a request can sometimes seem rude and unpleasant, even with a good reason for refusing; using 'softening language' can make an unpleasant task a little less unpleasant and avoid offending the other person or hurting their feelings unnecessarily.
- Play the audio again. Have the students listen for the words and phrases that Liam uses to soften his refusal and then work individually to fill in the gaps. Invite individual students to share their answers with the class.
- Ask the students to think about whether they agree with Liam and whether they think most young people would agree with him. Encourage all the students to participate in the discussion.

Answers
1 not sure **2** I'm sorry **3** I really can't **4** be honest **5** just that

D
- First, ask the students to read the instructions and the example conversation.
- Then put them in pairs. Have them take turns making requests and refusing politely. Remind them to use the words and phrases from Ex. C. Circulate and help as needed.

E
- Have the students work individually to match the words and phrases to their definitions. Give them time to compare their answers in pairs.

- After checking the answers with the class, invite different students to come up with a sentence that uses a word or phrase in the left column. Give immediate feedback on whether the target word or phrase is used appropriately in the sentence.

Answers
1 d 2 a 3 b 4 e 5 f 6 c

F
- Put the students in pairs, and assign each of them the role of Student A or Student B. Ask them to read the instructions carefully. Explain and clarify the instructions to the class if necessary.
- Remind each pair to include the softening expressions they heard in the conversation in Ex. B in their refusals. Elicit from the class ideas for phrases that Student A could use to try to persuade Student B to do something, and write them on the board. (*Oh, come on. / It won't hurt anyone. / Everybody does it. / It's not really a problem. / It's not a big deal. / Please? It would really help me out.*, etc.)
- Give the pairs a few minutes for the first roleplay. Then ask them to switch roles and remind them to change the situation, as well.
- Ask the students if there was a particular role they preferred. If so, have them explain why. Then ask for volunteers to perform their roleplay in front of the whole class and elicit constructive feedback from the audience.

Alternative
If the students are less confident speakers, assign specific situations, and put them into AA/BB pairs to prepare what to say before starting. Then put them into AB pairs and have them continue with the roleplay. After a few minutes, have them switch roles.

▶ Workbook p. 67, Sections 5 and 6

Pronunciation: intonation in cleft sentences (p. 135)

A 2.25
- See the Student's Book page for the **audioscript**.
- Play the audio, and have the students focus on the sentences. Ask them to pay attention to the small pause between the two clauses in each sentence. Then have them practise saying the sentences using the appropriate intonation.

B 2.26
- See the Student's Book page for the **audioscript**.
- First, ask the students to identify the sentences that begin with a rising intonation. Play the audio, and ask the students to put a tick next to those sentences. Check answers with the class.

- Play the audio again if necessary. Put the students in pairs to practise the target sentences. Encourage them to listen to each other, and provide feedback on intonation as they practise. Circulate and help as needed.

Answer
2 The place where I saw them in concert was a big stadium.
3 The year when he won a Grammy was 2014.

Writing: posting an opinion (p. 135)

Lead-in
Ask the students if they read online posts. Put them in pairs to discuss what types of posts they read (blogs, reviews, comments on articles, news reports or other posts, etc). Elicit the features they enjoy most about online posts and opinion pages, and encourage them to explain why.

A
- Direct the students' attention to the website question. Have them read the two posts and identify the points made for and against file sharing.
- When they finish reading, ask the students what kind of tone these posts use. (*They are written in a serious tone, even though the language is often informal.*) Then elicit as many points from the class as possible, and write them on the board in two columns titled *for* and *against*. (Do not erase this list, as it can be used later as a teaching aid in Ex. C. Alternatively, write the points on large pieces of poster paper and display them on one of the classroom walls.)

Answers
For: It's impossible to control the flow of information on the internet; musicians make a lot of money from concerts; people hear music and then pay money to go to the concerts.

Against: Musicians work hard and should be paid for their work; piracy destroys music careers; musicians won't keep creating music if we don't pay for it.

B
- Explain that the students will now write their own response to the two posts. As a pre-writing exercise, they will make notes to answer three questions to help plan and develop their responses.
- Ask the students to read the three questions carefully and answer them as decisively as possible. Encourage them not to be ambivalent about their decisions. Point out that they should write notes, not complete sentences, and that the tone should be informal. Where possible, ask them to include the softening language they have learnt.

C
- Ask the students to work individually to write their response to the two posts using the notes they have made, as well as the points for and against file sharing on the board. Circulate while the students are working, and help with the expression of ideas.

Music to my ears UNIT 11 107

- Display the responses on the classroom walls and invite the students to read and comment on their classmates' work.

Alternatives

- If the students need more support, work as a class to brainstorm more ideas for and against file sharing, and add them to the lists on the board. Then ask the students to work in pairs to make notes and write their posts.
- If time is short, ask the students to complete their posts at home. Display and discuss their responses during the next lesson.

Extra: speaking

- Write the title of the following debate topic on the board: *Illegal file sharing is destroying the music industry.*
- Select half the class to speak *for* the argument and the other half *against*. Put them in pairs or small groups to collaborate and discuss ideas.
- Organise the debate by having one or two representatives from each side take turns presenting their arguments. At the end of the debate, ask the students to vote on whether they are *for* or *against* the motion. Encourage them to vote based on the quality of the arguments presented, instead of automatically choosing the side they were assigned to.

LifeSkills: identifying bias (p. 136)

Step 1: Understand different types of bias. (Ex. A)
Step 2: Consider who a writer is and who or what they represent. (Ex. B, Ex. C)
Step 3: Look at the language a writer uses and what they emphasise or omit in order to decide whether their writing is biased or not. (Ex. D, Ex. E)

Lead-in

Read the target skill aloud, and invite the students to tell you what they think *identifying bias* means. Remind the students that they discussed bias in Unit 10 and elicit the meaning of *prejudice (in favour of or against one thing, person or group compared to another, usually in a subjective or an unfair way)*. Ask them if they can think of a situation where they might be biased, or what might cause that bias (e.g. dealing with a friend/family member as opposed to a stranger in a job interview). Then **highlight** the three-step strategy to develop the skill of identifying bias. Explain that sometimes writers appear to describe a situation objectively, but careful reading can show that they are biased. By looking at who a writer is, who/what they represent, what their personal interest is in the situation they are writing about, and what they emphasise or omit, you can identify the bias and understand what you are reading in that context.

A

- Refer the students to the instructions, and explain them if necessary. Have them read the text carefully.
- Put the students in pairs, and have them discuss the different types of bias they have just read about.
- When they finish, elicit from the class any examples they know of biased writing (e.g. a local newspaper that applauds the efforts of the local sports team although impartial reports say they performed badly).

Extra: class discussion

Put the students into three groups. Assign each group one of the following types of bias: bias by selection of facts, bias by labelling, and bias by exaggeration, emphasis or repetition. Have the students brainstorm issues that are important to them. Write their ideas on the board. Have the class vote to select one issue they would like to discuss. Then ask each group to make an argument for or against the issue using the bias that was assigned to them. Give groups a few minutes to organise their ideas. Then invite one person from each group to stand up and talk about the issue, reflecting their group's bias.

B

- Ask the students to read the instructions, and explain that each of the people described has a probable bias regarding the issue of music distribution based on their own interests.
- Ask the students to first read through Jake's profile, and then elicit their ideas about the bias that he is most likely to have. Then ask them to read the example describing Jake's probable bias.
- In the same pairs as in Ex. A, have the students study the other profiles and then discuss how each of these people is probably biased. Remind them to make notes on the ways they expect them to be biased.
- When the pairs finish, encourage the students to explain and discuss their ideas with the class. Accept all reasonable possibilities.

Possible answers

Blue: He might be biased in favour of more free music on the internet because more people could hear his music and discover him that way. He might be biased against more free music because he doesn't make much money yet, and he might argue that he needs people to pay for his music so that he can continue his career.

Megan: She is probably biased towards wanting everyone to pay for music because her job and her industry depend on people paying to listen to music.

Luis: He may be biased towards wanting more free music on the internet, especially if he is young and doesn't have a lot of money to pay for music.

C

- Refer the students to the instructions. Ask them to read the extracts carefully. Point out that there is one text for each person in Ex. B, including Jake. Remind them that they can choose more than one person as the writer of an extract, as long as they can justify their answers. Have them work individually to complete the exercise.

- Choose volunteers to take turns giving their answers to the class, and make sure that they explain how they arrived at their decisions. Encourage them to rank their choices if they have nominated more than one writer for any extract, and have them justify their ranking. Accept any possibilities that are well supported and reasonably logical. Emphasise that there are no wrong answers.

Possible answers

1 This was probably written by Luis, since it argues against the interests of both the music industry and musicians.
2 This was probably written by Jake, since it focuses on how hard life is for musicians and how important it is for them to continue to make money. It could also have been written by Blue or Megan.
3 This was probably written by Blue, since it concentrates on how current technology affects artists, particularly young artists. It could also have been written by Jake or Megan.
4 This was probably written by Megan, since it presents an overview of how the music industry is changing and how that affects different people involved. It could also have been written by Blue, Luis or Jake.

D

- Put the students in pairs to analyse the extracts again in order to judge how biased they are. Explain that they will be deciding on the amount (or degree) of bias in these texts.
- Draw their attention to the expressions in the **How to say it** box, and encourage the students to use them in their discussion.
- Check answers with the class, and encourage discussion when the students disagree on any point.

Possible answers

Extract 1: very biased, because it only mentions consumers' point of view and doesn't take into account the needs of musicians
Extract 2: very biased, because it only mentions the needs of musicians and doesn't take into account the needs of consumers
Extract 3: slightly biased, because it sees the important issue as supporting young artists, but not as biased as Extracts 1 and 2
Extract 4: not particularly biased, because it attempts to give both sides of the issue

E

- Ask the students to refer back to the types of bias in Ex. A. Explain that after deciding on the degree of bias in Ex. D, they are now going to decide on the type of bias each of these extracts might contain.
- Have them look back at the texts in Ex. C. As a class, discuss whether the writers demonstrate biases that fall into any of the categories in Ex. A. Point out that the students should look for evidence to identify each form of bias. If they have difficulty doing this, remind them that one of the texts does not display any obvious bias and that the other three do.

Possible answers

Extract 1: This extract only quotes one statistic, which supports the writer's view (bias by selection of facts).
Extract 2: This extract uses exaggerated language (*destroy the music industry*) and labelling (*anarchy*). (bias by exaggeration, bias by labelling)
Extract 3: This extract uses labelling (*stealing music*). (bias by labelling)
Extract 4: This extract seems well balanced and doesn't show any obvious bias.

F

- Ask the students to read the questions first. Then put them in small groups to discuss the questions, and encourage them to provide as much detail as necessary.
- Ask the groups to share their responses with the whole class.
- Ask the students how the skill of *identifying bias* might be useful to them in the domain of **Self and Society**, either now or in the future.

REFLECT

- Ask the students to read the **Reflect** question.
- Give them time to think about different situations in the domains of **Work and Career** and **Study and Learning** where the skill of *identifying bias* would be useful.
- Elicit the following ideas: *identifying the purpose of a text, weighing the merits of a claim, identifying the flaws in an argument, using an objective tone when writing reports or reviews, making fair decisions and choices*, etc.

RESEARCH

- Explain the task and make sure the students know what they have to do. First, they must select a controversial topic about which people might have several points of view.
- Have the students brainstorm possible sources for articles on their topic. Give them time to discuss their topic with others in the class who might know of websites or publications where they could look.
- Ask the students to present their research to the class in the form of a PowerPoint slideshow if possible. Each presentation should include a brief description of the article and its topic, a clear identification of the examples of bias (the underlined sentences should be included in the slideshow or given to the audience as hand-outs), an explanation of the article's content, and the ways the presenter thinks that it is biased. Encourage questions and comments from the audience at the end of each presentation.

Language wrap-up (p. 138)

For notes on how to approach the exercises in the Language wrap-up section, please refer to page 9.

1 Vocabulary

- Ask the students to read the whole paragraph first to establish the context before filling in the gaps with the words and phrases from the box. Remind them that they will need to change the forms of some of the words to make them fit grammatically into the gap.
- When they finish, ask them to read the paragraph again on their own to check that it makes sense overall and revise their answers if they wish.
- If many students have difficulty with item 2, explain that the word *worth* is always followed by a verb ending in *-ing*. Elicit other examples of this construction from the students (*worth seeing, worth doing, worth learning*, etc.).

2 Grammar

- Check that the students understand the instructions. Encourage them to read all ten sentences first before beginning the exercise.
- Point out that there is only one incorrect word in each sentence. After identifying the incorrect word in each sentence, ask them to cross it out and write the correct word just above it. Encourage the students to read their revised sentences to see if they sound correct.

Writing workshop: writing a review (p. 139)

Lead-in

Explain to the students that in this workshop they are going to write a review of a music album. Ask them to recall the outline template for a review that they learnt in Unit 8, and elicit the four parts to a review (*Introduction, What they liked, What they didn't like, Conclusion*). Point out that whether they are reviewing a play, a concert, a book or a music album, the four main parts of a review remain the same.

A

- Have the students read the assignment carefully, and then read the example review. Point out that the writer of a review is called *a reviewer*.
- Direct the students' attention to the four questions, and ask them to work individually to write a short answer for each one.
- Discuss the answers with the class. Ask the students to give their opinions on whether reading the review has made them interested in listening to the album, and encourage them to explain why or why not. (Note that these are responses to the fourth question and they will vary.)

Possible answers

1 In general, he liked the album. He says that it is worth paying attention to, and he gives it 3.5 stars.
2 He says the direction of the album is surprising because the style is very different from Coldplay's previous albums. He says that the optimism of *A Sky Full of Stars* is unexpected because the rest of the album is sad.
3 He likes the real emotions and the quality of the music and the lyrics. He also likes the fact that listeners get to know Chris Martin as a person.

B

- Ask the students to read the review again. Ask them to make notes about the review using the given format. Have them pay close attention to the format, and explain any vocabulary items as needed. Remind them that adjectives are words that describe nouns.
- Put the students in pairs to make their notes. Circulate and help as needed.
- Check answers with the class.

Possible answers

Adjectives used to describe the album in general or features of the album
surprising new direction, *different* style, *real* emotions, *lively, upbeat* dance rhythm, *unexpected, welcome* optimism, *depressing*
Background information (the musicians, the theme of the album, the style of the tracks)
Chris Martin's breakup with Gwyneth Paltrow, central theme about how the past affects the present and the future, *True Love* – favourite track and a theme that listeners can relate to, *A Sky Full of Stars* – lively dance track
The reviewer's opinion (good and bad points, and overall opinion)
Good – real emotions, technical perfection of the music, well-composed lyrics
Bad – a little too depressing
In general – he likes the album

C

- Ask the students to read the instructions carefully. Explain that they should first select an album to review. Then **highlight** the three categories of information in the format provided for the notes that they will make: adjectives that describe the album or elements of it, background information, and their own opinion.
- Remind the students that they should state the name of the album and the artist(s)/musician(s) in the title of their review. Direct their attention to the title in the sample review, if necessary, and ask them to imitate the format (i.e. *Title: Artist's name*). Also remind them to justify their final recommendation by providing reasons for their opinion.
- Have the students work individually to make their notes. Circulate and help as needed.

D

- Ask the students to use their notes to write their reviews. When they finish the first draft, ask them to revise their work to make improvements to the content and language.
- Have the students display their completed reviews on the classroom walls. Ask them to go around the class and read their classmates' reviews. Encourage them to say whether the reviews have made them interested enough to listen to the albums in question.

How are you doing?

- Ask the students to read the statements and tick the ones they believe are true.
- Ask them to discuss their review with another student in the class and identify things they could improve on next time.

▶ Workbook pp. 68–69, SkillsStudio

UNIT 12 DOWN TO EARTH

The expression *down to earth* means practical, or realistic. In this unit, the phrase relates to the fact that although many events which occur on Earth can be mysterious, there are usually ways to explain what happens.

Unit plan

Unit opener	(p. 140)	20 min.
1 **Grammar:** participle clauses	(p. 142)	40 min.
2 **Listening:** difficult situations	(p. 143)	30 min.
• Vocabulary: geology		15 min.
3 **Speaking:** talking about a mysterious phenomenon	(p. 144)	30 min.
• Vocabulary: adverbial modifiers		15 min.
4 **Grammar:** impersonal passive in the past	(p. 145)	40 min.
5 **Pronunciation:** stress shifts in parts of speech	(p. 146)	15 min.
6 **Reading:** a feature article	(p. 146)	30 min.
7 **Writing:** an editorial	(p. 147)	30 min.
LifeSkills: maximising your potential (Work and Career)	(p. 148)	50 min.
• Optional downloadable *LifeSkills* lesson (Self and Society)		50 min.
• Optional downloadable *LifeSkills* lesson (Study and Learning)		50 min.
Language wrap-up	(p. 150)	20 min.
Speaking workshop: giving a mini-presentation	(p. 151)	30 min.
Video and downloadable video worksheet		45 min.

Unit opener (p. 140)

Lead-in

Ask the students to look at the unit title and photos, and to predict what the unit will be about. Elicit the meaning of the title. Ask them to brainstorm features found on the surface of the Earth (*volcanoes, mountains, oceans, deserts, continents, rivers,* etc). Direct the students' attention to the points in the unit objectives box and review the information with them. Have students read and think about the questions in the cogs.

Listening: difficult situations

- Ask the students to brainstorm answers to the question, (*traffic noise, other people talking, wind,* etc). Ask them to think of a time when they could not hear well because of noise. What did they do to understand what was being said?

Writing: an editorial

- Discuss the questions with the class, especially the last one. Explain that some newspapers and magazines include editorials to voice opinions about a topic or a political candidate.

LifeSkills: maximising your potential

- Refer the students to the **LifeSkills** panel. Make sure the students understand the meaning of *potential* (*something someone seems capable of doing, but has not done yet*). Have the students suggest reasons why some people never reach their full potential (*they get ill or hurt, they get discouraged, they develop bad habits,* etc).

Common European Framework: unit map

Unit 12	Competence developed	CEF Reference (C1 competences)
Grammar	can use and understand participle clauses	Table 1; Table 2; Sections 5.2.1.2; 6.4.7.7; 6.4.7.8
Listening	can understand language in noisy environments	Table 1; Table 2; Sections 4.4.2.1; 4.4.3.1; 4.4.3.5; 4.5.2.2
Speaking	can talk about a mysterious phenomenon	Table 1; Table 2; Sections 4.4.1.1; 4.4.3.1; 4.4.3.5; 4.5.2.1; 5.2.1.1; 5.2.1.2; 5.2.3.2
Grammar	can use and understand past impersonal passives	Table 1; Table 2; Sections 5.2.1.2; 6.4.7.7; 6.4.7.8
Pronunciation	can correctly use stress shifts with different parts of speech	Section 5.2.1.4
Reading	can understand a feature article	Table 1; Table 2; Sections 4.4.2.2; 4.4.2.4; 4.5.2.2
Writing	can write an editorial	Table 1; Table 2; Sections 4.4.1.2; 4.5.2.1; 5.2.1.1; 5.2.1.2; 5.2.1.6; 5.2.2.4; 5.2.3.2

A

- Put the students in pairs and direct their attention to the photos. Ask the students to discuss which type of extreme environment they think would be the most difficult to survive in, and why.
- Before the students begin, elicit words that describe the four environments and write them on the board beside the geographical features listed in the Lead-in (*desert, drought, snow, ice, altitude, flood*, etc).
- Have the students discuss the photos and the questions. Circulate and help as needed.
- Discuss their ideas as a class. Take a class vote to find out which extreme environment the students feel would be most difficult to live in.

Culture note

- The Danakil Desert is a 100,000 km² tract of arid terrain in northeast Ethiopia. The area is known for numerous volcanoes and extreme temperatures, which often surpass 50°C. The local Afar people mine the salt which is created on the banks of lakes created by volcanic activity.
- Oymyakon is a remote village of about 500 people in northwestern Russia where the lowest temperature was recorded on February 6, 1933. The temperature there has never risen above freezing between October and March in recorded history.
- La Rinconada is a city high in the Andes mountains of Peru, three miles above sea level. It was originally built as a gold-mining camp and grew to become a city of over 50,000 people, most of whom work in the mine.
- Mawsynram is a village in northeastern India, close to the border of Bangladesh. The village has an unusually long monsoon season (nine months, compared with four in the rest of India) which causes an average of 12 metres of rain to fall per year.

B

- Keep the students in the same pairs as in Ex. A. Ask them to read the three questions and think about their answers. Then have them discuss the questions with their partner. Circulate and help as needed.
- When they finish their discussion, have the pairs share their answers with the class. Ask the students which type of harsh environment they would live in if they had to choose one (*hot, cold, high, wet*, etc) and why.

Extra: homework

Have the students do research on one of the extreme environments they would like to visit, as discussed in Ex. B. Ask them to find out more about the location and the factors that make that environment extreme, as well as information about what it is like to live there. Have them present their findings to the class.

Grammar: participle clauses (p. 142)

Lead-in

Write on the board: *I found what I was looking for. I went back home.* Ask students how they could link these two ideas, or clauses, into one sentence. One possible answer is to use a semi-colon; ask students if they can think of any others. Praise good guesses, but point out any grammatically incorrect forms, or sentences which sound inauthentic. If a student does phrase the sentence correctly (*Having found what I was looking for, I went back home* or vice-versa, with the clauses flipped) praise them. Tell the class this is the type of grammar they will be studying in this section.

A

- Direct the students' attention to the photo and the text. Ask the students to read the text with the question in mind.
- Elicit answers to the question.

Answer

They might like to see the amazing scenery or the ghost town. They also might be interested in the history of the local people; they may want to photograph the area or explore the local geological features.

NOTICE!

- Direct the students' attention to the **Notice!** box.
- Ask the students to look at the first sentence in the text and identify the main clause. Ask them what is the purpose of the other clause.
- Elicit answers from the class.

Answers

The main clause in the first sentence is 'Death Valley is the hottest, driest location in North America.' The other clause gives us extra information about Death Valley.

B

Form

- Have students read the homepage again, paying attention to clauses like the one they noticed.
- Ask the students to look at the information in the table, and then find examples from the homepage to fill in the gaps. Check the answers as a class.

Function

- Have the students read through all the examples. Tell them to choose the correct option for each of the three rules. Check the answers as a class.
  Direct the students' attention to the **What's right?** box and ask them to tick the correct sentence (*2*). Elicit why the incorrect sentence is wrong (*It makes it seem like the thought of Death Valley also booked the tour.*)

- Refer students to the two present perfect participle clauses in Ex. B. Elicit or point out that the first word following the phrase in each example is a noun or a pronoun (photographers, you). Then focus their attention on the correct sentence in the *What's right?* box. **Highlight** that the first word following the phrase is a pronoun (*I*).

Answers

Rules: active, passive, causes and effects
1 Housing up to 5000 people around 1908, ...
2 Named 'Death Valley' by prospectors during the California Gold Rush, ...
3 Having ventured into the desert, ...
4 Having faced one of the harshest environments that nature can throw at you, ...

Extra: grammar practice

Put the students in small groups. Ask them to write two sentences for each form. Circulate as groups work on their sentences and provide help as needed. Invite students from each group to take turns reading a sentence to the class. Have the class identify whether the sentence uses a present participle clause, a past participle clause or a present perfect participle clause.

C
- Have the students rewrite each sentence using a participle clause. Encourage them to refer to the table in Ex. B.
- Check answers with the class.

Answers

1 Looking for gold, the prospectors found nothing but rocks.
2 Founded in 1905, Rhyolite was once a thriving town.
3 Having visited Death Valley, you will never look at a desert in the same way again.
4 Located on the border between California and Nevada, Death Valley National Park was created in 1994.
5 Having heard how hot it was in Death Valley, I took plenty of water.

D
- Put the students in groups. Tell them to choose an area that they would like to attract tourists to.
- Tell each group to work together to write a travel advertisement that convinces people to visit the area. Remind them to use participle clauses and draw attention to the example.
- Suggest that the students in each group split up the work. For example, one could research tourist attractions, another could research scenery and a third could practise writing appropriate participle phrases, etc.

▶ Workbook p. 70, Section 1

Listening: difficult situations (p. 143 ◦ p.123)

Lead-in
Ask the students to read the information in the skills panel. Explain that not even native speakers can hear everything someone else says. Ask the students what types of language might be useful in noisy environments (*body language, gestures, facial expression, writing/reading*, etc).

A
- Put the students in groups. Ask them to list situations in which background noise could cause problems with understanding people's speech and discuss how they might deal with each situation.
- Have each group share its ideas with the class.

Answer

Possible situations include: cafés, restaurants and other places of entertainment; busy street areas; areas near roadworks, construction sites, etc.

B 2.27
- See p. 132 for the **audioscript**.
- Explain that the students are going to listen to four parts of a phone conversation about the subject of plate tectonics in which noise interferes. Ask them to listen for the statements and to write their best guess in each gap.
- Play the audio, repeating if necessary.

Answers

1 important 2 three 3 the lecture 4 volcano 5 wind and water

Culture note

Plate tectonics is the theory that the structure of the Earth's surface (its *crust*) is subject to the phenomena of large-scale processes involving movement of plates under the surface.

C 2.28
- See p. 132 for the **audioscript**.
- Explain that the students are now going to hear the complete phone conversation from which the examples in Ex. B were taken. Ask them to check their answers in Ex. B as they listen.
- Play the audio. Pause after each interruption, filling in the missing word as a class.
- Play the audio one more time. This time, have the students listen for and tick the phrases they hear used for clarification or repetition.
- Check answers with the class.
- Give the students time to practise repeating the phrases several times.

Answers

Sorry, how many?
Hang on, I didn't catch that.
Just a second. Was that water?

D
- Refer the students to the words and phrases in the box. Explain that these are all related to geology.
- Ask the students to label the picture, based on previous knowledge and what they learnt from the conversation in Ex. C.
- Check the answers with the class.

Answers

1 erosion **2** mountain range **3** earthquake **4** volcano
5 plate **6** crust **7** drift apart **8** collide

E
- Put the students in pairs. Direct their attention to the discussion questions.
- Give them time to read the questions and think about their answers before beginning their discussion. Point out that they are not expected to be experts at plate tectonics.
- When they finish, have a class discussion about the additional examples of the phenomena that the students came up with.

▶ Workbook p. 71, Sections 3 and 4

Speaking: talking about a mysterious phenomenon (p. 144)

Lead-in

Make sure the students know what *phenomenon* means (*an observable fact, event or circumstance whose cause or explanation is in question*). Ask for examples of mysterious phenomena the students know of. Ask them if they have ever seen photos of Stonehenge, the rock circle in England, or other large rock formations, such as the *moai* on Easter Island. Elicit how they imagine the rocks were moved.

Culture note

Stonehenge and the *moai* on Easter Island are two examples of mysterious phenomena that tourists visit every year.

Stonehenge is a prehistoric monument located in southern England. Archaeologists believe it was built between 3000 and 2000 BC and may have begun as a burial ground. It consists of two rings of massive upright stones, over 160 stones in total. Each stone weighs between 4 and 27 tonnes (4,000–27,000 kilograms). The stones in the outer ring are sandstone and probably came from local quarries. But the stones in the inner circle are bluestones, and archaeologists believe they were brought from quarries In Wales, around 220 miles (350 km) away.

Easter Island is an island in the South Pacific Ocean with an area of approximately 64 square miles (165 square km). Nine hundred giant stone figures – called *moai* – dating back centuries are found all around the island. Each *moai* measures around 40 metres high and weighs approximately 13 tonnes. Between 1050 and 1680, the stones were set on top of stone platforms that contained burial chambers, and archaeologists believe that the *moai* represent important figures deified after death.

A
- Direct the students' attention to the travel blog and photo. Ask the students to predict what kind of mysterious phenomenon this will be about.
- Have the students read the blog with the question in mind.
- Elicit the answer to the question.

Answer

The writer thought the most likely explanation was that the stones were moved by people.

B
- Direct the students' attention to the table and ask the students to look at the words at the top of each column. Ask them to read the text in Ex. A again, and underline these words as they find them. **Highlight** that these words are adverbial modifiers, and generally come before (or modify) an adjective.
- When they finish, direct their attention to the words in the box. Ask them to write each adjective in the box under the adverbial modifier in the table that the word naturally pairs with. Encourage them to refer to Ex. A as a guide, and point out that some words will pair with more than one adverbial modifier.
- Give them time to complete the table, and then check answers with the class.

Answers

incredibly: beautiful, difficult, dry, expensive, flat, good, important, interesting, surprising
completely: believable, different, dry, flat, new, surprising, wrong
totally: believable, different, dry, flat, new, surprising, wrong
slightly: different, difficult, dry, expensive, important, interesting, new, smaller, surprising, wrong
especially: beautiful, difficult, expensive, flat, good, important, interesting, surprising
somewhat: believable, different, difficult, dry, expensive, flat, important, interesting, new, smaller, surprising, wrong

C

- Ask the students to think of a place they know, and complete each sentence to describe that place. Have them complete the exercise individually. Circulate and help as needed.
- When they finish, ask volunteers to read their sentences to the class.

D 2.29

- See p. 132 for the **audioscript**.
- Direct the students' attention to the table. Explain that they are going to listen to a tour guide talking about the Racetrack Playa. The guide will describe different theories about the moving rocks mentioned in Ex. A. Ask them to take notes to fill in the table.
- Remind them that notes are quick words, phrases or abbreviations. Tell them if they miss one topic, they should go on and try to get the next.
- Play the audio, repeating if necessary.
- Check answers with the class.

Answers

1 Arguments for: Local winds can be very strong. There are short, but very powerful gusts of wind.
Arguments against: Nobody has observed this happening.
2 Arguments for: None
Arguments against: No local animals have the size or strength to push the rocks.
3 Arguments for: It's easy to imagine people moving the rocks.
Arguments against: There are no footprints or other signs such as tyre tracks of people moving the rocks.

E

- Ask the students to choose the theory or theories that they think most likely explain(s) the moving rocks, and prepare to present their theory to their partner. Explain that they may present their own theory, too.
- Remind them that they need to speak for two minutes. Encourage them to make some notes to help them stay focused and remember everything they want to say.
- Assign partners to keep time and listen without interrupting.
- Put the students in pairs and have them take turns explaining their theories.

F 2.30

- See p. 133 for the **audioscript**.
- Explain that students are now going to listen to the tour guide's explanation for the moving rocks. Ask them to note any similarities between the true explanation and their theories.
- Play the audio, repeating if necessary.
- Put students in pairs to discuss how similar their theories were, before discussing as a whole class.

▶ Workbook p. 70, Section 2

Grammar: impersonal passive in the past (p. 145)

Lead-in

Ask the students to review what they know about plate tectonics (*the Earth's crust has several large plates; the plates move; sometimes they collide with each other, which causes earthquakes and forms mountains; they're still growing*, etc). Make a list on the board. Ask them how they know these things. Ask them who first discovered each of these facts. Ask them if the answers are important (*no*).

A

- Direct the students' attention to the text and the picture. Ask if anyone knows what is pictured. Ask them to predict what the text will be about.
- Have the students read the text individually, with the question in mind.
- Elicit answers to the question as a class.

Answer

Scientists used to think that the Earth had formed by contracting, and so the mountains were the highest points because they were the last to contract. Now, scientists believe that the mountains were actually formed as a result of collisions between tectonic plates.

NOTICE!

- Direct the students' attention to the **Notice!** box.
- Have the students find two examples of the passive in the first two sentences. Ask them what form follows each one.

Answer

Both are followed by infinitives. The first is followed by a simple infinitive. The second is followed by a perfect infinitive.

B

Form

- Ask the students to read the text in Ex. A again, paying attention to the passive sentences.
- Have the students read the table. Ask them to complete the table with examples from the text and then check answers with the class.

Down to Earth UNIT 12 **115**

Answers

1 is thought to have created
2 were said to have been
3 are now known to have been

Function

- Have the students choose the correct option (*before*) to complete the rule.
- Check answers as a class.
- Direct students' attention to the **What's right?** box and ask them to tick the correct sentence (*1*). Discuss why the other sentence is incorrect.

Extra: practice

Have the students find two more examples of impersonal passive phrases in the text. Ask them whether they refer to present or past situations and facts.

Answers

... *the Earth's crust is considered to be composed of large, separate plates.* (present); *Mountains were said to have been the last parts to contract, ...* (past); *Mountains, earthquakes, volcanoes and other geological phenomena are now known to have been the result of the movement of tectonic plates.* (present)

C

- Ask the students to rewrite the sentences using an impersonal passive. Have the students refer to Ex. B for guidance.
- Put the students in pairs to compare answers, and then check answers with the class.

Answers

1 ... is estimated to have formed 4.5 billion years ago.
2 ... is understood to have first suggested continental drift in 1596.
3 ... are thought to have once formed one land mass.

D

- Put the students in pairs and have them read the instructions. Explain that they are going to use their imagination. Ask them to think about newscasts and news reports that they have heard. Ask them to work together to create a short news report about one of the three events.
- Give them time to prepare their reports. Circulate and help as needed. Remind the students to use the passive perfect infinitive where they can.

Extra: presentations

Have the students present their reports. Make a class tally of passive perfect infinitives used in the reports.

▶ **Workbook p. 72, Section 5**

Pronunciation: stress shifts in parts of speech (p. 146)

Lead-in

Write the word *are* on the board. Ask the students how many syllables it has (*one*). Add the letter *a* on the end of *are*. Ask how many syllables the new word – *area* – has (*three*). **Highlight** the pronunciation difference. Note that sometimes adding even one letter changes the stress and pronunciation of English words. Adding a syllable almost always changes the stress pattern of the word.

A 2.31

- See the Student's Book page for the **audioscript**.
- Direct the students' attention to the pairs of words.
- Play the audio, stopping after each pair of words so that the students can underline the stressed syllable in each one.
- Ask the students to explain what happened when each word in the left-hand column changed into the word in the right-hand column. Elicit that except for one pair – *reality-realistic* – each word increased by at least one syllable, and that the stress shifted one syllable to the right in the new word.

Answers

ge<u>o</u>logy – geo<u>lo</u>gical
<u>pho</u>tograph – pho<u>to</u>grapher
re<u>a</u>lity – rea<u>lis</u>tic
<u>pos</u>sible – possi<u>bi</u>lity
<u>ac</u>tive – ac<u>ti</u>vity
app<u>re</u>ciate – apprecia<u>tion</u>
ex<u>pect</u> – expec<u>ta</u>tion
<u>pro</u>gress – pro<u>gres</u>sive
<u>re</u>sident – resi<u>den</u>tial

B 2.32

- See the Student's Book page for the **audioscript**.
- Ask the students to listen to the sentences and pay close attention to the syllables that are stressed. Play the audio. Stop after each sentence and have the students repeat in unison.
- Have individual students repeat the sentences, correcting where necessary.

Reading: a feature article (p. 146)

Lead-in
Make sure the students know what *feature article* means. Ask them to think of and share examples of sentences using the word 'feature' as a noun (… the main feature), adjective (… feature attraction) and verb (… features a major film star).

Culture note
Fracking is the process of drilling down into the Earth before a high-pressure water mixture is directed at the rock to release the gas inside. Water, sand and chemicals are injected into the rock at high pressure which allows the gas to flow out to the head of the well. Although fracking can result in cheaper oil and natural gas supplies, it has proven to be a very controversial process which has caused a lot of environmental protest.

A
- Direct the students' attention to the definition and diagram. Discuss the question as a class, listing answers on the board.

B
- Give students time to read the article. Discuss the question, writing answers on the board.

C
- Refer students to the exercise. Give them time to circle the correct answers. Remind students that they may not be looking for exact matches, and so should consider how each of statements 1–4 could be paraphrased.

Answers
1 T 2 F 3 F 4 F

D
- Put students in pairs. Give them time to read the questions and think about their answers before they begin their discussion.
- Circulate and monitor while they discuss, assisting where needed.
- Discuss the answers as a class.

Writing: an editorial (p. 147)

Lead-in
Ask the students to read the information in the skills panel. **Highlight** that an editorial does not have a by-line (author's name), and is presumed to present the view of the editor and publisher of the paper. A column, on the other hand, also expresses an opinion but has the name – and often photo – of the author. A column expresses only the opinion of one person: the writer.

A
- Direct the students' attention to the instructions and the topic sentences. Elicit what a topic sentence is (*typically the first sentence in a paragraph*) and its purpose (*to state the subject of the paragraph*).
- Have the students read the five topic sentences and then the editorial. Ask them to choose the most appropriate topic sentence for each paragraph, reminding them that they will not use two of the topic sentences.
- Have them work individually, and then check the answers as a class.

Answers
Paragraph 1: 5
Paragraph 2: 1
Paragraph 3: 4

B
- Put the students in pairs and ask them to discuss the question and the purpose of each paragraph.
- Circulate and monitor, assisting where needed.
- Discuss the answers as a class.

Answers
1 The writer is for fracking.
2
Paragraph 1: To outline the current situation and describe how serious it is.
Paragraph 2: To outline the criticism of fracking and show that it is wrong.
Paragraph 3: To summarise, evaluate the arguments and justify an opinion.

C
- Direct the students' attention to the instructions. Tell the students they will now get their chance to write an editorial. Refer them to the skills panel, and ask what the three parts of an editorial are.
- Have the students choose one of the two viewpoints and make an outline for their editorial. Point out that they needn't feel strongly one way or the other about this issue to express an opinion on it. Circulate and monitor as they write. After a student has shown you his or her outline, allow them time to write their editorial.

Extra
Have the students read their editorials to the class. Post the editorials on poster paper around the classroom.

Extra: practice
Tell the students to write an editorial about a local subject that is close to their heart. Have them share the editorial when they are finished.

▶ Workbook pp. 72–73, Section 6

Down to Earth UNIT 12

LifeSkills: maximising your potential (p. 148)

Step 1: Understand the difference between hard skills and soft skills and the importance of each. (Ex. A, Ex. B, Ex. E)

Step 2: Assess your soft skills, and decide which areas you need to improve. (Ex. C, Ex. D)

Step 3: Consider practical ways in which you can continue to develop your life skills. (Ex. E, Ex. G)

Lead-in

Read the target skill aloud, and invite the students to tell you what they think *maximising your potential* means (*to make the most of what you have, or to be the best that you can be*). Then **highlight** the three-step strategy to develop the skill of maximising your potential.

A 2.33

- See p. 133 for the **audioscript.**
- Direct the students' attention to the instructions and the photo. Explain that they are going to listen to a conversation between a person looking for a job and a job counsellor. Ask them to listen for the answer to the question, and encourage them to take notes.
- Play the audio, repeating if necessary. Check the answer as a class.

Answer

hard skills, experience, soft skills

B

- Put the students in pairs. Ask them to listen to the conversation again, then discuss the three questions with their partners.
- Allow time for the students to read the questions.
- Play the audio. Give students time to discuss the questions. Circulate and monitor.
- Discuss the answers as a class.

Answers

1 No, he doesn't, because he thinks that he lacks experience related to his degree field.
2 He thinks that because Noel has gained work experience and developed his soft skills.
3 Hard skills consist of things you have learnt that are directly related to your field – job-specific skills. Soft skills consist of abilities such as problem-solving, critical thinking, time management, organisation, self-confidence, the ability to motivate people and so on.

C

- Focus the students' attention on the instructions and the example. Ask the students to include on their list any hard skill they have that might be useful in a job.
- Have the students compare their lists with a partner. Then ask them to decide which hard skills will be most important for their careers.
- Have students share their answers with the class. Make a list on the board.

D

- Refer students to the table and the words in the box. Point out that each label in the box describes a category of skills listed in the table. Have the students complete the first column of the table with the labels in the box. Check the answers as a class.
- Ask students to write one more skill in the gap at the bottom of each category in the table.
- Have students share their answers with the class.
- Next, ask the students to assess their own skills in each category, according to the instructions in their books.

Answers

1 Interpersonal
2 Critical thinking
3 Information literacy

Extra: practice

Write this list of jobs on the board: *construction worker, teacher, software company CEO, police officer, janitor, professional football player*. Add other jobs if you like. Put students in pairs or groups. Have each pair/group choose three of the jobs listed on the board. For each job, have them list the top three hard skills and top three soft skills they think would be required for each. When they are finished, have each pair/group share their thoughts with the class.

E

- Put the students into groups. Tell them they are going to work together to complete the table. First, ask them to think of two skills to write at the bottom of the *Soft skill* column. Then ask them to decide on one idea to write in each blank space in the *Ideas for development* column on the right.
- Circulate and monitor, assisting where needed. When students are finished, have each group share their answers with the class.

F

- Keep the students in the same groups. Ask them to discuss how each group member's soft skills might be useful in their future career. Each group member should share his or her top five soft skills. The other group members should take turns saying how one of those skills will be helpful. Tell them to suggest other soft skills if they wish.

G

- Discuss the questions as a class.

Possible answers

1 the importance of soft skills, how to assess soft skills, how to improve soft skills
2 improve soft skills, keep assessing them

REFLECT

- Ask the students to read the *Reflect* question.
- Give them some time to think about different situations in the domains of **Study and Learning** and **Self and Society** where the skill of *maximising your potential* would be useful.
- Elicit answers as a class.

Possible answers

Study and Learning – it can help you get high grades; it can help you learn more things, which makes you more versatile and a more valuable employee; **Self and Society** – it can help you be the best you can physically, mentally and emotionally; it can help society function at a higher level, because everyone will be doing the most they can.

RESEARCH

- Refer the students to the *Research* box. Have the students read through the instructions. Tell them to write a paragraph that describes the life skill they plan to develop, and a statement about how they will start developing that skill.

Language wrap-up (p. 150)

For notes on how to approach the exercises in the Language wrap-up section, please refer to page 9.

1 Vocabulary

A

Ask the students to read through the sentences before they fill in the gaps. **Highlight** that one of the answer choices in the box will not be used.

Alternative

- Ask the students to write their own sentences for each of the seven words or phrases, leaving a gap in each sentence for the word or phrase on the list.
- Have them swap sentences with a partner, and then have each partner complete the other's sentences.
- Have the students share some examples of their sentences with the class.

B

- Ask the students to read each sentence before they begin to fill in the gaps.
- Draw attention to the words in the box. Remind the students that there may be more than one correct answer per number.

2 Grammar

Explain that the text contains 12 mistakes with verb forms. Ask the students to find and underline each mistake, and then write the correct verb form on a separate piece of paper. Alternatively, ask the students to mark up the text as an editor would, crossing out the mistakes and using insertion marks (∧) to indicate where each corrected verb form should go.

Speaking workshop: giving a mini-presentation (p. 151)

Lead-in

Explain to the students that in this workshop they will practice giving a mini-presentation. Elicit that *mini* means short or brief.

Culture note

A mini-presentation is also known as a *pitch*. Explain this scenario: Imagine you have a great idea for a new product or service, but you need money. You have 60 seconds to convince them to lend you money. This is called making a pitch and it's practised in business schools globally.

A 🎧 **2.34**

- See p. 133 for the **audioscript.**
- Direct the students' attention to the photo and the three topics in the box. Ask the students what the person in the photo is doing. Elicit that they are giving a presentation.
- Explain that the students are going to listen to a woman making a short presentation. Ask them to choose the topic of her presentation from one of the three choices, and note the main points she makes.
- Play the audio. Put the students in pairs to compare their notes, and then check the answer as a class.

Answer

The speaker is presenting on topic C. The main points she makes are: English will be important for her in the future so she needs to continue to develop her abilities in English. She can do this by maintaining contact with other English speakers, both online and in person. She also recognises that she needs to speak to people from a broad range of cultures. She intends to read widely in English and also to listen to internet radio programmes and podcasts in English.

Down to Earth | UNIT 12 | 119

B

- Ask the students to listen again and focus on the phrases the speaker uses to link her ideas. Ask them to listen for the words or short phrases to fill in each gap.
- Play the audio, repeating if necessary. Check the answers as a class.
- Ask the students to explain what each of the phrases is used for. Ask them what other phrases they know that could be used in the same way, and make a list on the board.

Possible answers

1 As a consequence: used to describe results
   Other phrases: As a result, Consequently, etc
2 This implies: used to draw conclusions
   Other phrases: This means that, One implication of this is that, etc
3 First and foremost: used to introduce the first, most important point
   Other phrases: Firstly, and most importantly, etc
4 What's more: used to introduce a further point
   Other phrases: Furthermore, Moreover, etc
5 Besides that: used to introduce a further point
   Other phrases: Apart from that, In addition to that, etc
6 In a similar way: used to introduce another similar point
   Other phrases: Similarly, Likewise, etc
7 To briefly sum up: used to introduce a summary
   Other phrases: To summarise, In summary, etc

C

- Ask the students to read the instructions. Explain that they are going to give a brief presentation of their own. Ask them to choose one of the topics on the card and to use the planner to make notes.
- Give the students time to prepare their presentations. Circulate and help as needed.

D

- Schedule time for all the students to give their presentations to the class. Designate timers to time each presentation for one and a half minutes. At the end of each presentation, allow time for questions and answers.
- Have the class give a brief critique of each presentation. Have the students vote on the three best.

How are you doing?

- Ask the students to read the statements and tick the ones they believe are true.
- Ask them to discuss their presentation with another student in the class and identify things they could improve on next time.

▶ Workbook pp. 74–75, SkillsStudio

AUDIOSCRIPT

UNIT 1

Money-free

🎧 **1.03**

Speaker 1:
I can see the appeal of these freecycling websites for some people, but they're more or less a waste of time. You rarely find what you're looking for, so I'd say I was against the idea.

Speaker 2:
I've exchanged a few things on sites like that, and it worked out well for me. They're quite a good idea. I'm fairly sure that a site like that would benefit students, so I'm in favour of it.

Speaker 3:
I don't trust everyone on freecycling websites because it seems to me that not everyone is on there for the right reasons. Some people get things for free and then go on to sell them to make money. I'd be opposed to the idea on campus.

Speaker 4:
I don't have a lot of experience with freecycling websites, but I suppose they're generally a good thing. They reduce waste and they mean that someone gets some use out of things you don't need. I'm sure it would prove to be very popular with students, so why not?

Speaker 5:
I love those sites! I've given away lots of stuff, and I've even found a few things I wanted. I would argue that they're one of the most useful things on the internet. More people should use them, and I think we should definitely have one on campus.

Speaker 6:
More and more of these sites are appearing online, and I tend to think they might do some good. They aren't tackling the real problem, though, of how much we consume in the first place. What are the university authorities planning to do about that?

🎧 **1.05**

I = Interviewer, J = Jim

I: We're talking today to Jim Telfer, founder of *Barterrific*. Jim, tell us a little about your organisation.

J: Thanks, Claire. Well, very simply, *Barterrific* is a local community of people that barter. Bartering is a pretty old system, as old as, well, owning things. At the simplest level, bartering involves trading something you have for something you want. Or, something you can do for something you want done. You might trade an unwanted video game or DVD for one that you want. I noticed last week that someone traded a van for a boat.

I: Isn't that a pretty big trade?

J: Yes, it is. Big or small, doesn't matter – people barter things of all sizes.

I: And no money changes hands?

J: That's right. It's completely non-monetary. Members don't even pay to join.

I: But then … how do you, well, finance things, like your website? And advertising?

J: Barter, of course! The site was designed by a graphic designer who needs his lawn mowed, so I take care of that for him, and he updates the site. We do have a few ads on the site though. This acts as a subsidy for the cost of our service provider. But to members of the community, everything is free. Oh, and our local radio advert time, that's another barter. The radio station car park is on some land that belongs to my cousin.

I: So do people only barter second-hand goods?

J: Oh, no, not at all, although if they do, we encourage them to make sure they're in good working order. But people barter new items too. Also, it's not just physical products. I'd say a good 40% of our traffic is in services.

I: Give us some examples of what you mean, Jim.

J: Well, some people out there – students, retirees and so on – have plenty of time on their hands, so they might trade some of their time for some of your items. We have people who walk dogs, babysit children, paint houses, you name it.

I: I see. Can they trade services for other services?

J: Of course.

I: Isn't this just for individuals, then?

J: Not at all. We have a lot of businesses that are members. They are very keen on expanding the model. Apparently more than 30% of business done worldwide is through barter.

I: But why would a business not want to make money?

J: It does come down to money in the end, but in a different way. An example: say you're a small hotel and you usually charge £90 for a room. If no one is staying in that room, you're losing money, in the form of electricity, staff wages and so on. But that room doesn't really cost £90 and a lot of it's markup. Let's say it really costs you £8. Suppose you barter that room for some petrol from the service station down the road. The owner would usually sell the petrol for £50 so he thinks he's saved £40. But you've made £42 profit, rather than losing money. And, more importantly, the customer will be so happy with the price of his room, he'll spend more money in your hotel – maybe ordering dinner from room service.

I: So both sides are happy.

J: Exactly. When you barter, you're exchanging what you have or can do for what you want. It's a win-win deal. And that's why we're a community. People are also making friends. We set up a discussion forum on our website and people trade advice and just chat about things. Money creates huge pressure. Monetary systems are emotionally loaded. When you barter, whether at a local, national or international level, you escape some of that pressure.

I: Thank you Jim Telfer, founder of *Barterrific*. When we come back …

UNIT 2

Watch this space …

🎧 1.06

Speaker 1:
I'm really interested to hear what Professor Papadopoulos has to say, although I'm not sure I'm going to agree with him! He actually visited my university in Texas last year to give a lecture, but I didn't sign up in time, so I couldn't attend. I'm glad I'll get another chance today.

Speaker 2:
Oh yeah, I'm sure it will be fascinating. I actually know Professor Papadopoulos from Australia where I'm from – we worked together and when I heard he was in New York, I thought I'd come along.

Speaker 3:
Oh, that's interesting. I'm from New Delhi, but I'm over here in the States to chair a TV debate on space exploration programmes. I'm keen to get Professor Papadopoulos involved – perhaps you could introduce us later?

Speaker 4:
I'd love to buy Professor Papadopoulos's book – the photography is incredible! I've been fascinated by astronomy since I was a young boy. I actually grew up in the Australian outback where the view of the stars is amazing.

Speaker 5:
That must have been wonderful. I'm very envious – I'm from New York and so you don't see the stars very often here.

Speaker 6:
Our space programme in India is growing exponentially. For me, that's a worry, and so I'm intrigued to hear Professor Papadopoulos's views on that today.

🎧 1.07

Professor:
So, thanks everyone for listening to me. I'd like to open up the discussion and hear your views on the future of space exploration.

Speaker 1:
Professor, I think you make some good points, but if you ask me, space exploration is an incredible waste of money. I mean, we have so many problems here on Earth that we should spend that money on. You know, they were spending 200 million dollars a *month* on the space shuttle programme. That's unbelievable! Think of how many schools, hospitals and roads could have been built for that amount! I'm glad the programme has been cancelled, because it was an impractical use of money.

Speaker 2:
I see your point, but I believe it's very important to continue with space exploration. We have insufficient natural resources here on Earth, and we know that many asteroids and some of the other planets in our galaxy have large amounts of iron, platinum, magnesium and even gold. Just think, if we could extract them … their potential value is immeasurable. Who knows – there may be resources on other planets that are still unknown to us, and we'll never discover them if we stop space exploration. We're going to need to increase space programmes, not cut them, if we want to have enough resources in the future.

Speaker 3:
I agree. A lot of people think space programmes are a waste of money. They say we should spend the money here on Earth, but that's really an unacceptable argument. The fact is that we *do* spend the money here. Space programmes create jobs in science, technology and manufacturing. Just think: hundreds of scientists are working on new inventions; people in technical fields like robotics and IT are working on how to develop the scientists' ideas; and finally, thousands of people are employed in the factories that make the inventions. That's a lot of jobs!

Speaker 4:
It's true that space research creates a lot of jobs and it could be that there are more energy resources in space. However, I think it's more important to invest in researching more energy-efficient and environmentally friendly resources on Earth. Who's to say we can't create more jobs that way? I think it's more important to teach people to care for the Earth, rather than trying to look for ways to continue our unsustainable use of energy.

Speaker 5:
I always feel impatient with people who say we should stop exploring space. They know that the space programme costs a lot of money, but they are totally unaware of the benefits of it. Some of our common modern conveniences like mobile phone cameras, water filters or battery-powered tools might still be unavailable to us without the space programme. So if your phone takes good photos, or if you like drinking clean, filtered water, thank NASA. And we can expect that many more useful things will be invented in the future by scientists and technicians in space programmes around the world.

Speaker 6:
I know that the space programme has given us many important inventions, but those things could have been invented anyway. We are still incapable of providing enough food, clean water and medical services for all of the people on Earth. Many lives might be saved if more money were spent on helping poor people instead of sending a few people into space and collecting insignificant things like moon rocks. It's just impossible for me to understand why billions of dollars are spent on space exploration instead of on people.

🎧 1.09

Interviewer:
Dr Fisher, you are a biologist, and you are a member of the SETI Institute. For our listeners who may not have heard of SETI, it stands for Search for Extraterrestrial Intelligence. The SETI Institute conducts research and experiments to try to find out whether there is intelligent life in our solar system or in other solar systems. Dr Fisher, why do a number of scientists believe that there may be other intelligent life somewhere in the universe?

Dr Fisher:
Well, first is the simple question of probability. The universe is unimaginably big, and it is full of stars, planets, asteroids and moons. It is extremely improbable that among all of those, there would be only one single planet that had evolved to support life forms.
Second, there is evidence that a number of other planets have at least some of the conditions that caused life to begin on Earth. For example, organic compounds have been found in space, and there is evidence that some planets in our galaxy, the Milky Way, may have water. If a planet has organic material, water and temperatures that are not too extreme, there is no reason that life couldn't exist there as it does on Earth. If we know that there are planets with at least some of these conditions, then we can assume that there are planets that are still unknown to us where life already exists.
Finally, there have been so many reports throughout history of UFO sightings that they can't all be false. Now, it's true that 90 to 95 per cent of UFO sightings turn out to be aircraft,

weather balloons or some other identifiable phenomenon. However, there are many other cases that don't have simple explanations. Consider this. The first report of a UFO in America was in 1639, and there were a number of reports of strange, shiny objects appearing in the sky before the invention of aircraft, so the objects could not have come from Earth. Furthermore, there have been many reports of UFOs by pilots and military officers. These are professional people who know how to recognise man-made flying objects and who do not tend to invent fantasy stories.
Of course, at the moment, our ideas about intelligent life somewhere else in the universe are just theories, but I'm sure that intelligent life on other planets will be discovered some day. I just hope it's in my lifetime!

1.10

This drawing is an artist's concept of a future space colony. The information at the top of the picture says that the colony will float in space, so it won't be on a planet. The colony will be completed in the year 2060, and it will be colonised by people from several different countries.

The shape of the colony is oval, like a giant egg, and there are several structures that look like airports attached to the outside of it.

In the foreground of the picture, we can see life in the colony. These things in the air are similar to cars, but they fly. This long vehicle appears to be some kind of flying bus. There are some people on the ground, but many people are driving the flying cars or riding a type of flying bicycle!

There are lakes and trees on the ground, but all of the buildings are floating in the air! These big ones look like office buildings, and the smaller ones are probably houses. This strange oval structure appears to be some kind of stadium.

Except for the floating buildings and flying vehicles, life in this imaginary space colony looks pretty normal. I guess living in a space colony would be OK as long as it was designed to be as similar to Earth as possible!

UNIT 3

Password protected

1.11

M = Marta, C = Carly

M: Hey, Carly. Have you seen this notice?

C: Yeah. So our parents would be able to monitor our credit card purchases even if our credit cards are in our names and not our parents' names. I guess a lot of people will think it's an invasion of their privacy, but I actually think it's kind of a good idea. I mean, for most university students, our parents are paying all or most of our expenses, so I think they have a right to know what we're spending money on.

M: Maybe, but a lot of students will feel uncomfortable with that. I think it gives our parents too much control over the things we do and the decisions we make. Sure, some people make a lot of mistakes with credit cards. They spend too much and get into debt, or they fall for online scams and lose some money, but if we don't make mistakes, how are we going to learn? I think this will cause a lot of unnecessary arguments.

C: That's true, but I also think it might keep a lot of students from getting into trouble. Young people aren't always very careful about sharing personal data online, and irresponsible data sharing leaves us open to things like identity theft or internet scams.

M: I don't know. I just think parents should trust their kids and let them learn about managing money and credit. Just because they're parents doesn't give them the right to know everything going on in our personal lives. I think it will make people feel that their parents don't trust them.

C: I know what you mean, but a lot of the time parents end up paying for their kids' mistakes, and that's not really fair. If parents could monitor their kids' credit card use, it might save families a lot of money! Anyway, why don't you write to the website and tell them your opinion? I'm going to.

1.12

I = Interviewer, J = Justine

I: And now on *The Whole Story*, we turn to an issue which has been in the news a lot recently – identity theft. We called on the public to share experiences of identity theft with us, and today I'm joined by Justine Black, who's a manager with an international company. Now, Justine, you've been a victim of identity theft, haven't you?

J: Yes, that's right. I discovered that someone was using my identity to open bank accounts and take out credit cards, and that person had run up debts of over £200,000 in my name over the course of a year.

I: And, how did you discover that this was happening?

J: The first I knew was when I got a letter from a bank threatening to take me to court. They said I owed them a lot of money on a credit card, but I knew I had never spent that money because I didn't even have a credit card with them!

I: You must have found the situation very worrying.

J: Yes, I did. It ended up being harder than I thought to prove myself innocent. The person who was impersonating me had got hold of my address and my date of birth, and they used the information to open accounts. As far as the banks were concerned, Justine Black owed them money, and I was Justine Black. They seemed to think that I was making up the story to get out of paying my bill!

I: How did the person get your personal data?

J: Well, I consider myself to be pretty careful online, and I try to keep my personal details private. But I had bought things online, and so some of my details were stored in a database. It seems that the criminal managed to hack into the database and get my credit card details. Once they had my email address, they sent me a file that installed a program on my computer that connected to my keyboard and told them everything I typed. That's how they got my date of birth and other information when I signed into different websites.

I: And have you now solved the problem?

J: It's taken over two years, but I think I've cleared up most of the problems. In the end, the banks believed me and cancelled the debts. However, it's always possible that there's something else out there waiting to be discovered.

I: Justine, I know you've gone through a terrible experience with all of this. Thank you very much for joining us today and sharing your story. Tomorrow we continue with the topic of cybercrime, and we offer you some tips for how to avoid internet scams.

🎧 1.16

F = Fiona, A = Alina, D = Daniel

F: OK, so we've been asked to talk about how ideas of privacy in the information age differ. Why don't we begin by thinking about how we personally feel about privacy? Alina?

A: Good idea, Fiona. Privacy is very important to me. I personally don't want anyone to invade my privacy without my permission, either in real life or online. Is the same true for you, Daniel?

D: Uh … I guess not. I don't feel that it's that important. I'll usually share anything with anyone!

F: I agree with Alina. I think I'm a pretty private person. I guess I don't want to leave myself open to a lot of comments or criticism, so I don't put much information out on Twitter or Facebook. You just end up having problems if you share too much information.

A: OK. Maybe we should move on to talking about other people's ideas about privacy. For example, I know that my parents don't share as much information online as I do. I think they're afraid of people getting hold of their personal information to take out credit cards and run up debts. They don't like the idea of companies being able to monitor what they buy or whatever.

D: The same is definitely true for me. I often put things on Facebook or on Twitter that my parents wouldn't, or even that some of my friends wouldn't. For example, I was at a party last weekend, and I kept telling people on Twitter what I was doing and who I was talking to, and even what we were talking about, and I was getting all these replies from people who weren't even at the party, and I know my parents would find that a little strange, and …

F: Sorry to stop you, Daniel, but maybe we should focus on just our basic opinion; otherwise, we'll run out of time.

D: Oh, yeah. Sure. You're right. So, does anyone want to add anything on the topic of their parents' ideas of privacy?

F: I'd like to say that it's not just about different generations. It's also about different cultures. Ideas about privacy can be very different around the world.

A: Good point. I think it also depends on your personal experiences. I mean, anybody who has ever been through an internet scam or an identity theft situation probably has a different attitude to digital privacy than other people! So let's make a note of some of our ideas to share with everyone later.

UNIT 4

A new look at learning

🎧 1.17

I = Interviewer, DC = Dr Cowell

I: Welcome to *Consider This*. Today we're talking to Dr George Cowell about online university degree programmes. Dr Cowell, I understand you have some concerns about these.

DC: Thank you, Lisa. Yes, I do have some serious concerns about the growing trend of online education. In my book, *A Classroom is a Place*, I describe my research on this subject.

I: And you conclude that online classrooms are not that effective.

DC: Well, it's not quite that simple. In fact, I believe that online education is an excellent alternative for working older adults who want to further their education. There are many people who, for whatever reason, were not able to go to university when they were younger, or had to drop out before finishing their degree. They're now working and supporting families, so they don't have time to go back to university full time.

I: So they can work and study at the same time.

DC: Exactly. There's now a very broad range of courses and degree programmes offered online, and working adults can pursue their degree in their own time, at their own pace. However, I believe the situation is different for younger adults. We have to take into account the fact that the vast majority of 18- to 22-year-olds do not yet have the maturity to set goals for themselves or to discipline themselves to stick to those goals. When they're faced with total freedom to study – or not – whenever they want, most young adults just don't have the motivation and self-discipline to get the work done, and they drop out or fail.

I: But surely there are advantages to studying online, even for younger students. For one, it's cheaper and would stop so many students getting into debt, right? And without the distractions found on campuses, surely fewer online students would drop out.

DC: OK, yes, admittedly the cost of tuition is a factor, and it's true that some students do work better in an off-campus situation. There are students who feel stressed and uncomfortable in the social scene of a university. Others want to finish their degree more quickly, or take longer than they could afford to in an on-campus university. However, I feel that this is not the case for the majority of students.

A traditional university setting does so much more than just teach classes. It increases social skills, creates lifetime friendships and offers extra-curricular activities. Students learn to be independent, to organise their time and themselves; in short, young people make the transition from dependent teenagers to independent adults. That is simply not going to happen if a student isolates him- or herself to do an online degree.

I: Dr Cowell, our time is up, so we're going to leave it there. Thank you for coming in.

1.20

Conversation 1

M = Marcel, N = Natalya

M: How's your research paper going?

N: Not great. It's supposed to be on the effects of technology on education, but I can't find that much information on it, just opinions.

M: Most people say that technology is making education easier, don't they?

N: Yeah, but you read it in blogs and online editorials, so those are people who are really good at using technology anyway. And actually, I think technology has one very big negative side, though I can't find that much research on it.

M: Really? What's that?

N: Well, from what I've seen, technology is actually making students lazier. I mean, so many students just cut and paste material from the internet onto PowerPoint slides for their presentations.

M: Yeah, when students are faced with a big task like a presentation, they look for the easiest way to do it. Well, good luck with it!

N: Thanks.

Conversation 2

G = Giovanni, M = Mei

G: Hey, there, how's it going?

M: Fine! I've just finished my research paper – the one about the effects of rapidly changing technology on education.

G: And what did you conclude?

M: I think technology is making education easier and more exciting. Students now have such a broad selection of online resources that they can learn a lot more about any subject than they could before, which makes doing research papers more interesting. And students are also learning lots of other skills because of the more independent nature of working online.

G: Yeah? Like what?

M: They learn to do research at an early age, and they're faced with constant decisions – which website to use, which opinion to believe. Even young kids today are much better at finding out things for themselves.

G: I hadn't thought of that, but it's true. My little brother is teaching himself to play the guitar with an online class. It's amazing.

Conversation 3

A = Andrea, O = Omar

A: Look at this journalism assignment! Now we have to follow at least three TV network reporters on Twitter for a month!

O: Oh, that's an interesting assignment! It's so amazing how these sites aren't just social networks anymore. They're used by professionals as a way to keep up to date with things happening all over the world.

A: I know, but professors don't take into consideration the time it takes to do all this. I have to keep a blog for my writing class, follow Twitter for my journalism class, plus go to about a million websites for every essay I write. I think all this technology actually makes going to university harder, not easier.

O: I see your point. I like using different technology for my classes, but it's definitely time-consuming. Wasn't technology supposed to help us save time? Instead I feel like I have even less free time – because I'm using technology all the time!

A: Yeah, yeah, I know! And I'm sure it's the same in the workplace as well …

1.22

I would rather study in a traditional classroom setting than in an online class. There are three main reasons. The first is that I'm just not very good with technology. Whenever I'm faced with something to do on online, even registering for classes online, I always mess something up. For example, I forget my password, lose my student ID, click on the wrong link … The second reason is that I work better in small groups. When I took biology last year, the large lectures were really hard for me. It was hard for me to pay attention, and a few times I even fell asleep. But when I met up with other students in study groups, they asked me questions, I asked them questions, we went over problems together … whatever I was having trouble with, someone could help me. If I hadn't had those small study groups, I wouldn't have passed. In a large online class? I wouldn't stand a chance! Finally, I don't do very well without supervision. In an online class, it's up to you to read the materials, remember the deadlines, post your assignments … but even though I mean to, I just … don't. I need someone checking up on me all the time. Classmates, course assistants, the professor, my advisor, whoever … just somebody to help me keep on top of things, so I know where I stand. I have trouble setting goals on my own. That's why an online class really isn't for me.

UNIT 5

On the wild side

1.23

Lena's mother was an expert on plants, and she had already taught Lena how to identify many edible ones. They were examining a plant together one morning when Lena heard a loud noise and saw her mother fall to the ground. Lena was frightened, but she couldn't leave her. Suddenly, several men appeared and snatched Lena away from her mother.

This sounds like a horrible kidnapping story, and it is, but Lena is not a human child. She is an orang-utan, and her story is a common one in the forests of Borneo, one of only two remaining natural habitats of these gentle primates. A century ago, there were thought to be about 315,000 orangutans in Southeast Asia; today, orangutans are an endangered species with an estimated 45,000 to 70,000 remaining.

Lena's natural habitat, the Indonesian rainforest, is being destroyed at a frightening speed, and over half of the rainforest has already been destroyed. A second problem is that orangutan meat is very popular, despite the fact that it is known to be illegal to kill these animals. Finally, there is a large market for young orangutans as pets. Smugglers sell the young apes to people who don't care that these animals are not meant to be pets. For every six orangutans captured, five die before they are sold.

Fortunately, Lena was a survivor, but not before suffering great cruelty. She was sold to a vendor who tried to sell her in a street market. But the man was unlucky, and no one bought her. Days went by, and he gave Lena barely enough food and water for her to survive. Finally, she was too thin to be of any value to him, so he simply left her to die.

The good news, however, is that there are several orangutan sanctuaries in Borneo. That same day a young volunteer named Bakti was in the village buying some supplies for his sanctuary. He saw Lena and took her back to the sanctuary. After a few days of taking care of her, it was clear she would live, and she was named Lena, after a young Australian volunteer.

Lena made friends with other orangutans at the sanctuary, and gradually learnt social skills. The humans helped the young apes learn other essential orangutan skills that they would have learnt from their mothers if they had not grown up in captivity. In the wild, young orangutans stay with their mothers for eight years and learn from them how to identify which plants and fruits to eat, how to build nests and how to use sticks as tools to open fruit.

The staff at the sanctuaries are trained to interact with the orangutans so that they don't become dependent on humans. Orangutans are extremely intelligent and genetically very closely related to humans. They can learn to understand hundreds of words, and they can adopt certain human habits, which would obviously interfere with their ability to function in their natural state.

After three years, Lena and several of her companions were ready to return to the forest. They had completed a long rehabilitation process to learn to be independent. On the day of their release, they were taken deep into the forest, far away from the sanctuary. When they were released, they looked at the humans for a few minutes, unsure of what to do. But then, one by one, they climbed into tall trees and began their new lives as wild orangutans. Lena would go on to have four babies and live happily into old age.

UNIT 6

More than machines?

1.27

M = Man, W = Woman

M: Wow … listen to this. Yesterday an aeroplane actually flew past the airport – it missed it by 150 miles!

W: What? How? Was some equipment not working properly?

M: No … the equipment was working *too* well!

W: What is that supposed to mean?

M: Well, you know how most aeroplanes are automated these days. Machines do most of the flying and the pilots are dependent on them to control the plane. That's fine, but it means that the pilots can get bored.

W: So they missed the airport because they were bored?

M: Well, in a way. Because they were bored, they weren't aware of what was going on around them. And … they missed the airport.

W: Wow. They should have been focused on what was happening!

M: Yeah, but because the plane is automated, the pilots do other things, like check their laptops … it's too easy for them to be distracted by other things.

W: OK, I don't think you can blame automation for that. In fact, I'd be more alarmed by flying on a plane that wasn't automated. Machines don't get sleepy or depressed or make silly mistakes. They're not going to be overwhelmed by emotions if something goes wrong.

M: But depending on automation is dangerous. I know technology has its place. I guess I'm just suspicious of too much automation.

W: I still say that you can't blame automation for the problem. It was a human error. If someone had an accident while driving their car because they were talking on their mobile phone, you'd blame the driver, not the mobile phone.

M: But pilots can't choose whether or not to have all that automation in their planes. In a few years, more and more planes will have been equipped with automation like this. And I don't know if it's such a good idea.

W: In another few decades, we'll see that more lives will have been saved by automation than will have been lost by it. We might have to agree to disagree about this.

1.28

M = Man, W = Woman

Part 1

M: I'm so overwhelmed by all this housework. We need a robot to help!

W: Like one of those little robot vacuum cleaners? Yeah, they're pretty cool.

M: No, I mean a real robot, one that looks just like a person.

W: But you'd have to spend as much time making it do the chores as you would spend actually doing them yourself. I've seen you with the bread machine. You take all day!

M: Ah, but the robots of the future will be able to think for themselves. They won't need any human help. They'll just automatically be aware of what needs to be done, and they'll do it.

W: Yeah, that'll happen.

Part 2

M: Well, just look at how fast technology changes. A hundred years ago, a bread machine would have been unthinkable. Now I can set it in the evening to make sure I have fresh bread in the morning. See, it knows when I'm going to wake up …

W: Come on. It's a few pieces of metal and plastic. And you can't always depend on machines. They can break down any time.

M: OK, that's true, and it doesn't actually 'know', but it shows how quickly technology advances.

Part 3

W: But there's a difference between what's basically a fancy alarm clock and a machine that can think. Personally, I'm suspicious of these claims about programming a metal doll to have thoughts and feelings.

M: Isn't the human brain just a very complex machine though? I'm sure if scientists focused on figuring out how the brain works, they could replicate that mechanically. That would be wonderful.

W: Would it?

Part 4

M: Sure, why not? It would be amazing to have a machine that could think and had emotions.

W: Really? You wouldn't be at all alarmed by that? What if the machines decided they didn't like us, and rose up against us?

M: Oh, come on, that's science fiction.

W: Well, it's the natural outcome of what you're suggesting.

Part 5

M: But we would just program the robots not to be like that.

W: Then they wouldn't be 'thinking'. You can't have it both ways. Either you believe that machines can think and feel, and then you need to accept that they have free choice like humans, or you don't.

M: Well, no, I don't think those are the only two choices. If people are the ones who are creating the machine that thinks, then they can influence how it thinks.

W: But then that's not really 'thinking', is it?

M: OK … I see what you mean …

Part 6

M: But actually, I don't know. Couldn't you have a robot that could think, but that could still be controlled? Like dogs. They can think, but we train them to obey us.

W: OK, that's a good point. But being human is more than that. What about our soul? Do you think you can make one of those in a factory?

M: You want to know what I think? I think we're just getting distracted by these questions and issues. They're fun to talk about, sure, but I don't want to fight about it. OK?

W: You're right. Although, if we don't think about these things in advance, then we won't be able to make the right decisions in time.

M: You're so serious tonight! Come on. Help me with the dishes. Then let's watch a film. But, um, maybe not a science-fiction one. Maybe a comedy.

W: Let's do it!

....

🎧 1.31

OK. Well, let me see. This is a photo of some people working with robots in a factory. It looks as if the robots are doing the manual work, while the human workers are supervising. I would think that working with robots in this situation is probably quite interesting, as long as you've been trained for it. It's less tiring than actually doing the work yourself, and it probably means that you can be more productive. It means that the person can be more focused on making sure everything is done to a high standard. On the other hand, working with robots like this could make you anxious about your job. These robots are never distracted by things like human workers are, and they never need to take a break. The person may worry that before long they'll have been replaced by machines, which means this work situation could be more stressful than it seems at first glance.

The other photo is of a remote-controlled robot. My guess is that it's the kind of robot that is used for dealing with bombs. It looks as if the operator has sent the robot to examine something suspicious in the road. Working with robots in this situation probably gives you a feeling of security, since you can work safely at a distance. I'm sure it's still quite stressful – after all, you don't want to destroy an expensive robot – but at least you can be confident you're not going to get injured or killed. It's important that you can feel that you can rely on the equipment you're using, and a robot that breaks down might be more dangerous than having no robot at all. Unlike the first situation, you probably don't feel that your job is threatened, since I think it's very unlikely that robots will ever go into situations like this without a human operator.

UNIT 7

The critical consumer

🎧 2.01

C = Caitlin, H = Hanna

C: Hanna, don't forget we need to get lettuce for the salad. Shall we get a few bunches, in fact?

H: Well, lettuce is perishable, so we don't want more than we can eat in a few days. I can't stand old lettuce. It's barely edible. Let's just get enough for the salad tonight. There will be ... what, eight people? Ten? I think two heads of lettuce is about right. But now we have to decide what kind … There are so many varieties available!

C: Oh, that's easy. Get the organic. That's always the best choice. I wish it were more affordable, but … it's worth it to spend money on healthy food.

H: Well …, it's actually not such a simple choice. If you're thinking about the health of the planet, locally grown food can be a better choice than organic.

C: What do you mean? I don't care who grows it – I don't want to eat food that's been sprayed with chemicals.

H: Well, if the organic produce isn't grown locally, if it's flown or trucked in from far away, it leaves a huge carbon footprint.

C: Carbon footprint?

H: Yes. Aeroplanes, ships, lorries, and so on produce a lot of carbon gases – especially aeroplanes – so produce that is transported a long way has a large carbon footprint. We should try to buy more things that are locally produced. Of course, if you can find local *and* organic, that's great. But sometimes you have to just make the best choice possible.

C: I hadn't thought of it that way before, but you have a good point. Also, a lot of these organic products are in plastic packaging, and most plastic isn't biodegradable. So that's not good for the environment either.

H: I know! I can't believe that! They have strict standards for organic foods, but they don't hold the companies accountable for the kinds of packaging they use! The local lettuce, you'll see, isn't in any packaging at all. It's just loose.

C: OK, so local lettuce it is. Well, that's one thing I'm doing right. Also, I brought my own bags. Just because plastic bags are disposable, that doesn't mean you have to throw them away – they're still reusable ... And … Hanna?

H: Yeah?

C: After saying all that about packaging, you should really reconsider that fancy bottled water you just picked up. It isn't in a returnable bottle.

H: No … but it is recyclable – see, it has the symbol on the bottom.

C: I know, but why not just drink tap water? I read that most bottled waters aren't really any better than what comes out of your tap. I bookmarked a few links, in fact, which I can show you when we get home …

🎧 2.04

Al = Alex, M = Martin, A = Ana

Al: I'm in my overdraft again! Where does my money go?!

M: I know. Money seems to disappear like water. That said, there are things you can do to stretch your income.

Al: Well, I try to buy things on sale, and I don't buy a lot of clothes or whatever, but I just don't seem to have any extra money. I mean, I can never afford to go on holiday or do anything special. But then again, I guess I shouldn't complain because at least I'm always able to pay my bills.

A: Alex, do you make a monthly budget for yourself? I was having the same problem as you for

Audioscript 127

a long time. Then one month, having just received a *terrifying* credit card bill, I decided it was time for a change. I started following a monthly budget, and it's really helped me get my finances under control. Although actually, I haven't been sticking to my budget very well lately, so I need to be a little more careful.

M: Ana's right. I decided to keep a record of all the money I spent each month for a year. I wrote down everything, even things like a pen or a chocolate bar. Having kept that record, I realised that I was an impulse buyer. You know, you go to the shop to buy printer ink and you leave with about five other things that you hadn't even planned on buying.

A: Yeah, and you probably didn't actually need at least three of those things. I used to think it was too much trouble to make a shopping list, but if you make a list and stick to it, it keeps you from buying a lot of unnecessary stuff on impulse.

Al: Well, I thought I was fairly careful about what I bought, but having thought about it, I guess I probably do tend to buy stuff on impulse. On second thoughts, I need to budget my money a little better and cut down on buying little things I don't really need.

M: Yeah, it's the little things that we tend to waste money on. Of course, having said that, I do think you have to allow yourself a treat now and then, if you see something you really, really like. It isn't good to be *too* strict about money.

A: Yes, I agree.

UNIT 8

Artistic licence

🎧 2.05

Good morning. I'll begin this course on Surrealism by giving a brief introduction to the genre and to some of the most important Surrealist artists.

Surrealism was a European trend in art and literature that began in 1924. For some artists, it was a rejection of the harsh realities of war in Europe, first in World War I and later in World War II. Other artists used this style to present a critical illustration of those realities.

The school of Surrealism grew out of the theories of psychoanalyst Sigmund Freud, who believed that conscious thought accounted for only part of reality. He thought that our dreams represented a larger reality, or 'sur-reality', that exists in the subconscious part of our brains. The prefix 'sur', as you probably know, means 'over' or 'above', but also includes the meaning of 'additional' or 'beyond'. So something that is 'surreal' is 'beyond' our normal view of reality.

There were a number of extremely talented and famous Surrealists, but of all of them, the one you are probably most familiar with is Salvador Dalí. Dalí was a controversial and dramatic person, which meant he fit in perfectly with the unconventional Surrealist school. Nevertheless, many art critics and fellow artists felt he did not take art seriously.

At first, Dalí's work appears to be simply a strange and often humorous combination of unrelated objects. One painting features things like elephants and swans; another features people, eggs and dogs; and melting clocks with ants on them feature in another. Furthermore, the objects may be stretched out of proportion or cut into parts. You probably all recognise that first image, and you'll be writing tonight about what it could mean. The title gives a clue, doesn't it? *The Persistence of Memory*. Do you remember all events from your past equally well? Or do you perhaps remember some events of your childhood easily, while you can't remember everything you did last weekend? You'll probably want to explore that concept in your essay. Dalí also included a number of symbols in his paintings, and you'll see the same ones appear often. Ants, for example, represent decay or decomposition – the breaking down of materials.

Now, the next Surrealist painter is interesting for several reasons. First, although the Surrealists were primarily in Europe, there were several artists who moved from Europe to the Americas and brought Surrealist ideas with them. Dalí was one of them, as he spent time living in the United States; however, Surrealism had a greater impact in Latin America. This painting is by Leonora Carrington, who was originally from Britain but moved to Mexico after World War II. Two other artists were primarily responsible for the popularity of Surrealism in Mexico: Remedios Varo, originally from Spain, and Frida Kahlo, born in Mexico.

The importance of these last three artists cannot be stressed enough, first because they expanded the influence of Surrealism, and second because they were women. You'll be seeing much more of these three Surrealists during the course. Now, let's look at …

🎧 2.08

A = Asha, An = Anna

A: Oh, look. Here's a painting by Trinh Tuan. I've seen some other work by this artist.

An: Yeah, I'm just reading the description here. Hmm. I don't know if I agree with this interpretation. Often I wonder if the people who write these – and art critics in general – actually know very much about non-traditional art. What they say often seems unoriginal and uninteresting to me.

A: Yeah, and I often think that the stuff they write can be pretty incomprehensible, too. But still, the person who wrote this description makes some good points. For instance, it's true that Trinh Tuan has a recurring theme of strong emotions in his work.

An: Sure, I can see that from this painting. There definitely seems to be some emotion going on there, and it looks pretty negative. But it seems like too big an assumption on the part of the writer to say that this is an unloving, mismatched couple. I mean, where does the person get that from? I think the painting is misunderstood and misinterpreted on this label.

A: Yeah, OK, I get what you mean. I guess the people in the painting could be friends or relatives who are just disagreeing about something, right?

An: Exactly. Art 'experts' say such incredible things sometimes. And it's really just one person's opinion.

A: So what would *you* say about this painting?

An: Oh. Well, I guess I'd say that you get a sense of loneliness … like being isolated or apart, and maybe anger, but I don't think you can tell what the relationship between the people is. Maybe it's not important. And I don't think the black lines are meant to symbolise … an 'invisible wall'. Maybe the guy just likes to paint figures with black outlines.

A: What do you think about the title of the painting? The label doesn't explain that.

An: I don't know. Maybe Trinh has a really pessimistic view of what happens when people and relationships get older. But I wouldn't write that in a description like this because it's only one interpretation.

A: OK, OK, I get your point.

2.10

Visitors to our city admire the beautiful stone carvings on the historic buildings in the city centre. The carvings bring pleasure to both residents and tourists, and those tourists in turn bring money into the city. That's why it's important to protect our beautiful buildings from something that's threatening to destroy them: pigeons. These birds harm the carvings in several ways – they break off bits of the stone when they stand on the buildings and when they build nests on them, and their droppings contain chemicals that erode the materials. Three solutions to the pigeon problem have been proposed: poisoning the pigeons; hiring people to chase them away; and covering the carvings with metal nets. Poisoning pigeons is, in my opinion, a terrible idea. We can't be sure only one type of bird will eat the poison, and furthermore, larger birds and other predators will eat the dead pigeons and be poisoned themselves. Hiring people to chase them away is a better idea but costly and ineffective. It would require too many people and, as you know if you've ever chased pigeons away yourself, they come straight back. The best of these solutions is to protect the carvings with metal nets. Some people object to this because it will make the carvings a bit harder to see, but that is a better outcome than losing the carvings entirely. I have seen this solution implemented in other cities, and it doesn't look that unattractive. Let's protect our beautiful buildings so that future generations can enjoy them as much as we do.

UNIT 9

Just playing?

2.11

R = Radio presenter, B = Barbara

R: Welcome to *Then and Now*. Today, we're talking to people of different ages about their experiences of play. First up is Barbara. Now, Barbara, you're 64. How do you think children's play is different today?

B: Well, Greg, it's been a long time since I was a child, playing outside with other kids, and a lot has changed. You can see why. There's so much more traffic now than back then, and so many more threats that children face. So I'm not blaming parents, but it seems a shame to me. We had such fun making up our own games. One minute we were pirates, and the next we were cops and robbers. We didn't need all these electronic games that I see my grandchildren playing. We just used our imaginations, something children today don't seem to be very good at. And I certainly never told my mum that I was bored!

2.12

R = Radio presenter, B = Becky, M = Maarten

R: Thanks, Barbara. Next up is Becky. Becky, you're a mum. Do your children play differently from how you used to play?

B: Well, as far as electronic games, of course, children today do play different types of games from the ones I used to play because we only had very basic video games when I was a child. Some of the video games today are really great because they help kids with literacy and numeracy. However, I don't think the way kids play has really changed that much. My kids always spend a lot of time playing outside with other kids in the neighbourhood. They play sports and lots of other games that kids play, just like we did. They make up games and do all kinds of creative things, both indoors and outdoors, so I think if parents encourage them to do that, they will.

R: That's interesting, Becky. Finally, we have Maarten, who's 25. Maarten, how do you think play has changed?

M: There have been changes even since I was a child. I didn't spend much time outdoors – I would visit friends' houses – but we were free to do what we wanted. Our parents would just leave us alone to play, whether we spent time playing video games or making up our own games. These days, it's different. I have nieces and nephews, and their time is much more organised. Their parents take them to play centres. I'm sure they have fun there, but I wonder if they're missing out on some freedom and creativity.

R: Thanks, Maarten. That's a good point. We'll be right back after this break …

2.13

Conversation 1

P = Paolo, J-C = Jean-Claude

P: Hey, Jean-Claude.

J-C: Oh, hi, Paolo. What's up?

P: Not much. Hey, I'm getting a few people together to play some five-a-side after class this afternoon. You up for it?

J-C: Sounds great! I have to send a couple of emails after class, but that should only take a few minutes. Don't start without me!

P: OK, that's cool, but don't take too long. See you later!

J-C: Bye!

Conversation 2

DS = Dr Soares, P = Paul, O = Olivia

DS: Olivia and Paul, I wanted to talk to you because I'd like to invite you to a special event. Several of the top Latin American authors are speaking at the Newton Centre on Friday afternoon. Would you like to go?

P: Yes, I'd love to go. Thanks, Dr Soares. What time does it start?

DS: It's from four to six.

P: That's fine. I'll definitely be there.

DS: Oh, I'm glad. It's important that you be there a few minutes before four in order to get a good seat. What about you, Olivia?

O: I'd really like to go, but unfortunately, I won't be able to. I'm going away for the weekend on Friday afternoon. Thank you very much for inviting me, though …

DS: You're welcome. I'm sorry you can't make it. Paul, I'll see you there.

P: Yes, and thanks again.

Conversation 3

L = Lin, S = Sarah

L: Sarah! Wait! I want to ask you something.

S: Oh, hi, Lin. Is everything OK? Do you want to borrow my notes again?
L: No, I think I'm up to date. Listen, I'm thinking about going to the cinema tonight. Want to go?
S: Sorry, can't do it tonight. I have to help my roommate with a project. Can I take a rain check?
L: Oh, come on. Can't you get out of it?
S: No. I promised to help her. She has to turn it in in a couple of days. Maybe later this week?
L: Yeah, sure. Maybe Thursday or Friday?
S: Yeah. I'll give you a call.

UNIT 10

Fact or fiction

2.16

Conversation 1

A: What are you looking at?
B: Oh, it's a travel article on China.
A: Oh, yeah, I see … yeah, the Great Wall. The only manmade monument that's visible from space. I'd love to see that some day.
B: You know, that's actually not true. It's a common misconception.
A: Are you sure? I've heard that more than once.
B: Sorry, it's a myth. In fact, according to this article, it's doubly false. Not only can it NOT be seen from space, but other manmade structures can.
A: So why have I heard it so often? Was it some sort of hoax? I mean, did someone just lie about it?
B: I don't really know, but I don't think so. I bet someone was just exaggerating, and then someone else heard it and thought it was true and told someone else, and so on. I don't think, you know, that anyone would tell a fake story like that on purpose, especially since it's something that can be shown to be wrong.
A: Well, I can see how that could happen. I mean, it sounds believable.
B: It does. But …
A: I know, I know! It's not true. I won't forget, I promise. And I still want to go there anyway.

Conversation 2

C: Isn't it funny how things you always accept as fact sometimes turn out not to be true?
D: Yeah, I know what you mean. People just repeat them so many times that everyone thinks they're valid.
C: Yeah, like 'You only use 10% of your brain.' Everyone said that when I was a kid. I was sure it was some kind of scientific fact.
D: Me too! How funny. I wonder where that came from.
C: Who knows? Maybe it's just the sort of thing that sounds true. But when you read articles about that, they always have to start out by saying, 'Now this story is not true. In fact, we actually use all of our brains …'
D: Yeah, you're right. There are still more people who believe the myth than the reality, I bet. Well, people are gullible, you know?

Conversation 3

E: Hey, have you ever heard that myth that if you shave, your hair will grow back thicker and stronger?
F: Wait … that's not true?
E: No, of course not. The hair that's on the outside of your body is dead. Nothing you do to dead cells is going to change them.
F: I don't know … I mean, I think I've noticed when I shave my face …
E: No, you only think you've noticed that. You believe it, so you see it. It's possible the new hair feels thicker, or something, but the reality is, the hair is just the same.
F: Well, I'm going to have to test that somehow.
E: Hey, if you don't believe me, look it up online and you'll see it's a phoney claim!

2.20

C = Carrie, M = Mary, E = Elsa

Part 1

C: Wow, I just read this really interesting book for my business class. I think you'd like it.
M: Uh … I dunno …I mean, I kinda doubt that … I'm not really much of a business person, you know?
C: Yeah, but you are a Twitter addict, Carrie. Elsa, you too, right?
E: Sorry, a what?

Part 2

C: A Twitter addict. Someone who uses Twitter all the time.
E: Well, not all the time …
M: Guilty! I do. So, what's the book about?
C: It's about viral loops. But it uses Twitter as a well-known example.
M: Is that like viral marketing?
C: It's a little different. It's a growing phenomenon that …
E: Wait. I don't know what 'viral marketing' means.

Part 3

M: Well, I don't know the exact accepted definition, but it's like a kind of advertising, you know, where, like, one person really likes a product or something, and then that person tells all her friends, and her friends tell all their friends, and so the news spreads really fast …
E: Hey, slow down! Sorry, can you say that again?
M: Oh, sorry. Imagine one person really likes, um, a new brand of jeans.
E: Jeans.
M: Yeah. And so she tells her friends, maybe ten friends. And each of those ten friends tells ten other friends …
E: OK, I see.
C: Yeah, companies love it, of course, because that kind of advertising doesn't cost them anything. And it works because people trust their friends.

Part 4

E: But you said … the other thing … is different.
C: A viral loop, yes. It's related, but … think of something like Twitter. If you join, it's only interesting if all your friends join. With Mary's example of the jeans, see, if your friends don't want to buy those jeans, you wouldn't be that upset. But with things like social networking sites, you know, Twitter and such, the more people who are on them, the more people want to be on them. So it's a never-ending loop – more and more people keep trying to join.
M: Um … I always get this feeling with you, Carrie, like you're being really clear and stuff, but then when I try to put it into my own words, I realise I'm totally lost.

E: OK, you just lost me.
M: Sorry! I know I speak really fast.
C: Yeah, I can confirm that!
M: I meant, that I think I understand you, and then I realise I don't really. I still don't really understand the difference between viral marketing and a viral loop.

Part 5
C: So … you should read the book, then. You can buy it at lots of bookshops.
M: What? You're not even going to offer to lend me yours?
C: Well, you know what they say, right, Elsa? 'Neither a borrower nor a lender be.'
E: Um … what does that mean?
C: Don't borrow things, and don't lend them. That way, you'll avoid a lot of arguments later on.
E: Ah, OK. We have a similar saying in my country.

2.21

In general, I'm firmly of the opinion that schools have a responsibility to teach pupils about internet scams and dangers. Not only do I believe that, but I would also argue that schools should do all they can to protect young people online. The primary reason for my opinion is the fact that young people are spending more and more of their lives online, leaving them open to all kinds of hoaxes, scams and potentially dangerous people. Only by learning how to judge the information they see can they avoid becoming victims. My opinion is also based on my own experience of becoming the victim of a phishing email. I have no doubt that a short time spent learning about scams such as this would have helped me avoid a very difficult personal situation. Of course, schools should spend the majority of their time on academic subjects. However, it seems to me that schools should also make pupils aware of potential dangers they face online.

UNIT 11

Music to my ears

2.22

A = Amy, E = Emma, An = Andrew
A: … and when he started playing, I couldn't believe it. He was amazing! I had no idea he was going to be so good.
E: What's that, Amy?
A: I was just telling Andrew about the street performer we saw the other day, Emma.
E: Oh, yeah. He was great. I wish I had that kind of talent. I guess you either have what it takes or you don't. Maths I can do, but music …
An: Is that what it is, though? Is it talent?
E: What do you mean?
An: Well, I'm not sure that the idea of talent is very useful. I've been reading about multiple intelligences. The idea is that we don't have just one intelligence. We have lots of different intelligences: verbal intelligence, visual intelligence, mathematical intelligence and so on. One of those is musical intelligence. It covers some of the things you might think of when you think of musical talent, but it also covers lots of other things.
E: What kind of things?
An: Well, suppose you had high musical intelligence. You might play a musical instrument, or have a good sense of rhythm. But you also might respond to sounds emotionally, or you might use rhythm to help you learn something. For example, if you had to learn some facts for a test, you might make up a short poem or a song to help you remember them.
A: Oh, I do that sometimes! Hey, maybe I'm a musical genius! So, there would be no point in learning an instrument unless you had musical intelligence?
An: No, no. It's a skill you can get better at. If you practise and if you pay attention to the right things, anyone can increase their musical intelligence.

2.23

A = Amy, E = Emma, An = Andrew
An: So, what do you each think about your own musical intelligence? What about you, Amy?
A: Well, I always thought I didn't have any musical talent, but now that you've explained musical intelligence, I'm not so sure. I don't play an instrument, but I love music and I've always got it on in the background while I'm working.
An: That's part of musical intelligence, yes. Do you like to have music while you work, Emma?
E: Definitely not. There has to be complete silence or I can't concentrate. I don't really have a lot of music, so I don't listen to it very often. It's just not a big part of my life.
A: Oh, I'm the opposite! I love going to concerts, and I've got tons of different kinds of music on my computer. I'll listen to anything. I always have a song going through my head.
An: You see? People think that if they don't play an instrument or write songs, then they don't have musical talent. But that's the wrong way of looking at it. Enjoying music is just as important. I do play an instrument – the piano – and I'm quite good at it, but I'm a terrible singer! So, you see, you can be good at some aspects of musical intelligence, but not at others.
A: That's really interesting, Andrew. Where did you say you found out about it?
A: In a book I'm reading. I'll lend it to you if you like.

2.24

N = Nicole, L = Liam
N: Hey, I heard about a great file-sharing website with all the best music. It's totally free and you don't need an account or anything.
L: Oh, yeah?
N: Yeah. Listen, my internet connection speed is really slow, so if I gave you the web address, could you download some stuff for me? Then I can copy it onto my computer.
L: Uh, I'm not sure. I have a lot of stuff going on this week.
N: No hurry, whenever you can do it is fine.
L: You know, to be honest, I'd feel kind of uncomfortable doing that.
N: Really? Why?
L: It's just that I don't think piracy is right. The thing is that it violates copyright laws, and well, that's a form of stealing. I mean, it's just my opinion, but I think we need to pay musicians for their work.
N: What if you downloaded just a couple of tracks?

L: I'm sorry, but I really can't. But listen, I recently subscribed to a new media service. You pay a monthly fee, and you can stream as much music as you want. Tracks can be stored for up to 30 days. Why don't you check it out? I can show you the site and help you set it up if you want.

N: OK, maybe I'll do that. Thanks.

UNIT 12

Down to Earth

2.27

I = Ivan, R = Rachel

I: Uh, yeah, it was quite important, I think. I mean, it's going to be on the test, so …

I: So it was on how mountain ranges and, well, individual mountains too, I suppose, are formed. And there are, let's see, three major ways.

I: OK, you were there for the lecture on plate tectonics, right? On Tuesday?

I: Well, sometimes the plates drift apart, too. Then hot rock from the Earth's crust comes up through the open space, bursts out through the top, and when the rock cools again, you have yourself a new mountain.

R: Oh, like a volcano, right? Like, oh, in Hawaii and that one in the Philippines?

I: And then there's erosion, like when coastlines get worn down by wind and water … that just wear away at the surface of the Earth and change its shape. OK, that's it.

2.28

I = Ivan, R = Rachel

I: Hey, Rachel, where were you yesterday? You missed the lecture.

R: Yeah, I know … I had a dentist's appointment. I couldn't get out of it.

I: Oh, that's a shame. I hope you're feeling OK now.

R: Yeah, I'm OK. So what did I miss? Anything, you know, incredibly important?

I: Uh, yeah, it was quite important, I think. I mean, it's going to be on the test, so …

R: OK, so can you explain it to me? Please?

I: Well … Actually, yeah, it'll help me remember it to explain it to you. Let me just get my notes. OK. So it was on how mountain ranges and, well, individual mountains too, I suppose, are formed. And there are, let's see, three major ways.

R: Sorry, how many?

I: Three.

R: Three … ways. And they are?

I: OK, you were there for the lecture on plate tectonics, right? On Tuesday?

R: Um, on plate tectonics, oh, the lecture, yeah, right.

I: Plate tectonics. So picture two of these plates, moving towards each other … slowly, yeah, but they're still moving, and then they collide. Like this. If one plate goes under the other, it pushes the crust up, and that makes a mountain range. Like the Himalayas. That's called subduction.

R: Sub … duction. Wouldn't that cause an earthquake, too?

I: Yes, it usually does.

R: OK, next?

I: Well, sometimes the plates drift apart, too. Then hot rock from the Earth's crust comes up through the open space, bursts out through the top, and when the rock cools again, you have yourself a new mountain.

R: Oh, like a volcano, right? Like, oh, in Hawaii and that one in the Philippines?

I: Exactly. A lot of islands are actually the tops of volcanoes.

R: Huh. I didn't know that.

I: And then there's erosion, like when coastlines get worn down by wind and water that just wear away at the surface of the Earth and change its shape. OK, that's it. Remember that …

R: Hang on, I didn't catch that. What's the third way?

I: Erosion. Wind and water.

R: Just a second. Was that water?

I: Yeah. Wind and water.

R: And that makes mountains? That's hard to believe …

I: Well, it changes the shape of the existing landscape, so … yeah. I guess. That wasn't completely clear to me.

R: Maybe it's in our book. Or I could just check online. Thanks so much!

2.29

T = Tour guide, M = Man

T: Welcome to Racetrack Playa, folks. Now, let's look at the famous moving rocks. As you can see, this one is pretty big. Not something you would think you could move on your own. What do you think causes these rocks to move such incredibly long distances? Anyone? Well one popular theory is wind. Not a steady breeze, but a short, powerful gust of wind. The wind here can blow – just briefly, of course – at speeds of up to 145 kilometres per hour.

M: Wow, that's strong. So has anyone ever seen this happen?

T: Well, no, it's never been observed.

M: Could animals be pushing the rocks?

T: Well, there's no reason why an animal would do this. To push a rock of this size would also take a great deal of strength, and no animals living here are big or strong enough. There isn't any evidence to support this theory, but it is one we hear from time to time.

M: You know, I bet it's kids or teenagers doing it as a kind of joke.

T: Well, it's certainly something I can imagine teens doing. But remember, all we see is the rocks and the tracks. If people were moving these, we'd see evidence like tyre tracks or footprints. Any other guesses …

2.30

T = Tour guide, M = Man, W = Woman

W: So what *is* the explanation?

T: Well, a long-standing theory was that the rocks actually slide along a sheet of ice, again possibly pushed by the wind.

W: Wait a minute. Ice? In the desert?

T: Well, it gets pretty cold here at night, especially in the winter. This land right here has been completely covered in ice before.

W: But I suppose no one had ever seen this happen?

T: That is correct, ma'am. Until December 2013, when two researchers observed the process. Their report showed that rare rainfalls created a shallow water layer on the dry terrain. This froze overnight, and then in the morning as the temperatures increased, the ice broke into thin sheets. Gentle winds pushed the floating ice into the boulders, in turn pushing the rocks over the wet, muddy ground.

M: Incredible. I guess sometimes the truth is stranger than fiction …

2.33

C = Counsellor, N = Noel

C: All right, Noel, let's look at your qualifications and assess what's out there for you.

N: The problem is that although I've had several jobs, I don't have any job experience related to my degree field.

C: That's not necessarily true.

N: My degree is in management and finance, but I've just had part-time jobs to help with my expenses while I was at school. For example, I worked in a doctor's office one summer, but I was just answering the phone and setting up the appointment schedules. Well, also I received payments and made bank deposits.

C: So you were in charge of the payment records and the appointment books.

N: That's right. And for two terms I worked in a restaurant as a waiter. So that's not really a great recommendation.

C: Noel, the biggest mistake people make is to underestimate the skills they develop in jobs that supposedly have no relevance to their field.

N: What do you mean?

C: I mean that you have a lot more to put on a CV than you think you do! First, you have what we call 'hard skills'. Hard skills are things that you have learnt that are directly related to your field. In your case, you have a degree from a university of high standing in the field of business. That means you have a very good knowledge of the most up-to-date theories in economics, you have excellent IT skills with programs related to your field and you have excellent maths skills. All of those things are hard skills that can be emphasised in your CV, and they are the job-specific skills that your potential employer will look for in order to decide whether you are qualified for the job.

N: OK, but how do my jobs fit in?

C: They fit in with two other important factors: experience and soft skills. You don't have work experience in your professional area, but you do have work experience. Do you have, or can you get, letters of recommendation from your former employers?

N: Of course. They told me they would be happy to give me recommendations.

C: Excellent. If you hadn't already proven yourself to be a good employee, you wouldn't feel so confident about getting those recommendations. OK. Now we come to the third factor, soft skills. I think you will be pleased to find out that your part-time jobs have helped you develop a number of valuable soft skills.

N: What are soft skills?

C: They're called soft skills because they are not as tangible and obvious as hard skills, and they're not related to a specific academic field or profession. Soft skills include abilities like problem-solving, critical thinking, time management, organisation, self-confidence, the ability to motivate people and so on. They are important in any field. There are many soft skills, and these days, employers often value these skills as much as or more than degree credentials or work experience. Your soft skills can make the difference between being good at what you do and excellent at what you do. You can imagine which type of candidate potential employers would like to hire eventually.

N: Wow. I didn't know that.

C: Yes. So now let's see where you stand in terms of soft skills. I'm going to ask you to stand back and look at yourself critically as I ask you some questions about your relationships with people, your life experiences and your work experiences. And by critically, I don't mean negatively. I mean objectively. If you are good at something, say so and give me an example. If you are not so good at something, be honest with yourself. There are things you can do to improve soft skills that you are weak in. OK?

N: OK. I'm ready.

2.34

Having studied English for a number of years now, I'm completely confident that it will play a big part in both my career and my personal life. As a consequence, I can see the need to develop my abilities in English away from the classroom and my formal education. This implies that I have to come up with practical ideas to use my English in a variety of contexts. First and foremost, it's important to maintain contact with other speakers of the language. This can be done through online groups and social networks, as well as by keeping in touch with my fellow students beyond the end of my course. What's more, I'm aware of the need to interact with people from a broad range of cultures to widen my knowledge and experience.

Besides that, reading a range of material in English will both broaden my vocabulary and inform me about current issues. In a similar way, listening to internet radio programmes or podcasts on different subjects will help me develop my own opinions, in addition to providing practice in understanding a variety of accents.

To briefly sum up, there are specific practical steps you can take to become responsible for your own learning, and we each need to decide what we think will work for us.

WORKBOOK ANSWER KEY

UNIT 1

Section 1
Exercise A
Paragraph 1: Those aspects of our lives that we really cherish are so valuable because they do not have a price attached.
Paragraph 2: Not surprisingly, most utopias were planned to succeed without money. Yet societies that went without it inevitably failed.
Paragraph 3: The problem is what we value in itself and what we put a price on are often inextricably linked.
Paragraph 4: The objects in our lives that we really value – the stuff we cannot bear to throw away – mark out relationships that we value: a memento from a holiday, a picture from a wedding and toys kept from childhood.

Exercise B
Possible answers:
Paragraph 1: Imagine, for example, asking, 'How much do I owe you for that?' after a friend gives you advice. / Poets do not write for stock options. / Good relationships do not need insurance policies. / People do not need incentives to love each other.
Paragraph 2: Cities have functioned without money … / experiments such as time banks and local economic trading schemes have been talked about rather than implemented.
Paragraph 3: The paid-for meals were simply a way of expressing our love. / The cover price of a great book never captures its value.
Paragraph 4: a memento from a holiday, a picture from a wedding, and toys kept from childhood/homes/huge social gatherings – festivals, carnivals, sporting events

Exercise C
1 T 2 NM 3 F 4 T

Section 2
1 sustainable
2 consume
3 forage
4 barter
5 factory farming
6 livelihoods
7 sweatshops
8 skips

Section 3
Exercise A
1 c in recent times
2 d on a daily basis
3 b online
4 e by exchanging things
5 a in order to save money

Exercise B
1 d on a regular basis
2 a across the country
3 h to fill your cupboards
4 g through a traditional barter system
5 b by looking for
6 e on our Events page
7 f on the final weekend of each month
8 c next Saturday

Section 4
Exercise A
1 throw in
2 drop, off
3 condition, in good working order
4 up for grabs
5 second-hand

What's right?
I'll throw it in, as an added incentive.

Exercise B
1 second-hand
2 throw it in
3 up for grabs
4 in good working order
5 condition
6 drop them off

Section 5
Exercise A
1 reluctant
2 politely
3 agrees

Exercise B
1 guess
2 argue that
3 pretty sure
4 tend to think
5 more or less
6 seems to me

Section 6
1 haven't, No
2 Don't, No
3 Isn't, Yes
4 Doesn't, No
5 shouldn't, Yes
6 Didn't, No

What's right?
B: Yes, I have.

SkillsStudio
Exercise A
1 T 2 F 3 F

Exercise B
1 a 2 a 3 b 4 a 5 a 6 b

Exercise C
1 c 2 a 3 a 4 b 5 b 6 c 7 c

Exercise D
Student's own answers

UNIT 2

Section 1
1 public relations
2 rivals
3 infrastructure
4 press conference
5 prototype
6 inspired
7 giant
8 gain a lead
9 launched
10 lobby

Section 2
Exercise A
1 be taken
2 be transferred
3 be docked
4 circle
5 wear

Exercise B
1 More people could be accommodated in the floating hotel in the future.
2 The plan is to launch the first guests next year, but critics say it may be delayed.
3 Tourists will be taken to space by an expert team of astronauts.
4 Tourists could be charged up to $5 million for a total of four nights in space.
5 If the four-day space trips become popular, the price could be reduced eventually.
6 In 15 years, these kinds of trips might be seen as normal by your children.

What's right?
Passengers will be taken into space by an experienced crew.

Exercise C
1 will be given; D
2 will be held; D
3 will not (won't) be expected; D
4 might be changed; P
5 may be offered; P
6 could be brought down; P
7 may be made; P
8 will not (won't) be seen; D

Section 3
Exercise A
the USA – 3
the UK – 4
Australia – 2
India – 1

Exercise B
a) Speaker 2
b) Speaker 4
c) Speaker 1
d) Speaker 3
e) Speaker 2
f) Speaker 4

Section 4
Exercise A
1 in-
2 un-
3 in-
4 un-
5 im-
6 im-
7 in-
8 in-

Exercise B
1 insufficient
2 unbelievable
3 impatient
4 insignificant
5 uncertain
6 inaccurate
7 improbable
8 incapable

Exercise C
1 incapable; insufficient
2 inaccurate; uncertain
3 improbable; insignificant
4 unbelievable
5 impatient

Section 5
Exercise A
1 d 2 f 3 a 4 b 5 c 6 e

What's right?
Unless you have been to space, it is hard to appreciate the beauty of it.

Exercise B
1 provided that
2 as long as
3 unless
4 in case
5 since
6 Provided that

Section 6
Exercise A
Paragraph 1 Introduction: B Children – and adults – dream of becoming astronauts. Mention why.
Paragraph 2 Advantages: A Present some of the positive aspects of being an astronaut.
Paragraph 3 Disadvantages: D Analyse some of the less appealing sides of the job, including training.
Paragraph 4 Conclusion: C I believe the effort is worth it. Summarise main reason for my opinion.

Exercise B
a) 3   b) 4   c) 2   d) 1   e) 3   f) 2

Exercise C
1 NR   2 A   3 A   4 D   5 NR   6 D

SkillsStudio
Exercise A
1 d 2 e 3 f 4 g 5 b 6 h 7 c 8 a

Exercise B
1 Mars
2 colonise
3 health
4 investment

Exercise C
1 200
2 4
3 200,000
4 8
5 1,000
6 6 billion

Exercise D
1 F   2 T   3 T   4 F   5 F   6 F

Exercise E
Student's own answers

UNIT 3

Section 1
Exercise A
c

Exercise B
Paragraph 2: A tenth of young people are turned down by employers because of material on their social network, according to a report.
Paragraph 3: There is a difference between what young people and employers think is reasonable online conduct, according to the report.
Paragraph 4: Employees are getting into serious trouble for things they say online, even with easy-going employers.
Paragraph 5: If you voice a negative opinion about your job, your employer could see it.
Paragraph 6: Young people should be careful about what they write online.

Section 2
1 information age
2 invaded
3 monitor
4 compiled
5 database
6 scam
7 theft
8 hack into
9 blackmailing
10 leaving yourself open

Section 3
Exercise A
1 Too many of us consider our personal information secure.
2 When a virus destroyed my database, Peter helped me recover it.
3 The man described identity theft as an easy crime.
4 The images from the security camera proved she was a thief.

What's right?
She described him as an honest man.

Exercise B
1 find it
2 reporters as
3 make celebrities really angry
4 rude
5 it strange
6 as the main problem
7 describe them as
8 photographers

Section 4
Exercise A
1 e 2 a 3 d 4 h 5 g 6 c 7 b 8 f

Exercise B
1 ended up
2 run up
3 get hold of
4 clear up
5 taken out

Workbook answer key 135

6 got out of
7 go through
8 calls on

Section 5
Exercise A
1 b 2 b 3 a 4 b 5 b 6 a
Exercise B
1 I don't imagine there's anything
2 I guess not
3 I don't suppose the kids want it
4 they don't feel they have anything
5 I hope I don't have anything
6 I don't think I understand
What's right?
I don't suppose they are interested.

Section 6
Exercise A
1 d 2 h 3 f 4 b 5 i 6 c 7 a
8 e 9 g
Exercise B
a) 3, 4, 9
b) 1, 5, 7
c) 2, 6, 8
Exercise C
1 (Why don't we start by discussing what we all learnt about privacy …)
2 (Who wants to start?)
4 (I don't mean to interrupt you, … but can you speak up a little?)
7 (Maybe we should move on to discussing whether this loss of privacy is a problem …)
8 (So, does anyone else want to add anything before we start writing …?)

SkillsStudio
Exercise A
1 Europe
2 Europe
3 the USA
Exercise B
1 data protection, b
2 fundamental right, f
3 private information, c
4 sensitive data, c
5 strict agreement, a
6 tax records, e
7 postcode, d
Exercise C
Paragraph 1 e
Paragraph 2 j
Paragraph 3 c
Paragraph 4 a
Paragraph 5 i
Paragraph 6 k
Paragraph 7 f
Paragraph 8 d
Headings b, g, h are not needed
Exercise D
Student's own answers

UNIT 4

Section 1
Exercise A
1 c 2 f 3 e 4 b 5 d 6 a
Exercise B
1 dropped out of
2 had been/were faced with
3 getting
4 set
5 am, faced with
6 offers a broad range of
7 take, into
8 get

Section 2
Exercise A
1 wherever
2 whatever
3 Whoever
4 However
5 whenever
What's right?
Whatever you cook for dinner, I'm sure it will be delicious.
Exercise B
I hope you don't mind me writing to you. My name is Pascale Dubois, and I took your film studies class last term. I enjoyed it very much! <u>Whatever we studied topic</u>, you always stimulated the class. So, I'd really like to take your class again, but I have some questions.
This coming term, I see that you're teaching Advanced Film Studies, but it's an online class. So, does that mean we can view each week's material <u>whoever</u> we want, or is there an assigned meeting time for viewing? Also, I noticed that there are four essays we need to submit across the term. Do we have to submit online, or can we submit <u>whenever</u> we want (for example, giving to you in person, leaving in your postbox, and so on)? Finally, whoever wants to join the class <u>are</u> able to – is that correct? I'm asking because my friend is actually studying economics, but he's heard really good things about your class and he wants to take it too.
1 Whatever topic we studied, you always stimulated the class
2 So, does that mean we can view each week's material whenever we want, or is there an assigned meeting time for viewing?
3 Do we have to submit online, or can we submit however we want (for example, giving to you in person, leaving in your postbox, and so on)?
4 Finally, whoever wants to join the class is able to – is that correct?

Section 3
Exercise A
Speaker 1: Germany
Speaker 2: Brazil
Speaker 3: United Arab Emirates
Exercise B
1 c 2 a 3 b 4 a 5 c 6 c

Section 4
Exercise A
1 b 2 a
What's right?
If I had paid more attention in IT, I would know more now.
Exercise B
1 hadn't
2 would
3 had
4 wouldn't
5 would
6 hadn't
Exercise C
1 would have chosen / would choose
2 hadn't invested
3 would have preferred / would prefer
4 wouldn't lose / wouldn't have lost
5 hadn't promoted
6 would stay

Section 5
1 standing
2 stand a chance
3 It stands to reason
4 where, standing
5 standards
6 stand out
7 outstanding
8 stood back

Section 6
Exercise A
1 Because; And
2 however; Even though
3 Although; since
4 Therefore, but
Exercise B
1 Because the young are more interested in the life of reality show celebrities and other so-called stars, they don't care about important issues anymore.
2 I sort of agree with you; however, has it occurred to you that the fault lies with the media itself, not with the young or the parents?
3 Even though the majority of people want to be informed about important issues, a lot of media attention is on scandal and gossip.
4 Although you're right to say students could help themselves more, it's unfair to blame them since the cost of getting a degree is huge.

136

5 Therefore, it stands to reason that today's parents are the parents of tomorrow's leaders.
6 You blame the young, but maybe you should stand back from the situation and take a good look at today's parents!

SkillsStudio
Exercise A
1 b 2 c 3 a
Exercise B
1 g 2 a 3 e 4 c 5 b 6 d 7 f
Exercise C
1 d 2 b 3 c 4 d 5 b
Exercise D
1 15
2 subsidies
3 quality
4 150
5 (>) 70
6 90
7 71
8 900
Exercise E
Student's own answers

UNIT 5

Section 1
Exercise A
1 is believed that
2 is reported to be
3 is understood that
4 are assumed to make
5 are (in fact) said to make
6 is known that
What's right?
Owls are thought to be unlucky in some cultures.
Exercise B
1 considered to be
2 thought that
3 believed to be
4 understood to
5 assumed to be
6 said that
7 claimed to be
8 it can certainly be said

Section 2
Exercise A
1 endangered species
2 wild
3 in captivity
4 smugglers
5 release
6 natural habitat
Exercise B
1 natural habitat
2 wild
3 endangered species
4 in captivity
5 release
6 smugglers

Section 3
Exercise A
1 Pr 2 F 3 Pa 4 Pr 5 Pa 6 F
What's right?
The elephants ought to have been released into the wild.
Exercise B
1 been taken away
2 protected
3 looked after
4 be released
5 be brought up
6 set them free
7 be found
8 be given

Section 4
Exercise A
b
Exercise B
1, 2, 3, 6
Exercise C
Correct order - 4, 3, 2, 5, 1

Section 5
Exercise A
1 a 2 c 3 c 4 a
Exercise B
1 under
2 well
3 over
4 badly/poorly
5 highly

Section 6
Exercise A
1 F 2 T 3 F
Exercise B
2 (or)
4 (a list of examples – Iberian lynx and western gorilla)
5 (– –)
6 (that is)
7 (– –)
8 (known as)
9 (which is)
12 (That is)
14 (a list of examples – African elephant and black-footed ferret)

SkillsStudio
Exercise A
1 plankton
2 plankton
3 bees
Exercise B
1 insight
2 disperse
3 predator
4 diversity
5 evolution
6 bacteria

Exercise C
1 B 2 B 3 A, D 4 B, C 5 A, C
6 B 7 A, B, C 8 A 9 C 10 B
11 C 12 B 13 A 14 D 15 B
Exercise D
Student's own answers

UNIT 6

Section 1
Exercise A
1 will have taken over
2 will have been replaced by
3 will have been improved by
4 won't have invented
5 will have been significantly enhanced by
6 will have developed
What's right?
By the time I graduate, my IT skills will have become obsolete.
Exercise B
1 will have been invented
2 will have been replaced
3 will have made
4 will have been improved
5 will have forgotten
6 will not have lost / won't have lost

Section 2
Exercise A
1 by 2 by 3 on 4 of 5 on 6 of
7 by
Exercise B
a) 7 b) 5 c) 3 d) 1 e) 6 f) 4
g) 2
Exercise C
1 dependent on
2 are, aware of
3 Are, distracted by
4 am suspicious of
5 are alarmed by
6 focus on
7 am, overwhelmed by

Section 3
Exercise A
1 b 2 c 3 a
Exercise B
1 Not really.
2 I didn't know that.
3 I don't agree with you.
4 That will never happen.
5 That's not OK.
Exercise C
1 c and a
2 a
3 c
4 b
5 c and a

Workbook answer key 137

Section 4
Exercise A
1 go after
2 point out
3 pick up
4 go on
5 come about
6 rely on

Exercise B
1 pick up
2 pointed out
3 come about
4 went after
5 going on
6 relying, on

Section 5
Exercise A
1 In 2017, we will have been using ATM machines for 50 years.
2 By the time I retire, I will have been teaching for 20 years.
3 I will have been working for eight hours when I leave the office.
4 In September, we will have been living in this house for 17 years.

What's right?
When I retire, I will have been working for 50 years.

Exercise B
1 will have been studying
2 will have been playing
3 replaces / will have been waiting
4 comes (has come) / will have been working
5 will have been using / buys
6 will have been playing

Section 6
Exercise A
c

Exercise B
1 Robot to Expose Hidden Secrets of the Pyramids
2 Stuart Fox
3 www.technewsdaily.com
4 12th August

Exercise C
1 II 2 MI 3 MI 4 RSI 5 RSI
6 MI 7 II 8 MI 9 RSI 10 RSI
11 RSI

Exercise D
1 The robot will travel very deep in the Great Pyramid of Giza.
2 The room at the end of the Queen's tomb has been closed for thousands of years.
3 The robot has a fibre-optic camera, ultrasonic probe and releasable mini-robot.
4 The robot can fit through spaces as small as 1.8 cm in diameter.
5 This is the third attempt to reach the end of the Queen's tomb shaft.
6 Previous attempts found large doors blocking the way.
7 The robot is especially designed to fit into very tight spaces.
8 Small red marks have been found on the walls of the shaft.
9 The red marks might have religious importance, or could just be ancient graffiti.

SkillsStudio
Exercise A
1 g 2 c 3 d 4 f 5 e 6 a 7 h
8 b

Exercise B
1 Robots that check your health
5 Robots that perform operations
6 Robots that find bombs
8 Robots that help fight crime

Exercise C
1 c 2 a 3 b 4 a 5 d 6 a

Exercise D
1 carry out
2 will have been made
3 point out
4 pick up on

Exercise E
Student's own answers

UNIT 7

Section 1
Exercise A
c

Exercise B
1 Take
2 The implication of this is that
3 What this means is
4 or
5 which means that
6 Examples include
7 such as
8 which

Exercise C
1 unplanned purchases
2 whole shop
3 eye level
4 fewer items
5 regular customer

Section 2
Exercise A
1 b 2 a

What's right?
While I was paying at the checkout, a shop assistant finished packing my bags.

Exercise B
1 when shopping
2 Before going
3 When walking
4 Before buying
5 After seeing
6 While shopping

Section 3
Exercise A
1 edible
2 affordable
3 disposable
4 perishable
5 recyclable
6 biodegradable
7 returnable
8 accountable

Exercise B
1 accountable
2 edible
3 perishable
4 affordable
5 biodegradable
6 recyclable
7 disposable
8 returnable

Section 4
Exercise A
1 Wanting
2 having
3 Being

What's right?
Not wanting to spend too much money, I bought the cheaper T-shirt.

Exercise B
1 Having moved house
2 Being returnable
3 Not understanding
4 Shops, being
5 Knowing
6 Not wanting

Exercise C
1 Owning
2 knowing (*having learnt* is also possible)
3 having done
4 earning
5 being
6 having learnt (*knowing* is also possible)

Section 5
Exercise A
1 e 2 d 3 a 4 f 5 b 6 c

Exercise B
1 F 2 F 3 T 4 T

Exercise C
1 That said
2 Although actually
3 having said that
4 But then again
5 having thought about it
6 On second thoughts

Section 6
Exercise A
1 cut down
2 credit
3 broke
4 stick
5 stretch
6 afford
7 on sale
8 budget

Exercise B
1 afford
2 broke
3 sale
4 credit
5 stretch
6 cut down
7 budget

SkillsStudio
Exercise A
a

Exercise B
1 to no regard
2 let alone
3 spoken up for
4 zero tolerance
5 sacrifice
6 rational
7 conscious
8 well-informed
9 spread the word
10 regulation and policy

Exercise C
1 F 2 T 3 NM 4 F 5 F 6 T
7 F 8 NM 9 F 10 T

Exercise D
Student's own answers

UNIT 8

Section 1
Exercise A
1 b 2 f 3 e 4 d 5 a 6 c

Exercise B
1 too simple
2 didn't try
3 against
4 Paris
5 thinks
6 different from

Section 2
Exercise A
1 school
2 unconventional
3 controversial
4 concept
5 represents
6 symbol
7 in proportion
8 illustration

Exercise B
1 controversial
2 school
3 unconventional
4 proportion
5 concept
6 illustration
7 symbol
8 represent

Section 3
Exercise A
1 Had he not sold his first painting, he might have given up.
2 Had the artist lived longer, he would have produced many more masterpieces.
3 Should you take this art course, be sure to attend every class.
4 Should you want to be an artist, be prepared to work hard for little financial gain.
5 Had Van Gogh not gone to Paris, he wouldn't have met the artist Gauguin.
6 Had we known how talented he was, we would have gone to see the exhibition sooner.

What's right?
Had she not become a lawyer, she would have been an artist.

Exercise B
1 Had the concept ~~have~~ been clearer, more people might have appreciated the work.
2 Should you ~~decided~~ decide to display this controversial work, you're likely to get many complaints.
3 ~~Hadn't the artist~~ Had the artist not included such strong symbols in his paintings, the impact would have been reduced.
4 ~~Should~~ Had you tried a more conventional approach, perhaps the establishment would have been more welcoming of your work.
5 Should the images ~~are~~ be out of proportion, you might have to start again.

Section 4
Exercise A
1 non-
2 un
3 mis
4 un
5 in
6 un
7 in
8 im

Exercise B
1 unable
2 unwilling
3 uninteresting
4 incomprehensible
5 impossible
6 misunderstood

Section 5
Exercise A
1 It's difficult to know where this trend started.
2 It's not easy to tell how he achieved such an intricate effect.
3 It's important for you to explain who you thought would see this graffiti.

What's right?
It's difficult to know if/whether people will like her work.

Exercise B
1 Where can I see interesting exhibitions this weekend?
2 Did the sculpture take a long time to complete?
3 Why do so many people like this sort of art?
4 Who sculpted this?
5 How much would this painting have cost 20 years ago?

Section 6
Exercise A
a) 4 b) 3 c) 1 d) 2

Exercise B
a) 6 b) 4 c) 3 d) 5 e) 2 f) 1

Exercise C
b

SkillsStudio
Exercise A
1 h 2 c 3 a 4 g 5 f 6 e 7 d
8 b

Exercise B
b treatment where patients express and explore themselves through creating art

Exercise C
1 d 2 c 3 b 4 d 5 a 6 b

Exercise D
1 20th
2 feelings
3 connection
4 behaviour
5 depression
6 tiredness
7 life
8 hourly
9 effort
10 usefulness
11 relationship

Exercise E
Student's own answers

UNIT 9

Section 1
Exercise A
1 b 2 e 3 d 4 a
Exercise B
1 d 2 c 3 a 4 b

Section 2
1 outlet
2 imitate
3 Engaging in
4 literacy
5 numeracy
6 open-ended
7 outcome
8 emerge

Section 3
Exercise A
1 not stay
2 have
3 not spend
4 allow
5 not lose
6 not protect
7 keep
8 don't recommend
What's right?
She insisted that he stop playing football in the office.
Exercise B
1 children not grow up
2 a child take risks
3 don't propose
4 your child visit
5 not bring
6 have

Section 4
Exercise A
1 Would you like to try it out?
2 Are you up for it?
3 Yes, I'd love to.
4 Sorry, can't do it.
5 Can I take a rain check?
6 Want to go?
Exercise B
a) 6 Want to go?
b) 4 Sorry, can't do it.
c) 1 Would you like to try it out?
d) 5 Can I take a rain check?
e) 2 Are you up for it?
f) 3 Yes, I'd love to.

Section 5
Exercise A
1 declined
2 accepted
3 declined

Exercise B
Conversation 1: Phrases 2, 5
Conversation 2: Phrases 6, 3
Conversation 3: Phrases 1, 4

Section 6
Exercise A
1 d 2 a 3 e 4 f 5 c 6 b
Exercise B
1 to exercise
2 playing
3 concentrate
4 to do
5 doing
6 play
What's right?
I recommend that he play this game.
I recommend playing this game.
Exercise C
1 to complete
2 do
3 work
4 processing
5 play
6 doing

SkillsStudio
Exercise A
To persuade
Exercise B
1 f touch people
2 a perceived as unproductive
3 g a catalyst for positivity
4 i through their perspective
5 h boosting our productivity
6 d cultivate healing
7 j serious benefits
8 c facilitate deep connections
9 b a guilty pleasure
10 e legendary physician
Exercise C
1 C 2 B 3 F 4 G 5 A 6 D
Paragraph E is not needed
Exercise D
Student's own answers

UNIT 10

Section 1
Exercise A
1 misconception
2 fake
3 hoax
4 gullible
5 phoney
6 myth
Exercise B
1 gullible
2 fake/phoney
3 misconception
4 myth
5 hoax
6 fake/phoney

Section 2
1 Never <u>have I met</u> such gullible people. Tricking them was too easy!
2 The tourist handed over his credit card, but little <u>did he know</u> it was all a hoax to get his money.
3 Only <u>when you</u> start to look into these conspiracy theories do you realise how crazy some of them are.
4 Not only <u>is the story</u> completely fake, it's also offensive to the people mentioned in it.
5 No sooner had he read the article, <u>than</u> he shared the link on his Facebook page.
What's right?
Little did I know, it was all a scam.
Exercise B
1 Only when
2 Barely
3 Never
4 Under no circumstances
5 No sooner

Section 3
Exercise A
1 dismis<u>sal</u>
2 valid<u>ates</u>
3 verifi<u>cation</u>
4 confir<u>med</u>
5 debun<u>king</u>
6 support<u>ed</u>
7 disprov<u>es</u>

Section 4
Exercise A
1 c ✓
2 d ✓
3 e ✓
4 f
5 g ✓
6 a
7 h ✓
8 b ✓
Exercise B
1 What, by
2 could, again
3 Sorry, what
4 You've
Exercise C
1 likes
2 hasn't
3 won't
4 his home encyclopedia
5 come into contact with a virus
6 thinks
7 can't

Section 5
Exercise A
Borley Rectory was <u>builded</u> (*built*) in east America (*Essex*) <u>on</u> (*in*) 1963 (*1863*) by Reverend H. D. Bull. It was a small house (*huge mansion*) <u>surounded</u> (*surrounded*) by trees.

At first, not only is (*was*) the ghost of a nun seen, but also shadowy figures were spotted in the garden (*children's bedrooms*). However, the ghosts were not violent. Over six (*sixty*) years later, william (*William*) Price (*Gregson*), who was the owner, reported poltergeists in the house. Price (*Gregson*) burned the hosue (*house*) down and then tried to collect insurance money, but he didn't get it. the (*The*) house is gone now, but the legend has never been completely disproval (*disproved*).

Exercise B
Borley Rectory was builded (*built*) in east America (*Essex*) on (*in*) 1963 (*1863*) by Reverend H. D. Bull. It was a small house (*huge mansion*) surrounded (*surrounded*) by trees. At first, not only is (*was*) the ghost of a nun seen, but also shadowy figures were spotted in the garden (*children's bedrooms*). However, the ghosts were not violent. Over six (*sixty*) years later, william (*William*) Price (*Gregson*), who was the owner, reported poltergeists in the house. Gregson burned the hosue (*house*) down and then tried to collect insurance money, but he didn't get it. the (*The*) house is gone now, but the legend has never been completely disproval (*disproved*).

Exercise C
1 spelling
quite → quiet
2 factual
Harry Price → William Gregson
3 no mistake
4 no mistake
5 grammar
destroying → destroyed
6 punctuation
labelled, phonies → labelled phonies

Section 6
Exercise A
1 I'm
2 Do you
3 It's
4 is that
5 That's
6 that's
7 Is it
8 It
9 that was
10 There are
11 Are you
12 who is
13 I
14 It's
15 It

Exercise B
1 I think so.
2 I don't think so.
3 I suppose not.
4 I imagine so.
5 Well, I can't see any, so I guess not.
6 I suppose so.

What's right?
Had an email telling you you've won the lottery?

SkillsStudio
Exercise A
1 g 2 e 3 a 4 i 5 j 6 f 7 b
8 c 9 d 10 h

Exercise B
1 g 2 b 3 d 4 a 5 h 6 e

Exercise C
1 b 2 a 3 d 4 c 5 b

Exercise D
1 English-language
2 outrage
3 evidence
4 Pranks
5 1564
6 Calendar
7 New Year
8 trick
9 left-handed
10 ingredients
11 hundreds
12 gullible

Exercise E
Student's own answers

UNIT 11

Section 1
Exercise A
c

Exercise B
1 I 2 A 3 A 4 I 5 A 6 I 7 I
8 I 9 A

Exercise C
1 E, I, K
2 C, H, J
3 D
4 F
5 A, B
6 G

Section 2
Exercise A
1 If
2 I wish
3 Suppose
4 It's time
5 unless

What's right?
What if you had all the money in the world? What would you spend it on?

Exercise B
1 suppose
2 were
3 believed
4 wouldn't
5 were (also possible: *was*)
6 if
7 unless

8 had
9 time
10 got

Section 3
1 it takes
2 seriously
3 into account
4 for granted
5 out of context

Section 4
Exercise A
1 It was Rob Fusari who produced her early songs.
2 New York was the place where she lived for 20 years.
3 The reason why she divides opinion is because of her dress sense.
4 2008 was the year when she released her first album.
5 Musical integrity is the thing that distinguishes her from her contemporaries.
6 It was Beyoncé who sang on her hit *Telephone*.

What's right?
It was her mother who inspired her to start singing.

Exercise B
1 The people *who influenced her when she was growing up were Michael Jackson* and *Madonna*.
2 The year that *she wrote her first song* was *1999*.
3 It was *NYU that offered her a place* when she was just *17*.
4 The reason *why she got the name was* because she sounded like *Freddie Mercury*.
5 It *was The Fame, released in 2008, that launched her career.*
6 The place where *Lady Gaga now lives* is *Los Angeles*.
7 The thing *that most people admire is* Lady Gaga's *dedication to her art*.

Section 5
Exercise A
1 know
2 thing
3 sure
4 just
5 sorry
6 really
7 kind
8 honest
9 opinion

Exercise B
1, 3, 4

Exercise C
1 I'm not sure.
2 To be honest,
3 It's just that
4 I'm sorry, but I really can't.
5 The thing is,

Section 6
Exercise A
1 copyright
2 track
3 stream
4 piracy
5 file sharing
6 subscribe

Exercise B
1 stream
2 piracy
3 copyright
4 file sharing
5 subscribe
6 track

SkillsStudio
Exercise A
a, d, e

Exercise B
1 resurgence
2 superior
3 format
4 like-minded
5 jewel
6 intimate

Exercise C
1 b 2 a 3 d 4 d 5 a 6 a

Exercise D
Student's own answers

UNIT 12

Section 1
Exercise A
1 ~~Lived~~ Having lived for so long in such a cold environment, he now wants to move somewhere warmer.
2 Now ~~forgetting~~ forgotten by most people, this quiet town used to be the centre of trade.
3 He was alone on the island for 6 months, ~~survived~~ surviving on the fish he caught.
4 ~~Knew~~ Known for its hot springs, Japan is rich in volcanic activity.
5 ~~Get~~ Getting lost in the desert was one of the scariest experiences of my life.

What's right?
Looking through my binoculars, I saw an elephant appear from behind the trees.

Exercise B
1 Flying
2 Running
3 Struck
4 having experienced
5 preparing

Section 2
Exercise A
1 slightly
2 especially
3 somewhat
4 completely
5 totally
6 incredibly

Exercise B
1 incredibly
2 especially
3 completely
4 somewhat
5 totally
6 slightly

Section 3
Exercise A
1 [1] Did you say 'Milan'?
2 [4] Hang on, I didn't catch that.
3 [2] Sorry, could you repeat that?
4 [6] What was that?
5 [3] Sorry, how many?
6 [5] Wait, what did you say?

Exercise B
1 Japan
2 diving
3 pyramid
4 25
5 thinks
6 Yonaguni

Section 4
1 earthquake
2 mountain range
3 crust
4 plates
5 drifted apart
6 collided

Section 5
Exercise A
1 to have erupted
2 to have caused
3 to have left
4 to have inhabited
5 to have been formed

What's right?
The volcanic eruption is said to have inspired many local legends.

Exercise B
1 An earthquake approximately 70 km off the coast of Japan is known to ~~cause~~ have caused the tsunami that struck Japan in 2011.
2 The scientist is said to ~~be falsify~~ have falsified his data about the rock formations.
3 ✓
4 ✓
5 The Arctic researcher is believed to ~~dead~~ have died when he got lost on his way to the North Pole.

Section 6
Exercise A
Paragraph 1 Topic sentence: a
Paragraph 2 Topic sentence: a
Paragraph 3 Topic sentence: b

Exercise B
General issue: They [glaciers] are on the verge of disappearing due to global warming.
Proposed solution: The glaciers are to be wrapped in synthetic blankets the size of a football field to prevent the top snow layer and the ice below from melting.

Exercise C
1 against
2 3
3 for
4 3

Exercise D
a) 3, 5
b) 3, 4
c) 1, 3
d) 2
e) 3

SkillsStudio
Exercise A
1 d 2 i 3 b 4 h 5 c 6 j 7 e
8 a 9 g 10 f

Exercise B
Grand Canyon, USA E
Bali, Indonesia D
Ngorongoro Conservation Area, Tanzania B
Gobustan National Park, Azerbaijan F
Gran Salar de Uyuni, Bolivia C
Puerto Princesa, the Philippines G
Seljalandsfoss, Iceland A

Exercise C
1 Sentences b, c, e
2 d 3 a 4 b 5 b 6 c

Exercise D
1 atmosphere
2 ecology
3 thousands
4 lions
5 mud
6 salt
7 underground

Exercise E
Student's own answers